What Is Religion?

D1291283

Starting from the premise that religion is a human endeavour that can be analysed and compared across time and cultures, *What Is Religion?* brings the most up-to-date scholarship to bear on humankind's most enduring creation. Religious belief is one of the most pervasive and ubiquitous characteristics of human society. Religion has influenced human lives since prehistoric times, shaping the world views of cultures from isolated tribes to vast empires.

The book opens with a brief history of the idea of religion, then divides the study of religion into four essential topics – types, representations, practices and institutions – and concludes with a final, eye-opening chapter on religion today. Packed with case studies from a wide range of religions, past and present, *What Is Religion?* offers a very current, comprehensive, yet intellectually challenging overview of the history, theories, practices and study of religion.

Thoroughly updated throughout, this second edition provides an accessible, wide-ranging, engaging and concise book for undergraduate students in the study of religion. It is also invaluable for students of anthropology, history, psychology, sociology and theology as well as anyone interested in how and why humans became and continue to be religious.

Jeppe Sinding Jensen is Interacting Minds Centre Research Associate and Emeritus Associate Professor in the Department of the Study of Religion, Aarhus University, Denmark. Trained in Arabic and Islamic culture, history of religions and philosophy, his work now focuses on theory and method in the study of religion.

What Is Religion?

Second edition

Jeppe Sinding Jensen

 Routledge
Taylor & Francis Group

LONDON AND NEW YORK

Second edition published 2020
by Routledge
2 Park Square, Milton Park, Abingdon, Oxon OX14 4RN

and by Routledge
52 Vanderbilt Avenue, New York, NY 10017

Routledge is an imprint of the Taylor & Francis Group, an informa business

© 2020 Jeppe Sinding Jensen

First edition published by Acumen 2014

British Library Cataloguing in Publication Data
A catalogue record for this book is available from the British Library

Library of Congress Cataloging-in-Publication Data
Names: Jensen, Jeppe Sinding, 1951- author.
Title: What is religion? / Jeppe Sinding Jensen.
Description: Second edition. | New York : Routledge, 2019. |
Includes bibliographical references and index.
Identifiers: LCCN 2019007866 (print) | LCCN 2019010330 (ebook) |
ISBN 9780429504167 (e-book) | ISBN 9780429996085 (PDF) |
ISBN 9780429996078 (ePub) | ISBN 9780429996061 (Mobi) |
ISBN 9781138586338 (hardback : alk. paper) |
ISBN 9781138586345 (paperback : alk. paper)
Subjects: LCSH: Religion. | Religions.
Classification: LCC BL48 (ebook) | LCC BL48 .J45 2019 (print) |
DDC 200--dc23
LC record available at https://lccn.loc.gov/2019007866

ISBN: 978-1-138-58633-8 (hbk)
ISBN: 978-1-138-58634-5 (pbk)
ISBN: 978-0-429-50416-7 (ebk)

Typeset in Sabon
by Taylor & Francis Books

Contents

Preface
What is this thing called religion?

Religion is the subject of this volume. Not any particular religion, here or there, now or then, but religion *in general* as a human social and cultural fact. Religion is a human activity. If humans did not behave in those ways which we usually deem religious there would not be much religion. The gods might have existed but they would have been alone with no one to indulge or punish, to afflict or heal, and no one to communicate with. Whatever one may think of religion, praise or blame, it is a fact that religion is abundant in this world and that religion has been an integral part of human cultural and social history for a long as the historical records may take us.

Now, there are many books about many religions, in many historical and contemporary shapes and sizes, but not many on religion as an object of general and comparative investigation. This volume intends to help redress that situation and provide the reader with an introduction to what the academic study of religion has to say about the question 'What is religion?' Scholars and scientists from many academic disciplines study religion and so it should be interesting to look into what they *find*, *how* they find it and *why* they find it. These questions obviously involve theoretical issues and in that respect this volume is a contribution, however modest, to *theorising* about religion in general.

The term *religion* is used here to indicate that religions (in the plural) have so much in common, in spite of all apparent differences, that it is meaningful to talk about religion *in general* and use the term as the label of an abstract category that covers a wide range of human behaviours. In this sense, the term 'religion' and its associated categorising functions – analogously to 'sport', 'art', 'language' or 'economy' – other abstract terms used to broadly classify modes of human behaviour. Like those other modes, religion consists in recognisable forms of human social behaviour and that alone should be reason enough to venture a general and comparative study of religion in 'its' many variations, and of the components and phenomena that make up actual religious traditions. Each of these can be said to exemplify various aspects or dimensions of the total 'universe' or 'world' of religion. Not that all religions share *all* the same features, but typically they include ideas about superhuman agents, ritual purity, human fate after death, morality, ideas about the order of nature and the cosmos, conceptions of an 'other world' and – not least – how humans are to behave and think in this world. It is a book about those phenomena in the lives of humans which we characterise as religious. In that sense, more closely explained below, it is a *phenomenology* of religion – that is, an '-ology' about religious phenomena. Given the breadth of the motley assortment of such phenomena, the concept of religion applied in this book is *intentionally* extensive, for reasons to be explained. When I use the term 'it' about religion, it really is against my own best judgement. We should be aware that human language and human thought tend to make us believe that when there is a word, there must also be a corresponding object, a 'thing' that the word refers to. But we should not talk about consciousness in the same way as we talk about tomatoes. In consequence, when used about religion, the 'it' is at most a pragmatic label, a handy term (Jensen 2017).

In terms of the methods and theories applied, the approach of this book is novel, deliberately complex and inclusive. It ranges from cognitive science, moral and evolutionary psychology, across social and cultural anthropology, semiotics, historical textual studies to the philosophy of language ... and then some. The many approaches of the comparative and general studies of religion are necessary in a toolkit for explaining and understanding religion more fully as one of the most pervasive and universal characteristics of humanity. In today's media- and market-driven world, religion is a domain of human thought and behaviour that attracts much attention across cultures. An enquiry into the nature and function of religion is as relevant as ever, and surely, as the history of research tells us, more can be said now than before.

Religion appears to have been with humanity for a very long time. It certainly has changed over time, but some of its main characteristics trace back into early human cultural evolution. However, the secular study of religion as a human endeavour is quite recent and it is a result of historical, scientific and philosophical changes in modern intellectual history. It has not been equally welcomed in all places. Some think that religion should be studied religiously because that is the only possible way to understand it, some that it is impossible because of the variations among particular religions, and some that it is impertinent as it does not adequately respect religious sentiments. Still others opine that 'religion' is a specific social formation with particular social entailments, that is, 'religion' is a modern ideological construct used to classify, colonise and dominate politically and economically. This book is an attempt to present religion as part of human practice in a religiously and politically unbiased manner. However non-apologetic, it is not *theoretically* unbiased, as will become evident below. I have aimed to produce a book that will assist the concerned reader in understanding both the complex phenomenon of religion and how religion has become and is an object of scholarly enquiry more than a way of life to follow. In the passing, I shall just note that I am not a religious person myself.

Thus, the main idea of this book is that religions, in all their apparent diversity, are products of the human mind and of human activity. For those reasons alone it is plausible that they do have something in common and that it is possible to conduct comparative studies of religions and craft a general study of religion. The general hypothesis is that, as religions are made by humans, then not only the study of religion but also other human sciences, from psychology to philosophy, can provide important contributions to our understanding and explanation of religion and religions. As a human social construct, religion is, in principle, no more mysterious or less accessible than politics, language or sports. The anthropologist Clifford Geertz once noted that culture consists of 'social events like any other; they are as public as marriage and as observable as agriculture' (Geertz 1973: 91). The same holds for religion and religions. We may use a helpful distinction here between 'e-religion', which consists of mind-external, objective social and public forms of religion on the one hand and 'i-religion', which consists of individual mental phenomena such as representations, intentions and beliefs on the other. But again, those individual mental phenomena are only interesting when objectified, made public, written down or communicable in other modes of externalisation. Therefore, religion is not ontologically mysterious nor is it epistemically intractable: religion consists of beliefs and behaviours held and performed by humans. That is all that there is to it. The fact that many religious beliefs and behaviours refer to imagined entities or agents with strange and mysterious properties is well known. However, they are imagined entities and agents and it is as such that they can be studied: namely as objects of the human imagination, the ability to have and hold objects in the mind. This epistemological position may disappoint some but there is nothing that can be done about these conditions. Ever since the days of Immanuel Kant (1724–1804) all that we can talk about as humans is what and how things *appear* to us – not what they really are 'as such' in and of themselves. Now, objects may appear to our minds without being ontologically existing material entities. One example: of the ancient Chinese 'celestial animals' only turtles are objects of contemporary zoology; the others: dragons, phoenixes and unicorns are not. However, as objects of thought, reverence and ritual observance they are real enough – because they matter.

The materials covered in this exposition of religion as a feature of human life and history consist of case studies and illustrations from a wide range of the world's religions, past and present. The choice of these cases and illustrations reflects both specific aspects of religion as well as important and focal issues in the study of religion. Theoretically, this book is based on the recent cognitive science of religion, on dimensions in cultural, social and moral psychology, on aspects of social anthropology and sociology, and with inspirations from linguistics and semiotics. This composite theoretical and methodological 'conglomerate' is necessary to give a reasonably comprehensive coverage of 'religion' – a topic of tremendous complexity. This is also the place to apologise to fellow scholars for the near impossible condensation of many of their contributions to the journey through the world(s) of religion. However, I chose to include many items very briefly rather than omit them. The concerned reader is thus given a chance to pursue the issue, through the references and electronic resources.

This book is written for anyone with an interest in religion *and* how it can be studied and researched with current methods and theories. This makes it especially relevant for undergraduate students in the study of religion and in other subjects where religion is, can or should be a significant topic, such as (in alphabetical order) anthropology, archaeology, classics, cognitive science, history, political science, psychology, sociology and theology – and the study of religion, of course. With a breadth of information and covering a range of approaches, the book is intended to be accessible to any interested reader. This means that I shall sometimes need to explain what may seem trivial to some, but certainly is not to others. The decisions that needed to be made along the way are based on more than thirty years of teaching experience, undergraduate as well as graduate and doctoral students coming to the study of religion from a range of other subjects. It is also a result of my own participation in decidedly cross-disciplinary Aarhus University research settings, the MIND*Lab* research conglomerate and the Interacting Minds Centre, in which I am currently a research associate. They have been able to attract attention, scholars and scientists from all over the world that have truly enriched our scholarly vistas and agendas. My own visits to many attractive environments have also been instrumental. Here, I wish to thank the members of faculty who have been especially welcoming at the Rijksuniversiteit Groningen, the University of Turku, the University of Western Michigan (Kalamazoo), the University of Toronto, the University of Bergen, the University of Trondheim, the University of Manchester, the University of Colorado (Boulder), Université de Lausanne, the Aristotle University of Thessaloniki, the University of Alabama (Tuscaloosa), the University of Georgia (Athens), the University of Vermont, and the two University of California campuses in San Diego and Santa Barbara. They have been critically influential in the development of the theoretical platform that serves as the basis here. Thanks go to my colleagues and friends in the Department of Culture and Society at Aarhus University in Denmark, my home institution, especially Lars Albinus, Hans Jørgen Lundager Jensen, Anders Klostergaard Petersen, Andreas Roepstorff, Jesper Sørensen, and Uffe Schjødt. They have been very supportive over the years and encouraged the teaching of innovative courses on matters related to my own research interests. So many thanks are due also to the *many* students who have taken part in seminars, participated in projects and helped develop new perspectives in the study of religion and culture. Some of them now form the next generation, as they have become faculty members in the research unit Religion, Cognition and Culture, which my long-time friend and colleague Armin W. Geertz and I founded almost two decades ago. Outside my home turf I have had the good fortune and privilege of arguing, debating, studying, talking and working with good friends and clever colleagues from a number of scholarly fields: Greg Alles, Veikko Anttonen, Pascal Boyer, Joseph Bulbulia, Terrence Deacon, Merlin Donald, Esther Eidinow, Steven Engler, Tim Fitzgerald, Chris Frith, Mattia Gallotti, Ingvild Gilhus, Terry Godlove, Paul Heelas, Edwin Hutchins, Hans G. Kippenberg, E. Thomas Lawson, Gabriel Levy, Luther H. Martin, Robert N. McCauley, Russell McCutcheon, John McGraw, William E. Paden, Ray Paloutzian, Hans H. Penner, Ilkka Pyysiäinen, Bryan Rennie, Andrea Rota, Benson Saler, Kevin Schilbrack, Robert Segal, Chris Sinha, Ted Slingerland, Michael Stausberg, Ann Taves, Robert Yelle, Harvey Whitehouse, Donald Wiebe and Alan Williams.

I heartily thank all the above. Their contributions have been truly invaluable and if they detect some of their own work here below this is no coincidence, as bits and pieces of interesting materials have been piling up over the years in teaching notes and research scraps for as long as I have had the ambition to write a book like this. During more than three decades, I have benefited immensely from working with anthropologists, archaeologists, cognitive scientists, historians and historians of religions, linguists, philosophers, political scientists, sociologists, psychologists and theologians. I would be grateful if this book could also be of some use to them in return for all that they have offered me. Sincere thanks also go to the anonymous reviewers of the manuscript; their critical, acute and helpful comments have been highly valuable in the attempts to make this project as precise and accessible as possible. The staff at Routledge, Fiona Hudson Gabuya and Jack Boothroyd, and Liz Hudson at the Little Red Pen have encouraged and aided me all along in the process of turning a heap of complex academic thoughts into an approachable book. Special thanks go to my subject area editor Rebecca Shillabeer. Finally, gratitude goes to my family, and above all, to my sagacious and loving wife, Merete.

1 Introduction
Some ideas about religion

Religion is a puzzling social and individual phenomenon to many people in the modern world. It can be favourably associated with agreeable human qualities such as ethics, morality and spirituality, or negatively with superstition, stifling tradition, rejection of scientific knowledge and human progress in general. Religion has come in many shapes and held great power over minds and bodies, cultures and societies. It seems to have been ever-present in human history, but only over the past two centuries has religion become an object to study rather than a power to obey. This book aims to meet many of the questions about religion: What is it really? Where does it come from? What does it consist of? Does it help individuals cope? Does it provide meaning in life? Will it become obsolete and go away by itself? If not, why? What will religion be like in the future?

Other related questions are relevant to the *study* of religion: How does one study religion academically, rationally and scientifically? That is, how can scholars go beyond simply reporting what believers believe? Can religion really be explained? Why are religions so diverse and yet they obviously appear as religions? Is it meaningful and legitimate to compare religions? What are the moral or political concerns of scholarly and scientific studies of religion and religions? Should scholars be critics or caretakers? These are some of the highly significant questions in the study of religion.

One should remember that 'religion' is a term referring to a concept and not to any 'given' fact. It is a term used to cover certain ranges of human behaviour, empirically as well as theoretically. The term 'religion' is used not only in contemporary religious discourses but also in the media and politics, as well as in scholarly works, methods and theories, though with quite distinct ramifications. Additionally, the history of the concept of religion reveals a complex legacy from antiquity, influenced later by the Renaissance, the Enlightenment, the Romantic movements and finally by the modern scientific world view. Philosophers, theologians and others have toiled with religion before it became an academic subject – as the History of Religions – in its own right in the nineteenth century, beginning in both the Netherlands and Switzerland in 1876. Today there are competing as well as complementary methods and theories employed by (in alphabetical order): anthropologists, classicists, historians, philologists, philosophers, political scientists, psychologists, scholars of religion, sociologists and theologians, to name the most frequent. Thus, although 'religion' is a very commonplace term in the modern world, it would be inappropriate to attempt to describe, explain and interpret religion without due attention to intellectual history and scholarly theory. Some have wished to abolish the term because of its roots in Christian and European contexts (e.g., Dubuisson 2003). The use of the term is convenient, however problematic it may be theoretically (Saler 2015) It is a handy term, one that helps getting a grip on complex ideas, one could call it an 'epistemic placeholder' (Jensen 2017).

Five views of religion to think with

Thus, I will use the term 'religion' as the common-sense reference to that entire gamut of human practices, which we normally call 'religion'. In the discussions below, the various features of religion will be elaborated upon because the concept of religion *is* manifestly theory-dependent. To substantiate that point, here are five types of influential definitions of religion from various perspectives, which I will use as reference points later on. The definitions are from the modern era and presented in a roughly chronological order. They exemplify the expanse of thinking about religion, and I will point to the reasons and consequences of their differences. We shall use them to discuss and think with as we go along.

The first definition is by the French sociologist Émile Durkheim (1858–1917) in his 1912 book *The Elementary Forms of the Religious Life*. Durkheim focused on religion as the social construction of the ethics and morality of groups. He strives to be neutral and descriptive in his definition: 'A religion is a unified system of beliefs and practices relative to sacred things, that is to say, things set apart and forbidden – beliefs and practices which unite into a single moral community called a Church, all those who adhere to them' (Durkheim 2001: 46). Here Durkheim introduces the distinction between sacred and profane as primary and not between gods and humans as most people who are brought up in religious traditions would intuitively imagine. In that way, he is also able to include ancient Buddhism in the category of religion – where it belongs – because there are sacred 'things set apart', that is, the Buddha's teachings or the monastic order. However, the most important criterion in Durkheim's view is the 'moral community'. For Durkheim, religion is an eminently social fact, which consists of beliefs and practices that unite a community. For Durkheim, no religions are false, because they all fulfil human needs, and so he says that 'our entire study rests on this postulate: that the unanimous feeling of believers across time cannot be purely illusory' (Durkheim 2001: 312).

The second definition, presented by the psychoanalyst Sigmund Freud (1856–1956), is emphatically critical of religion. His definition is typically Western with belief in a monotheistic 'Father God' as its main feature. Below that surface of belief, there are neurotic depths, and Freud views religion as a kind of immature behaviour related to illusion and wishful thinking: 'Religion would thus be the universal obsessional neurosis of humanity; like the obsessional neurosis of children, it arose out of the Oedipus complex, out of the relation to the father' (Freud 1961: 42). Freud's own wish, then, is to remove religion from humanity as it matures and relinquishes 'what constitutes the root of every form of religion – a longing for the father' (1961: 42). The main merit of Freud's view of religion is that it points to complex, subconscious, psychological and emotional processes and introduces us to a critical view of the authority of religion that has become quite widespread in the Western world. It focuses on belief, on the individual and not on the group.

The third, and very different, view of religion comes from German-American theologian Paul Tillich (1886–1965), who focuses on faith rather than religion in the broader sense. Tillich maintains that the essence of the human religious attitude is 'ultimate concern' because humans are concerned with the conditions of their own existence. Thus, 'Faith as ultimate concern is an act of the total personality. It is the most centered act of the human mind … in the dynamics of personal life' (Tillich 1957: 5). In Tillich's view, faith is not opposed to emotion and reason but transcends them both. The modern version of sin is alienation, which leads to meaninglessness if not countered by faith as ultimate concern. Even atheists have 'ultimate concerns'. As faith, religion helps humans cope existentially. Consequently, Tillich's view of religion is functional. Looking at the religious traditions of the world, the concept of ultimate concern is apt in many ways. For, although indubitably Christian in origin, this idea does provide an insight into the very fundamental cognitive and emotional functions, that religious convictions have as the normative conditions for how humans of perceive themselves and their world.

This view of the religious perspective is also present in the fourth definition. In 1966, the American anthropologist Clifford Geertz presented a definition of religion as a 'cultural system' consisting of symbols through which humans bestow meaning on their existence. To Geertz religion is:

> (1) […] a system of symbols which acts to (2) establish powerful, pervasive, and longlasting moods and motivations in men by (3) formulating concep-tions of a general order of existence and (4) clothing these conceptions with such an aura of factuality that (5) the moods and motivations seem uniquely realistic.
>
> (Geertz 1973: 90)

The definition is thus both substantial and functional; it tells us what religion consists of, namely a system of symbols (and their meaning), and what it does in its mostly psychological, that is, cognitive and emotional functions. There are no gods or other superhuman beings in this definition, so it may apply equally well to ideologies or other social formations with authority. Whether this is a strong point or a weakness of the definition will depend on how it is used. Geertz emphasised how the human experience is importantly shaped by religion and as part and parcel of human culture. Like languages, religious cultural systems exist outside newborn human individuals and as they become internalised they come to guide human perception and cognition. The 'religious perspective', as Geertz calls this mode of cognitive governance, rests on a conviction of what is 'really real' through the 'imbuing of a certain specific complex of symbols – of the metaphysic they formulate and the style of life they recommend – with a persuasive authority which, from an analytic point of view, is the essence of religious action' (Geertz 1973: 112). Geertz's view of religion has become influential; it ingeniously incorporates aspects from the philosophy of language on meaning and symbols, as well as from sociological and anthropological theories about social experience. To this, he added psychological perspectives. Geertz's general view of religion, then, may best be quoted directly:

> For an anthropologist, the importance of religion lies in its capacity to serve, for an individual or for a group, as a source of general, yet distinctive, conceptions of the world, the self, and the relations between them, on the one hand – its model *of* aspect – and of rooted, no less distinctive 'mental' dispositions – its model *for* aspect – on the other. From these cultural functions flow, in turn, its social and psychological ones.
>
> (Geertz 1973: 123)

The final perspective of religion to on display here presents ideas from the more recent cognitive science of religion as formulated by the anthropologist and psychologist Pascal Boyer. In his approach, religion is an evolutionary by-product (a 'spandrel') rooted in the propagation of attention-grabbing representations that violate ordinary and psychologically intuitive perceptions of the world. Boyer has formulated a whole research programme on religion, ranging from beliefs about superhuman imagined agents to religious ritual as parasitic on human danger detection systems in the brain (Jensen 2009c). According to Boyer, there is nothing 'true' about religion. It may function in some ways, but mostly negatively as superstition and deceitful 'false' consciousness. Believers do not know *really* why and what they believe: they are, so to say, deceived by their own brains. If Boyer is right, this will have the profound consequence that believers' views are invalidated as first-person authority. The scientist, like the doctor or the psychoanalyst, really knows *better* and so religion is now to be understood through third-person analyses. His work concentrates on the 'evolutionary origins of religious thought': evolution provided humans with large brains and vivid imagination and so they have come to imagine certain kinds of things that are not real. Humans have gods and spirits as partners – they have imaginary companions just like children may have 'invisible friends'. Humans did not acquire religion and any odd belief because they had flexible and open minds:

> On the contrary, because they had many sophisticated inference systems, they became vulnerable to a very *restricted* set of supernatural concepts: the ones that jointly activate inference systems for agency, predation, morality, social exchange, etc. Only a small range of concepts are such that they reach this aggregate relevance, which is why religion has common features the world over.
>
> (Boyer 2001: 324–5)

In Boyer's view, the cognitive study of religion provides better knowledge of human mental processes by looking at the 'human propensity towards religious thoughts. One does learn a lot about these complex biological machines by figuring out how they manage to give airy nothing a local habitation and a name' (Boyer 2001: 330). This is the last sentence in the book. On Boyer's view, religion is in the world because human minds are designed so that they can hardly avoid having religious ideas. We shall return to some of these themes below. Suffice it now to note, with Boyer and others of the same persuasion, that religions are *of course* dependent on the nature of human minds and whatever the gods may think about us humans, *we* study what humans think about their gods and how humans behave towards them.

Views of religion and intellectual 'turns'

These five very different views and ideas about religion were chosen because they have been very influential, and so we may find stronger or weaker echoes of them in many places. They are also important because they refer to intellectual and cultural patterns beyond the more narrow concern with religion; they each represent a 'turn' in modern intellectual and academic history. First, Durkheim's theory not only shifted the focus in the study of religion from doctrine and history to the social functions of religion, but it also contributed broadly to the creation of sociology as an academic enterprise. With Durkheim, we have the 'functional turn'. With Freud we acquired the 'psychoanalytic turn', one that was not only critical of religion as a psychological phenomenon but also part of a whole 'hermeneutics of suspicion' movement (i.e. 'things are not what they seem') which swept across the modern world in the twentieth century. Tillich's theology and view of religion tapped into the existentialist movement in philosophy and so represents the 'existentialist turn' after the Second World War. Geertz combined the tradition of American cultural anthropology with inspirations from the philosophy of language and symbolic forms in the 'linguistic turn' and so introduces us to a new way of handling the 'problem of meaning' in religion and culture. Boyer takes on the new radical naturalistic views of the human mental world in the 'cognitive turn' and applies this to the study of religion. This 'naturalistic turn' builds on recent advances in cognitive science and offers compelling evidence that religion may be an entirely human invention.

Then, these theoreticians have not only presented influential views of religion they also mirror some of the major 'turns' in the more recent academic and cultural histories. We shall use them to 'think with' in the presentations, analyses and discussions that follow. To sum up, the theories and perspectives that we have just reviewed evidently hit upon very diverse origins, functions and meanings in and of religions. It really does matter what colour spectacles you put on, as the meanings of the term 'religion' seem to be as flexible as the meanings of the terms 'house' or 'sport'. It is obvious that one must not confuse words and objects, since a term or concept is not what it refers to. Formulated as a philosophy of science rationale: the concept of 'religion' is theory-dependent and not a 'given'. But this is all too often forgotten in ordinary language use where we tend to reify many concepts and so ask, for instance: 'What is religion really?' The historian of religions Jonathan Z. Smith has repeatedly stressed the philosophical point that 'map is not territory': an analogy which should be instructive: the *concept* of religion is a kind of map of the 'thing' religion, that is, all those human activities which we classify as having to do with 'religion'. There are also cases of fuzzy borders: how does one distinguish between magic and religion on the one hand and between ideology and religion on the other? There is only one solution: to acknowledge that these terms are terms for concepts and not for realities; they are *analytic terms* that are constructed in the service of analysis, of interpretation and as tools for our heuristic and investigative purposes, that is, to help *us* find out about things. Our terms and concepts will aid us more in some instances than others; some cases are clear-cut, some are very 'fuzzy', but without our concepts we would not even *know* that the fuzzy cases are fuzzy. Our terms and concepts are tools and if they do not do the job properly, then they must be honed or replaced. The best tools ultimately lead to a plethora of more finely crafted tools and more specialised tools (Jensen 2011b). Over recent decades, the term 'religion' itself has become disputed in postmodernist criticism as a Western, European or Christian invention that is used to promote the view of the modern world as more rational than religious traditions. Some find that the term is thus used to perpetuate hegemony and domination of the 'Other' (e.g., Campany 2018; Dubuisson 2003; Patton and Ray 2000). To the degree that this is correct, it will remain more of a political problem and one that is not solved by discarding the term. It seems wiser to be pragmatic and use a terminology that is broadly understandable. For better or worse, the term 'religion' is with us. It may be fuzzy, but that means broad too. Kevin Schilbrack points out that a label reflects the purpose of the labeller, the labels are also 'interactive kinds' in the sense that those being labelled may also embrace, edit, or discard the labels: 'With social realities, if people find the term useful and live in its terms, this agreement is all that is needed for the alleged thing to exist' (Schilbrack 2014: 104).

A practical and stipulative definition of religion

For now, then, the term 'religion' will serve as a practical one (Saler 2015). To make matters a bit clearer, let me introduce a *stipulative* definition that spells out a specific view of religion that reflects a reasonable consensus in contemporary research. Additionally, it includes relevant elements and aspects in relation to the theoretical platform of this book. It is also a *polythetic* definition in the sense that it stipulates a number of such elements and aspects that may be more or less important in any given actual religious tradition. ('Polythetic' means 'having many things in common but not necessarily all.') It draws recognisably on the five views of religion reviewed above with the added emphasis on the semantic dimension – that is, the dimension of *meaning*. If religions were not 'full of meaning' then they would not exist or function (Jensen 1999). This will be explained in the box below.

Thus, specific religions at specific times may have any weighted combination of the sets of elements and components. Some religions are high on sacrifice, others on purity or ethics. Some are very dogmatic and others not. Some have a special ritual language which only few can master, or esoteric lore for the initiated, where others are open or egalitarian. The advantage of polythetic definitions, classifications and typologies is that they demonstrate the kinds of 'family resemblance' that we find among religions. We rarely doubt whether some social formation 'counts as' religion even though there may not be any single decisive element in the case in question, as there should to be according to a monothetic ('setting up one thing') definition. For instance, 'worship of a single deity' or 'authority of sacred scriptures' are not exclusive criteria for whether a social formation is religious or not, as such views rather point to an ethnocentric view of religion *from* within a specific tradition. Some religious traditions are *so* religious that they may at first seem not to be religious at all: they may be sanctifying every aspect of life to such a degree that whatever should appear as profane is hardly distinguishable (Zuesse 1992). It is analogous to sports and games, which is where the philosopher Ludwig Wittgenstein got the 'family resemblance' idea from: some sports are very strenuous, like running a marathon or cycling the Giro d'Italia, but others are low on exertion, such as playing billiards. Some games are team games, and some depend totally on fortune and yet others on cunning (Wittgenstein 1993). The category of 'food' is even more unrestricted, but I think the examples suffice for now. We shall see many more and very different instances of religion below; they have some things in common, for sure, but not all.

Box 1.1 Religion

Semantic and cognitive networks comprising ideas, behaviours and institutions in relation to counter-intuitive superhuman agents, objects and posits.

Explanation

Typically religions include such elements or components as explanations of the origin (cosmogony) and classifications of what makes up the world (cosmology); ideas about matters, objects and agents that are sacred, ultimate and inviolable; beliefs in spiritual beings such as superhuman agents; special powers and knowledge that such beings and agents have and which humans may gain access to; beliefs concerning human fate and life after death; ritual actions of various kinds (from silent prayer to bloody sacrifice) that ensure the communication with the sacred or 'other world'; institutions setting the limits and conditions for such communication and containing rules for human conduct in systems of purity, hierarchy and group relations; ethics and morality.

Who is 'right' about religion?

Another continuing problem in the study of religion concerns the differences between the views of insiders and outsiders (Jensen 2011a). Insiders characteristically insist on the truth and uniqueness of their tradition, faith or belief whereas outsiders may be anything from curious to sceptical and critical. Some Buddhists do not consider Buddhism a religion because they focus almost exclusively on the philosophical and psychological dimensions of the vast assemblage of doctrines and learning that comprises the Buddhist scriptural traditions. They may regard popular practice and worship as a sort of inauthentic Buddhism. Similarly, some Muslim groups do not consider rival groups as 'Muslim' at all, and Christians often disagree on the status of the sacraments. Some of them, in the tradition of Lutheran 'dialectic theology', maintain that Christianity is not a religion because religions are produced by humans out of their own needs, whereas the Gospel has 'descended from above'. Again, in many other traditions, 'our religion' is just what *we* do: everybody else may be totally wrong but we do not care. One thing is certain though, as history tells us: it is always those that are closer to us and most like us, who cause the most trouble – the neighbours, in short. Then, a logical question arises: what is the scope of a religious tradition and where are its borders? Here I venture an idea that I have contemplated and used in teaching: 'a semantic space where the interlocutors may meaningfully disagree'. We know that humans do not all and not fully agree on their traditions and so instead we may point to the confines of a semantic universe within which they may meaningfully *disagree*. This occurs when there is so much congruent semantic space that they agree on certain 'ultimate sacred postulates' (Rappaport 1999: 287). On a large scale, Jews, Christians and Muslims may agree or disagree on whether they have the 'same god' or Jesus is a prophet or divine, but to a Japanese Shintoist that discussion will entirely beyond the point, that is, outside the relevant semantic space of 'meaningful disagreement'. On a smaller scale, Roman Catholics and Protestants may disagree on the number and nature of the sacraments, but Jews would not consider this relevant. Inuit groups may discuss the powers of the shaman's helping spirits, but that is beyond the space of meaningful disagreement for any other ethnic or religious group. 'Meaningful disagreement' is a useful analytic tool.

Now, it is obviously not the scholar's primary task to judge the value of any one or all religion, but on the other hand, it is difficult to remain ontologically and epistemically neutral. Ideally, any academic study in the humanities or the social sciences should be unbiased and value-free, but it is impossible to avoid all normative concerns as the modern scientific project espouses certain epistemic virtues by itself. Philosopher of science John Dupré has noted some of those features in what he terms a 'virtue epistemology'. These are 'sensitivity to empirical fact, plausible background assumptions, coherence with other things we know, exposure to criticism from the widest variety of sources, and no doubt others. Some of the things we call "science" have many such virtues, others very few' (Dupré 1993: 243). Epistemology for the study of religion need not harbour concerns that are different from those that apply to the study of other kinds of human thought and behaviour. Religions typically attribute authority to invisible or abstract powers but it is *not* those powers that we study, but the human thoughts and behaviours in articulated in *relation* to them. For, whatever the gods may be, they are certainly beyond the reach of science and academic scholarship. The study of religion is not *theology* – it is the study of human behaviour (e.g., Wiebe 1999). This epistemic stance invites, unavoidably, questions from and confrontations with insiders as the religious traditions' caretakers. Scholars are not caretakers. They are critics, whether they want to be or not, there is no escape. They may personally believe in some things but they cannot logically believe in *all* things. Scholars are under the obligation to heed what Peter L. Berger called the 'Heretical Imperative': knowing, respecting and reflecting upon what it means that there are so many different ways of conceiving and practising human life (Berger 1980). Thus, scholars must self-critically evaluate the theoretical, philosophical and political commitments that drive and underwrite their scholarly endeavours (McCutcheon 2003). Kevin Schilbrack's astute conclusion is that:

> there are no terms whose history or implications are free of politics. None of our thinking is without ideological baggage. None of our perspectives are neutral. There is no way to study what we now call religious rituals, histories, experiences, institutions and so on, without the acts of classification that make possible value judgments between cultures. This is why I argue for retaining the word 'religion', though now conscious of the shadows it casts.
>
> (Schilbrack 2014: 105)

The making of comparability

I wish to end this introductory chapter with a few reflections on the necessity and validity of comparison and generalisation as necessary for the scholarly and scientific study of religion. We know that it is quite common for adherents of a specific religious tradition to decry the comparability of their own tradition with others, except perhaps for the conclusion that the others are false or futile. However, such an exclusivist stance is not a productive strategy in the study of either religions (in the plural) or religion (in the singular) as academic topics. We must leave religious or political value judgements aside and focus on the purposes of academic investigation: the pursuit of knowledge. Now, if the things we are concerned with could only be compared partially or not at all, we would not be able to produce any scientific evidence or scholarly knowledge at all. The comparability of things related to all that which we call 'religion' hinges on careful selection of the aspects and dimensions for scrutiny and comparison so that they make sense (Jensen 2003, 2019). We can only compare specific aspects or dimensions and not religions *in toto*. Pascal Boyer offers some perceptive thoughts on this issue:

The study of religion is an 'impure subject', that is, a subject where the central or official topic is not a scientific object. True, there is 'religion' around and there may well be 'religions' as well. And there are mountains and giraffes, too. But neither giraffes nor mountains constitute proper scientific objects. Only particular aspects of mountains and giraffes qualify as scientific objects, and those particular aspects are shared with non-mountains and non-giraffes. It follows that there is no privileged 'method' or 'theory' in the study of religion as such, although there may be particularly adequate theories and methods in the study of specific aspects of religious ideas and practices.

(Boyer 1996: 212)

Thus, for similar reasons, religion can be said to be *both* a complex and an 'impure subject' because any one religion is a mixture of 'substances', that is, of world views, morality, beliefs about life after death, in spirits, in the effects of ritual actions and many more of the elements normally found in the 'inventories' of religious traditions. It is these *elements* that we normally compare and which we will be much more concerned with in this book. Fraught with difficulties as comparisons may be, it is only comparison that makes the study of religion (and many other things) possible. The 'problem of comparison' is a returning topic in the study of religion (e.g., Hughes 2017; Stausberg 2011). We also know, and should remember, that the objects of our comparisons are models and *not* objects and maps, *not* territories: if we wish to compare different forms of, say, sacrifice, we still need *some* model of sacrifice to be able to carry out the comparison. The events and behaviours that we classify as 'sacrifice' in the model depend on a set of selected criteria for them to make up a 'sacrifice'. As we cannot have models without implicit theory ('What are you thinking about when you say religion?'), it follows that the entire enterprise depends on the soundness of our theoretical reflections (Jensen 2009b). It also follows from the concerns about comparison that we should be careful about our generalisations, but not that generalisation is impossible. Indeed, we are already generalising as soon as we use the term 'sacrifice' because any term is also a kind of definition, however rudimentary or brief. The anthropologist Claude Lévi-Strauss (1908–2009) used the expression 'generalised interpretation' to indicate what it is that anthropologists have in mind when they talk ('generalise') about 'sacrifice' and present an abstract model of the activities they identify as 'sacrifice'. Subsequently that abstract model may be compared with particular examples of sacrifice and the models become validated, expanded, criticised, reinterpreted, or even rejected: but without the models, we would *not even know* that we were talking or disagreeing about sacrifice in the first place. Consequently, it all depends on the level and scope of investigation and the theories and methods involved in the process. Not least, it depends on scholars and scientists having ideas about that range of human behaviour that it is informative to call 'religion' – even if it may amount to having an 'impure subject' that is theoretically highly sensitive. Therefore, it is not surprising that there have been many ideas about religion in the past. A very short history of those ideas will be presented here so that we may get a sense of where *we* are now – and why.

2 A very short history of the idea of religion

There is no way of knowing anything intellectually sensible about religion without knowing something about the study of it. In this sense, the study of religion resembles philosophy: if you have no idea of the history of philosophy, you cannot do contemporary philosophy. Already, the examples of definitions and ideas of religion presented above stressed the theory-dependence of any awareness about religion: if you have *no* idea of what it is you cannot even recognise it. For that reason, here is a brief history of the image or imagination of religion.

Let us begin with the etymological uncertainties: the term 'religion' comes from the Latin 'religio' with two possible meanings. One is 'religare', to chain or tie 'again', and the other is 'relegere', to collect or read 'again'. Whichever is more correct, the Roman use of the term implied meticulous observation of the traditions for ritual exchanges with the gods. The correct, prescribed behaviour towards the superhuman was to be carefully observed, something the Romans were well known for in those days. Very little could be done without the proper rituals, consulting oracles, sacrificing or praying. The Roman calendar was divided into days for profane events and for sacred events. This only indicates the careful and fastidious nature of traditional religion. The peoples of antiquity, like other peoples all over the world, had systems of conduct and networks of belief where the participation of the gods in all affairs was commonplace. For instance, any town in classical Greece had its added population of superhuman beings who were taking care of all kinds of affairs for their human community. (Larson 2016). Over the years, the Latin term 'religio' changed from the early Christian meaning 'idolatry' to the now more common global usage, and in such diverse cases as the Universal Declaration of Human Rights and in the popular media. As we saw above, the 'subject matter' of the *idea* of religion is dependent on theory and so the development of discourse on religion is important. The interest in religion as an object of study did not appear out of nowhere. The history of this interest is closely linked to the emergence of first enlightenment and later modernity in the Western world (see, e.g., Preus 1987; Kippenberg 2002). Now, there are several significant issues to consider in a history of the idea of 'religion'. I shall not present these in a strict chronological order. That would prove inextricably muddled since there is no single clear and linear progression from one set of approaches to the next. Rather, a set of topics have mingled and become woven together over time.

Truth in religion versus criticism of religion

In Europe and especially from the Middle Ages onwards, the world views of the Christian churches dominated for centuries with schisms and quarrels over the right and true interpretations of the scriptures. In other literate traditions, there were also differences of opinion over religious, metaphysical and political matters, such as between the Sunni and Shi'a branches of Islam or different branches of Judaism. The traditions in South Asia, for example Buddhism and Hinduism, also diverged and branched out in many philosophical, ritual and institutional directions. Many critical voices and movements arose over time in those traditions, but they remained religious *within* the religious traditions themselves. many philosophical schools and religious movements wanted and caused schisms and reformations in Hindusim, Buddhism, Islam and the Chinese traditions. After any such event there is always the problem of the truth of what was before and what now comes after – which is or were more right or true? The most important intellectual effect of such breaks is that truth becomes *relativised* and knowing that others think differently means that choices are (in principle) possible.

As the story here leads on to the formation of the non-apologetic academic study of religion there is a different strand that attracts attention, namely that which wanted freedom from religious authority and dogma altogether. For the growing scientific world view in the intellectual history of the Western world it was problematic to accept the claim to truth of the biblical scriptures as 'revealed religion'. Instead of simply repeating religious conviction, the philosopher René Descartes (1596–1650) demanded critical intelligence; he analysed the possibilities for acquiring reliable knowledge and developed the process of systematic doubt as a philosophical method. Importantly, with Descartes, the source of knowledge turned from God and revelation to the human mind and its relation to the world. The philosopher David Hume (1711–76) was prominent among the critics of religion in the early modern age. In the essay *An Enquiry Concerning Human Understanding* from 1748 he concludes section 10, 'Of Miracles', with this critique of Christian belief in biblical miracles:

> So that, upon the whole, we may conclude, that the Christian Religion not only was at first attended with miracles, but even at this day cannot be believed by any reasonable person without one. Mere reason is insufficient to convince us of its veracity: And whoever is moved by Faith to assent to it, is conscious of a continued miracle in his own person, which subverts all the principles of his understanding, and gives him a determination to believe what is most contrary to custom and experience.
>
> (Hume 2008: 95)

Other Enlightenment philosophers contributed greatly to this growing scepticism and criticism of established religion. Among them, François Voltaire (1694–1778) advanced some of these novel British ideas in France and wrote scathing satirical works on religious fanaticism. For him, free thought and reason were to be the means to end religious wars that had tormented Europe for centuries: 'It is the spirit of philosophy that has removed this plague from the world'. Religion must be depoliticised, declared the philosopher John Locke (1632–1704) in his writings on tolerance and politics. He was a religious man himself, but he also firmly articulated the view that religion was a private personal matter and that politics and religion should be kept apart. There could still be truth in religion, but the sphere of religion must be restricted and it should not be all-encompassing.

One fundamental question occupied these Enlightenment philosophers: if religion does not emanate from God, where, then, does religion come from? In which human domain does religion have its origin? Is religion primarily an intellectual phenomenon concerned with human thought and reason? Or, is it principally an ethical and moral matter concerned with duties and obligations towards the gods and fellow human beings? Or, again, is religion an emotional and aesthetic disposition concerned with the sense of beauty and harmony? Regardless of the apparent difference there is one common denominator that we should notice: these are truly *revolutionary* ways of thinking about religion because they ground the explanation of religion in human nature, and *not* in the will of the gods. In that sense, they are all *naturalistic* explanations.

Such views of religion were serious blows to the established scriptural claims to truth based on revelation, doctrine and church authority. Many learned people could now view religion as natural, and so they did in the Christian theological movement characterised as 'Deism'. This philosophical-theological position became quite influential in the seventeenth and eighteenth centuries. It was involved both in the Enlightenment and in the growing scientific revolution as an attempt to explain religion in a manner that might preserve religion but did not compromise reason and science. Deists were critical of the more mystical and magical points in religion, but they were not critical of religion as a whole. Instead, they redefined how religion *should* be regarded. Deism entertains a number of distinct ideas. It is monotheistic, and God exists as a wholly transcendent being that does not mix in the affair of humans. He created the universe so that it runs according to the laws of nature. As humans have been given the ability to reason by God, then they may know God by observing the natural world. Further, the human soul is immortal, it realises that piety and virtue are the right ways of worship, that there is a Day of Judgement and rewards and punishments in the afterlife. The emphasis on the latter serves as warning and admonition for a life based on ethics and morality. These are the main ideas, and although they differed in importance to the followers, they also did much to contribute to very common understandings of religion today. It is also noteworthy how Deist ideas resemble classical Islamic theology on many points as well as creationist ideas in certain forms of contemporary Christianity.

Romanticism and emotional religion

In the eighteenth century, Romanticism began to appear in the Western world, with an ever-more keen fascination with the ancient and the distant. Some

Romantics hallowed the ancient myths, legends and bards of their own nation (e.g., Saxon or Scottish) while others delved into the books of the Orient and revered the wisdom of the age-old Indian sages in the Vedic scriptures. The Romanticists were largely and quite loosely positive towards religion. Their interpretations of religion followed their whim because for them the truly defining aspect of religion was *feeling* and the proper modes of religion were driven by human emotion. The focus was on piety and experience, and thus personal *religiosity* and intuition belong so intimately together in the romantic view of religion that the philosopher and theologian Friedrich Schleiermacher (1768–1834) could proclaim in his 1799 work *On Religion: Speeches to Its Cultured Despisers* that 'Religion's essence is neither thinking nor acting, but intuition and feeling' (1996: 22). That is because:

> Intuition is and always remains something individual, set apart, the immediate perception, nothing more ... The same is true of religion: it stops with the immediate experiences of the existence and action of the universe, with the individual intuitions and feelings ... it knows nothing about derivation and connection, for among all things religion can encounter, that is what its nature most opposes.
>
> (Schleiermacher 1996: 26)

Throughout his writing career, Schleiermacher used different terms to denote religious feeling and intuition; he was not always lucid in his statements. But they are interesting because he is in a sense almost our contemporary in some of his views which easily translate into current conceptions of individual experience and spirituality. In the early works he disclosed an almost *pantheist* character and talked about feeling or intuition 'of the universe' and consciousness of 'the infinite and the eternal within the finite and the temporal' – in an almost classical Indian philosophical sense. In the later works he developed the idea of the feeling of 'absolute dependence' and of 'createdness' by God. In *On Religion*, he discussed how religion is the miraculous outcome of direct relationships with the infinite or with God and that doctrines are but the reflections of this 'miracle'. He also teasingly wrote to the 'despisers' that:

> In the second place, just as little do I consider that I have the right to hold the conceptions and doctrines of God and of immortality, as they are usually understood, to be the principal things in religion. Only what in either is feeling and immediate consciousness, can belong to religion. God and immortality, however, as they are found in such doctrines, are ideas. How many among you – possibly most of you – are firmly convinced of one or other or both of those doctrines, without being on that account pious or having religion. As ideas they can have no greater value in religion than ideas generally.
>
> (Schleiermacher 1996: 96)

The truth of religion thus resides in the subjective experience, and this, by itself, qualifies as proof, validated by first-person authority because the experiencing and feeling subject *knows* best (e.g., as will follow below in the work of Rudolf Otto). The legacy from romanticism concerning (1) religion as subjective experience and emotion; and (2) the validity of first-person authority on religious truth is still thriving. (Just ask around ...) Although more critical of Enlightenment ideas than of religion and the established churches, the romanticist emphasis on religiosity, experience and emotion inadvertently turned religion into a truly human affair. This, in fact, helped pave the way for ever more naturalistic explanations of the nature and origin of religion.

'Positive knowledge', science and the critique of religion

As the Romantics had found religion on the side of emotion and subjectivism, then a more critical emphasis on perception and objectivity could lend a critical blow to their view of religion and religiosity. Such a stance came with the introduction of 'Positivist Philosophy' by the philosopher Auguste Comte (1798–1857). He divided the intellectual history of humanity into three main stages, or 'phases', in a law-like schema where human intellectual life had passed through distinct theoretical conditions which he termed (1) the 'theological or fictitious', (2) the 'metaphysical or abstract' and (3) the 'scientific or positive'. The theological stage, in which the religious specialists exerted the highest authority, was further divided into 'fetishism', 'polytheism' and 'monotheism'. In the metaphysical or abstract stage philosophers and philosophy provided the authority on how to interpret the world. In the final stage, the 'positive', science rules and has the final word on the matters of the world – now based on positive knowledge instead of doctrine or metaphysical speculation. In a sense, Comte really hit the nail on the head, because this view of religion and 'its' conflict with science is quite prevalent in many places. We should note that this distinction between religious knowledge as fictitious and scientific knowledge as valid focuses exclusively on religion as an intellectual activity, and so it is an *intellectualist* theory about religion: religion as an attempt to explain the world and so satisfy the inquiring intellect. True, many mythological themes revolve around questions of the origins of things, but it is unwise to consider this side of religious narrativity the very foundation of religion. On further consideration, this view may owe its popularity to the fact that children's religious upbringing mostly begins with and is scaffolded by just such explanatory origin narratives and what we learn first often becomes what we consider foundational. Thus, intellectualist theories about religion may in turn be explained by child psychology and developmental science.

Evolutionary theory, as presented, for example, in the work of Charles Darwin (1809–82), also contributed to the disrepute of traditional religious claims to explain the world, humanity and history. Now it became obvious that humankind was not created a few thousand years ago. New academic fields in the nineteenth century such as history, philology and archaeology also provided evidence that humankind had invented its gods in its own image. One curious example among many of the traditional Bible-based ways of explaining events in human history was given in the explanation about the Maoris of New Zealand as being originally Jews from Israel! When everything had to be explained on the basis of the Christian bible, where else could humans come from (Pybus 1954)? This single example demonstrates how the explanatory frameworks of religious doctrines (in a literate tradition) were considered both as the adequate and the sufficient sources of true knowledge: nothing more needs to be known than what the doctrines say.

With the increasing modern scientific and evolutionary explanations of the material world, irreconcilable stances towards religion became even more marked than in the earlier Enlightenment era. With time, the philosophical 'critique of religion' gained ever stronger momentum. The anti-religious approaches to religion were intensified by three prominent German philosophers. The first of them, Ludwig Feuerbach (1804–72), must be considered an important key figure in the early critical study of religion. In his view, religion was false and delusional, and it held humans captive in a world of make-believe that prevented them from changing their own fate in life. If religion had any essence, it was an illusion, the result of a psychological projection with imagined gods that could help humans cope in a harsh world. These projective illusions have this-worldly consequences when they are provided with authority and power. Historian of religions Walter H. Capps has succinctly summarised Feuerbach's outlook on religion's deceptions that:

> frustrate all human attempts to promote and take responsibility for better society. By according highest status to a supernatural deity, humankind forfeits the opportunity to improve its own lot. Poor people remain poor; the hungry stay hungry; society remains in a state of disrepair; and God is given all honor and glory … This only demonstrates to Feuerbach that religion is the product of misplaced enthusiasm.
>
> (Capps 1995: 37)

The second 'cultured despiser' of religion here is Karl Marx (1818–83). He was appalled by the social conditions of poor in the early industrial society time, and, as a confessed atheist, he followed Feuerbach in the view of religion as projection and 'false consciousness'. He also notoriously opined, as the *full* quote from 1844 says, that: 'Religion is the sigh of the oppressed creature, the heart of a heartless world, and the soul of soulless conditions. It is the opium of the people' (Marx 1977: 127). So religion is not only a sedative, it is also a 'sigh', a small-scale revolt with at least the possibility of imagining a better and more just world. In the same year, 1844, Marx also stated that the critique of religion had now been concluded [*sic*]. In a more sociological vein he also declared that, 'The ideas of the ruling class are in every epoch the ruling ideas' (Marx and Engels 1973: 54) – perhaps a truism, but one not to be overlooked in any historical, sociological or anthropological analysis of matters religious, ideological or cultural.

The third influential German philosopher was Friedrich Nietzsche (1844–1900). He was almost militantly atheistic in his view of religion. Religion is simply fraudulent to this nihilistic thinker: there is no meaning given in life, neither in heaven nor in holy books. On the positive side, it is because of this void of given meaning and the collapse of religious authority that humanity can finally free itself of religious repression and create its own values and ideas. There is no truth in religion. In Nietzsche's view, religion is a means of exercising power. In the 1895 essay *Anti-Christ*, he articulates this catalogue of mistakes and errors to be found in Christianity:

> In Christianity neither morality nor religion come into contact with reality at any point. Nothing but imaginary *causes* ('God', 'soul', 'ego', 'spirit', 'free will' – or 'unfree will'), nothing but imaginary *effects* ('sin', 'redemption', 'grace', 'punishment', 'forgiveness of sins'). A traffic between imaginary *beings* ('God', 'spirits', 'souls'); an imaginary *natural history* (anthropocentric; a complete lack of the concept of natural causes); an imaginary *psychology* (nothing but self-misunderstandings, interpretations of pleasant or unpleasant general feelings – for example, the condition of the *nervus sympathicus* with the aid of the sign-language of religio-moral idiosyncrasy, 'repentance', 'sting of conscience', 'temptation by the devil', 'the proximity of God'); an imaginary *teleology* (the 'kingdom of God', 'the Last judgment', 'eternal life') – This purely *fictitious world* is distinguished from the world of dreams, very much to its disadvantage, by the fact that latter *mirrors* reality, while the former falsifies, disvalues and denies actuality. Once the concept of 'nature' had been devised as the concept antithetical to 'God', 'natural' had to be the word for 'reprehensible' – this entire fictional world has its roots in *hatred* of the natural (– actuality! –), it is the expression of a profound discontent with the actual ... *But that explains everything.* Who alone has reason to *lie himself* out of actuality? He who *suffers* from it. But to suffer from actuality means to be an abortive actuality ... The preponderance of feelings of displeasure over feelings of pleasure is the *cause* of a fictitious morality and religion: such a preponderance, however, provides the *formula* for *décadence*.
>
> (Nietzsche 2003: 137)

Summing up, it is easy to see how these sceptical and negative views of religion are also common in public affairs and political opinions in many secularised societies today, especially in relation to the role of religion in issues concerning human rights, multiculturalism, education and politics. In other parts of the world, there are precariously maintained borders and balance between the influence of religion and other spheres of society and, in yet others, religion and religious authorities exercise considerable political power.

However, disbelief and doubt are not modern and Western ideas alone. All scriptural traditions have their own critics and sceptics, individual and collective movements, for example in Buddhism, in Chinese philosophy, in the Hindu traditions, in Islam and in Judaism. Traditional societies also have their individual sceptics but mostly the political and economic conditions are so intertwined with religious and cultural frameworks that it is difficult for critical individuals to survive 'outside the law'. So, when the focus here seems Western or 'Eurocentric', it is because we find the most radical criticism of religion there and so also the bases for the developing scholarly interests in studying religion. In the Western world, the history of institutionalised religion led to increased secularisation, separation of church and state and to situations where the 'sacred canopy' of religion – originally suspended over all spheres of life – was increasingly questioned and largely removed. The sociologist Peter L. Berger offers a simple definition of this process: 'By secularization we mean the process by which sectors of society and culture are removed from the domination of religious institutions and symbols' (1990: 125). Later we shall return to this issue, which has since proven to be more complex. However, the 'condition of secularisation' has led to widespread philosophical and theological discussions concerning the validity of religious belief and the truth-conditions of religious language. For most contemporary philosophers, religious language, symbolism and discourse are simply erroneous and futile forms of reasoning (see, e.g., Frankenberry and Penner 1999). As a reaction to these negative stances, others hold that religious language should not be judged simply as an outdated and pre-scientific mode of explaining the world but as a form of coming to grips with the conditions of human existence – 'coping', as noted above, in the views of Paul Tillich (1957).

Essence of religion versus functions of religion

Theological approaches to religions mostly agree that religions have a 'common essence' and refer to something metaphysically real (e.g., 'God') that is considered the origin and cause of religion. Taken at face value, some questions then arise. Are there universal truths in all religions or more in some than in others? Are they all equal? Are religious traditions unique? Will comparisons demonstrate differences more similarities? The Orientalist and scholar of religion Friedrich Max Müller (1823–1900) became famous for his slogan on the merits of the comparative study of religion: 'He who knows one, knows none', and so suggested that to know about religion in general one should not only know one's own but others' as well. Müller was a romantic universalist to who held most religions to be true. Not all were convinced: the German theologian Adolf von Harnack opined (in 1906) that for the study religion in general it was enough to study Christianity and its history and said that, 'Who does not know this religion, knows none, and whoever knows Christianity and its history, knows all.' In von Harnack's opinion, Christianity was exclusive, the only true religion, and so there was no need to compare. In addition, in the end, how should one go about proving the validity of one or the other view? Neither value judgement (for that is what they are) is empirically tractable in any way.

The agnostic, academic approaches in the study of religion handle such matters differently: they acknowledge that religious traditions are made by humans as social constructions. What else (Engler 2004)? Now, the question arises: what is the essence of social constructions? Very simply stated, *they are social* – shared by human groups that have ideas and values in common. Thus, the question of the truth of religion recedes and the value of the function of religion increases. Already in antiquity, philosophers judged religion and piety to be good for morality, individual and public. The philosopher Immanuel Kant (1724–1804) held that religion (in his case Christianity) was directly related to and sustained the ethics of humanity. He rejected theological and metaphysical speculations about proving the existence of the divine, God, because this would be to talk about something that is beyond the limits of human experience. However, Kant saw the *ideas* of God, the soul and the world to be effective as 'regulative', that is, suitable for guiding humans towards moral and ethical modes of conduct. This moralistic stance also meant that for Kant, the inner life was more important than the outward ritual quest to please God, which Kant somewhat condescendingly termed 'statutory religion'. In Kant's view, religious representations become symbolic instead of revelatory: Jesus symbolises moral perfection, the Devil symbolises the evil tendencies in humans, and God and 'eternal life' are symbols for ideas that we cannot express otherwise. According to Kant, religious representations have this symbolic character because religion springs from the desires of the human mind. This is Kant's 'Copernican Turn': religion comes from human nature and not 'from outside' in the form of revelation. Needless to say, he had problems with contemporaneous religious authorities. In his time, he was a moralistic rebel. He was also a functionalist in his view of religion: religion is good for morality, and morality is good for an orderly society and so it secures also the lives of individuals.

A more psychological and emotional evaluation of the function of religion was given by Ludwig Feuerbach (as above). In his view, religion is existentially useful as humankind has posited another, ideal 'second' world where they can find comfort and justification, over and above this 'first' material world in which many live miserable lives. Religion is a human projection and basically a lie, but a comforting one. Thus, with the functionalist views epitomised in these three philosophers the focus shifts from what religion 'is' to what religion 'does' for humans, for better or worse, and how and why it does so. The effects of their revolutionary insights continue to guide research today.

Intellectualism: religion as explanation

The functions of religious traditions can also been seen as 'epistemic', that is, religion serves an intellectual purpose by providing world views and explanation of the world (as briefly noted above). In short: religions may provide cosmologies with explanations of the origins, functions and values related to the natural, social and supernatural realms. However mythical or inadequate such cosmological explanations may seem from a scientific perspective, they do have cognitive functions by providing more or less ordered world views. This development in theory arrives later, however, and enters the theoretical stage in the late nineteenth century primarily with two British scholars: Edward Burnett

Tylor (1832–1917), the first professor of anthropology, and the classicist James George Frazer (1854–1941). Tylor's heritage in anthropology has been substantial. His minimalistic and consciously simple definition of religion is: 'The belief in spiritual beings'. In a qualifying statement that let his social evolutionist convictions shine through, he added: 'Animism characterizes tribes very low in the scale of humanity, and thence ascends, deeply modified in its transmission, but from the first to last preserving an unbroken continuity, into the midst of high modern culture'. So 'Animism is, in fact, the groundwork of the Philosophy of Religion, from that of savages up to that of civilized men' (1871: 10). Tylor was firmly committed to the idea of the 'psychic unity of mankind', as originally termed by the German ethnologist Adolf Bastian (1826–1915). The basic idea is that all humans have the same cognitive abilities functions but that the use of these abilities depended on society and culture. The 'ancient savage philosophers' were curious and so, to Tylor, 'primitive man' was a rationalist thinker. The belief in spiritual beings was the outcome of rational thought processes in attempts to explain life and death, dreams, and unexplainable events as, for example, when the ancient Egyptians believed that the ram god *Khnum* was responsible for the annual fluctuations of the surface level of the river Nile. Animism was popular in anthropology for several decades, but then it faded and was forgotten – or methodologically 'forbidden' because of the imagined implicit scale of evolutionist social evaluation – ranking cultures and societies from low to high. Unexpectedly, some of the ideas of animism have now surfaced in the cognitive science of religion (more below) and somewhat vindicated Tylor's position.

Sir James George Frazer's ideas were in many ways similar. He wrote about 'our primitive philosopher' who first resorted to magic back then in primordial time because he believed the universe to be ordered and therefore could be manipulated in ways similar to the cause-and-effect relations now known from science and technology. However, magic proved erroneous and its tools useless and so Frazer characterised magic as the 'bastard sister of science'. When at some point in Frazer's fictive history of humankind the 'primitive philosopher' realised that magic did not do its job properly, he turned to religion. And religion involves a fundamentally different world view, for as Frazer explains:

> if religion involves, first, a belief in superhuman beings who rule the world, and second, an attempt to win their favour, it clearly assumes that the course of nature is to some extent elastic or variable and that we can persuade or induce the mighty beings who control it to deflect, for our benefit, the current of events from the channel in which they would otherwise flow. Now this implied elasticity or variability of nature is directly opposed to the principles of magic as well as of science, both of which assume that the processes of nature are rigid and invariable in their operations.
>
> (1993: 51)

And so the primitive philosopher 'came to rest … in a new system of faith and practice, which seemed to offer a solution of his harassing doubts and a substitute, however precarious, for that sovereignty over nature which he had reluctantly abdicated' (Frazer 1993: 58). This conjectural history reveals Frazer's view of religion as not only intellectualist but also as instrumentalist in the view of religion as a coping mechanism: religion assists humans in their lives, from the practical to the cognitive and the emotional. The intellectualist understanding of religion as explanatory has been quite enduring, and it is still current, for the simple reason that most (if not all) religions have a cosmology (i.e. world view) at their centre and that is, as noted above, what most children learn bits and pieces from. The systems of beliefs, practices and institutions would not make sense if they were not embedded in a cosmology. Not all religious traditions construct the same cosmological dimensions, of course, but that is no reason to wholly reject the intellectualist point of view. The function of religions, religious traditions and beliefs and practices can be many, and the intellectual, explanatory functions are among them.

The history of religions: origins, developments, texts

The non-confessional study of religion in the secular university came into being in the late half of the nineteenth century, first in Switzerland and the Netherlands (both in 1876). It was known then as 'the history of religions'. Like many other academic fields, it arose slowly and because of its subject matter the academic development was fraught with struggles and controversies. Note the 's' in 'religions', indicating that this study went beyond the Judaeo-Christian tradition, and that it was different from both the theological scrutiny of Christian doctrine and from the previous philosophical speculations about religion in the singular that almost exclusively drew on Christian traditions. The first approaches in the history of religions focused on history and sacred texts; this was a logical extension of critical textual studies in liberal theology which had demonstrated that the composition of the Bible was a result of historical conditions and not of divine intervention. Thus, the Pentateuch, 'The Five Books of Moses', were not written by Moses as dictated by Jahweh, but were later compilations influenced by neighbouring cultures and religions (dates and conditions are still being debated). Already in 1835 the theologian David Friedrich Strauss (1808–74) had scandalised the German theological community with the highly controversial work *The Life of Jesus, Critically Examined* (2012). The biblical accounts were purged of the supernatural and miraculous elements which Strauss considered mythological inserts that were the results of wishful thinking in the earliest Christian communities intended to support the conviction that Jesus was indeed the Messiah. However, Strauss considered religion to be real enough and that it did have an essence, namely *ideas* and *thoughts*, instead of a divine being. Strauss insisted that the methods he applied to the study of early Christianity were also, in principle, applicable to all religions with textual sources, and his work engendered a new approach to historical and textual sources in the study of the world's literate religious traditions in general. With Strauss's historical critical philological method, the 'history of religions' was born as an academic pursuit, if not yet institutionalised as an independent discipline. Table 2.1 presents an overview of some important differences between literal religious readings and the historical critical philological method (as it has been labelled since).

The late nineteenth century witnessed the rise of a keen interest in historical studies of individual religions, from antiquity as well as from Asia and in the general public as well as in the academy. The philological mastery of ancient and Asian languages became a hallmark of erudition because the method demanded that the scholar should be able to read the sources in the original language to fully grasp their meaning in the original historical and social contexts. Consequently, the history of religions became a very language-oriented discipline focusing mainly on origins and developments in doctrinal and elite religion as these had been recorded in the world's literate religious traditions. In this manner religion turned out to be primarily a 'textual object' for many scholars, not a social one nor a psychological one. The history of religions consisted mainly in the study of sacred, normative texts and their interpretations. These are still prominent tasks, not least because many of the literate religious traditions are extremely rich in materials that can be very difficult to work with (e.g., the study of Buddhism may involve knowledge of languages such as Pali, Chinese and Japanese). With the widened perspectives on religion spurred by the new knowledge of the many traditions came an ethos of research with considerations on how different religious traditions could or should be treated. The emphasis has mostly been on impartiality, irreducibility and

Table 2.1 Comparison of literal religious readings and historical philological method

Dimension of discourse	Literal method	Philological method
Origin/source of discourse	Supernatural (to be obeyed)	Human imagination (to be analysed)
Chronology/importance of historical dimension	Ahistorical/time does not matter: eternal validity	Historical: elements must be analysed in their time
Criticism/doubt	As heresy	As foundation for study
Ontology (what there is)	Includes the supernatural	Only natural (includes human thought)
Epistemology (knowledge of what there is)	Knowledge as accepted through authority	Knowledge of what can be verified
Medium of distribution	Divine language	Philological sources in original language
Method of reading/ interpreting discourse	Literal: 'God's own words'	Critical: Situated historical expressions of human concerns
Interpretive community	Devout insiders	Critical academic scholars
Ultimate sacred authority	The supernatural source	None

understanding the traditions 'from within' without passing judgements on the traditions studied: attitudes that may land the historian of religions in problems with relativism. This is definitely different from the critique of religion as referred to above (see, e.g., Cox 2010: 48–72).

Religion and the individual

When Feuerbach, Marx and Nietzsche launched their critiques of religion as 'false', they based their views primarily on introspection into a familiar tradition, the Christian Protestant one and their own ideas about individuals' projections, reflections and actions. Before the influential work of Émile Durkheim, most theory of religion was 'individualistic' in the sense that it viewed religion as a phenomenon in and for humans as individuals. The general attention was turned towards 'i-religion' (see p. viii above). From a historical perspective, it is obvious that this orientation is an outcome of the Christian theological effects on European intellectual history. It has had a lasting influence, ranging from (for example) Paul's letters in the New Testament, the teachings of the Puritan Fathers, the works of the Christian philosopher Søren Kierkegaard (1813–55) and on to contemporary interests in individual spirituality. The first-person 'bias' is also a straightforwardly intuitive result of introspection: 'I act because of the beliefs I have' – and therefore individual belief intuitively appears primary. A more problematic corollary of the individualist perspective is that of 'first-person authority': that the believing person herself best knows her religion. In this manner, 'insiders' are intuitively and 'naturally' privileged (Jensen 2011a).

The individualistic approach to religion fell into two broad categories. One was not confined to any one specific academic discipline or field but mainly looked at religion as *religiosity*, that is, the religious beliefs and practices of individuals, whereas the other was related to a more specialised psychology of religion (and, in more recent years, the cognitive science of religion). Actual psychological investigations into religion only began around 1900 with the pioneers Wilhelm Wundt (1832–1920) and William James (1842–1910). Wundt was the first to call himself a 'psychologist', and he also counts as the inventor of experimental methods in psychology (in 1879). Wundt took a deep interest in the relationship between culture and mind and how the study of mythology and religion could clarify how the human mind functions, individually and collectively. His work on 'folk psychology' investigated the mutual relations between individuals and their socio-cultural environments. Thus he became the main creator of cultural psychology, which later had noted influences on cultural anthropology and studies of religion and culture in native traditions of North America (Cole 1998: 27–35).

The German liberal theologian Rudolf Otto (1869–1937) espoused an entirely different psychological approach, one that influenced the later experiential phenomenology of religion. His ideas about religious experience are fully meshed with his Christian Protestant theology as can be seen from his main work *The Idea of the Holy: An Inquiry into the Non-rational Factor in the Idea of the Divine and Its Relation to the Rational* (1923). By the title, it would seem to belong to systematic theology but contemporary German theologians considered it to be more psychological about human experience than theological about God. Instead, it achieved profound influence in and on the growing field of religious studies and later notable pro-religion scholars such as Joachim Wach, G. V. D. Leeuw, Mircea Eliade and Paul Tillich(Alles 1996). Although now a classic and a must-read for scholars of religion, *The Idea of the Holy* is a quite peculiar work as it concerns not so much what a potentially theological question of what the holy might be in itself but focuses on the human responses to the felt experience of the holy. Otto assumed that these responses were not based on empirical perception nor on conceptual thought, but on a special kind of intuition, the 'sensus numinis' – a sense of 'The Numinous', that is, the sacred stripped of its moral and ethical dimensions but that which strikes humans with awe and wonder. It is a mystery, Otto says, one that fascinates human but also makes them tremble, so he characterises it as the *'mysterium tremendum et fascinans'* which reflects the holy as an experience of the 'wholly other' (*'das Ganz Andere'*). To make matters more complicated, Otto declared that it was *'arrethôn'*, Greek for something that you cannot speak about, but which he then wrote several hundred pages about! Otto also believed that this kind of experience was universal and global where it now obvious that it was Christian and ethnocentric (Fujiwara 2017). He also held that religion was a unique phenomenon *'sui generis'* (of its own kind) and thus it should and could only be understood in its 'own terms'. How that belief might lead on to a secure epistemic footing for the study of religion is also a mystery, but the history of the history of religions has been a peculiar at times quite religious one and views analogous to Otto's have surfaced in many contexts (Ambasciano 2019).

Quite different was the work of William James. He was primarily a philosopher, but he also did significant work in the psychology of religion, not least in *The Varieties of Religious Experience* (1902). James's approach was decidedly individualistic, as he suggested that religious experience and religious experts ('virtuosi') should be the primary topics in the study of religion rather than religious institutions as the latter are but the social products of experience and experts. He drew a sharp distinction between personal and institutional religion. James further held that intense and extreme (if not outright pathological) varieties of religions or religious experience, such as those of mystics, were of deep concern to psychologists as they may help elucidate the normal mental functions. As a pragmatist philosopher, he had an ingenious solution to the problem of the truth of the reported experiences of mystics: they are true for the experiencer but for others they are just ideas to be considered and so there can be no claim to truth without the personal experience. There is, however, a deep difference between having an experience and claiming that the object of the experience exists beyond individual experience (dreams come to mind). Like most scholars in the recent cognitive science of religion, James was interested in the 'inside-out' processes as his focus was on the 'producers' of religion, with less emphasis on the internalisation of religion. Interestingly, the sociologist Max Weber (1864–1920) paid close attention to the psychological functions of religion in individuals, how they were motivated by their joys, fears and doubts: Weber's analyses of sociological and economic matters are often both historical *and* psychological, for instance that Puritan Protestants in New England acted as they did because they believed, felt, hoped and feared in specific ways conditioned by their religious tradition(s).

The controversies over the psychological human 'value' of religion were clearly displayed in the theoretical oppositions between Sigmund Freud and Carl Gustav Jung (1875–1961). Freud's scathing critique of religion has already been dealt with in the introduction above. He was not really interested *in* religion; his theoretical object was neurosis, and his main concern with religion was to free humans from it, and so his stance is avowedly emancipatory. Aspects of Freud's work are at best applicable to the study of 'i-religion': how individual lives are moulded by childhood experience and other psychological and socio-cultural factors such as authority, sexuality and repression. It is more difficult to build a theory of religion on Freud's understanding of religion as 'illusion' (Freud 1961). Universities are not likely to fund and host departments of 'comparative illusions'.

On the contrary, Jung's idea of religion was positive but also normative as it also concerned the esteemed value of the right *kind* of religion. For Jung, the religious traditions mirrored the workings of the human psyche. Religions are filled with collective mythologies about referents (gods, ancestors, etc.) that do not exist but are to be understood as *codes* for psychological features in the development of the 'ego', the individual psyche. The actual theoretical object of his work on myths and religious beliefs is psychological. Therefore, religious beliefs and their referents ('Gods', etc.) are reinterpreted as *really* being psychological in the light of his premises concerning 'depth psychology' and 'archetypes'. Although some archetypical ideas and motives are undoubtedly found in many myths and cosmologies, it turns out that Jung's work (like Freud's) is problematic to apply to the study of religion. Both, however, have become leading figures in circles that have adopted their creeds. The cross-field of psychology and religion has witnessed more than its fair share of players with emancipatory or nostalgic agendas, as either critics or caretakers of religion. The focus on individual religion is important and necessary, but the academic study of this subject must definitely be more scholarly and scientific than religious. The psychology *of* religion should not be confused with any *religious* psychology: religious traditions have their own theories about the 'inside' of humans. Such theories can be extraordinarily interesting, but not a topic for analysis here.

Individual religiosity is a sensitive subject and one that is theoretically and methodologically complicated, difficult to assess, measure and control for (e.g., in experiments). Insiders and outsiders may disagree profoundly, and believers may be affronted by what they conceive of as reductionist approaches and attempts to explain their belief and convictions 'away'. Auspiciously, over the past generation the psychology of religion has reasserted itself as a non-apologetic and more sober academic enterprise (Wulff 1997; Hood et al. 2009; Stausberg 2013). Of special recent interest are research subjects such as religious development, the relevance of attachment styles in childhood, the development of personality traits in adolescence and adulthood, the influence of authority, suggestibility, and ritual, religion and health (Paloutzian and Park 2013). The question of whether and how the religiosity of individuals depends on their social environments is also complex: do certain social or individual forces lead to religiosity or to specific kinds of religious orientations? Are individuals' personality traits responsible for their religious orientation or, conversely, does religion influence personality? The problems in the contemporary psychology of religion are many and the field has just begun to move out of the Western and Christian domains in which it has traditionally worked. Religion *is* individual and if it were not, there could be no collective or social religion, no institutional or traditional religion. To this we now turn.

Religion, collective and social

In contrast to the individualistic perspectives in and of psychology, sociological and anthropological approaches to religion have been heirs to Émile Durkheim's programme (see Chapter 1) in their focus on the *social* levels and dimensions of religion. That is, they focus on 'e-religion' as the collective representations and practices of groups and the institutions that the practices refer to in Durkheim's 'moral community'. It is *all* social and all shared and so, on the social level, groups would reason that, 'We act the way we do because of the beliefs that *we* have.' In this perspective, the most indicative factors of religiosity are social conditions and norms: individuals become religious because others around them already are and so individuals become members of a religious community – a social entity.

As one of the founding figures of sociology, Émile Durkheim can be said to have basically *invented* the social level of analysis. He discovered how human life can be described as governed by social realities, 'social facts', and that society could be studied as an entity in itself. Roughly in the same epoch, the linguist Ferdinand de Saussure (1857–1913) discovered how language in *general* could be studied as a system, as a theoretical entity, separately from its history and the practice of it (Saussure 2012). Taken together, the perspectives of Durkheim and Saussure demonstrate how language is an eminently 'social fact', and so is religion. Consider the analogy with the game of chess: the rules have been invented, they have a history, but to play chess the set of rules is a 'social fact' to be followed; just moving the pieces around without knowing the rules would be meaningless. Likewise, social life, language, culture and religion become meaningful because the sets of rules exist (have histories) and because there are systemic relations involved in human action, speech and cultural life, and so also in religious beliefs and acts. This is not to claim that religions (or other social and cultural phenomena) are neatly ordered as stable systems but only that a certain measure of systemic relations and constraints must be present or they become meaningless. Table 2.2 shows possibilities in method and theory in the study of these subjects, which may help indicate the many sides of the study of religion and religiosity.

Table 2.2 Possible modes for the study of e- and i-religion

Religion	General hypotheses	Specific analyses	Social: e-religion	Individual: i-religion
Genetic: origins of religion	Origin in evolution, mind, society or...?	History, archae-ology, language history, migrations, etc.	Externalising religion: creating rules	Religious development: cognition and emotion
Functional: functions of religion	Religion in culture and society: causes and effects	Anthropology, sociology, politics, etc.	Systems of institutions, rules, norms, values	Religious practice: motivation and action

Table 2.2 demonstrates how religion (like language, music or chess) may be studied in a genetic dimension: how did religion arise in cultural evolution? How did a particular religion emerge in history? Functional investigations at the social level will analyse how religion relates to society, politics and economy. Genetic questions at the individual level investigate how religion is acquired, and functional questions at the individual level address how religion 'works' in the mind or how 'it feels'. The study of how it feels to play chess is obviously different from a study of the rules and combinations of moves. Similarly, the study of individuals' mastery and use of cultural codes is different from the study of the systems of codes. It is important to keep these distinctions in mind in order not to confuse the modes of investigation.

Anthropological and sociological approaches have been abundant and influential in the study of religion conceived as collective and social patterns and networks of norms, rules and meanings that provide social cohesion and structure, from the early theories of the social and moral nature of religion as social 'glue' (e.g., Durkheim), across studies of functions of magic as communal technology in farming and fishing and the emotional and cognitive functions of religion (Malinowski 1992) to how religious systems provide semantic and symbolic means and patterns in complex collective world views (Evans-Pritchard 1956). Others have focused on the relations between religion, politics and social structure in the theories of 'symbolism' or correspondence that were prevalent in British *social* anthropology for many decades (e.g., Morris 1987). Both theories focused on how religion 'symbolises' or 'corresponds' to social order, structure and function. Central issues concerned beliefs and behaviours in and of groups as well as their systems of classification, that is, how world views are constructed and organised as cultural and mental 'grids' (e.g., Douglas 1966). Both British and French social anthropology were very productive during most of the twentieth century, theoretically as well empirically, because the colonial situations allowed anthropologists to work almost wherever they wished, and often they did so as actual members and employees of the colonial administrations. North American *cultural* anthropology developed differently with many studies of the disappearing native American cultural and religious traditions. Many American anthropologists took their inspiration from folklore studies, linguistics, philosophy and psychology. Cultural anthropologists advanced the 'interpretive turn' in anthropology with studies of symbols and meanings in culture and religion as sources of 'conceptions of the world' for individuals and groups (e.g., Geertz; see Chapter 1). In France, Claude Lévi-Strauss combined ideas from cultural anthropology and linguistics in structural anthropology as a way to discover universal aspects and 'hidden' codes in human culture in general. Lévi-Strauss studied culture as consisting of ideas and pointed out how the universal aspects of the *'ésprit humain'* are not in the head (the English translation 'human *mind*' blurs this idea) but in culture. (e.g., Lévi-Strauss 1969, 2004).

As the linguist who discovers a new language strives to analyse its rules and meanings, so may anthropologists study cultures and religions, and discover the elements, such as the symbols, norms and values that cultures and religions are composed of, and how they work in practice. There is a clear analogy here to Saussure's distinction between *'langue'* and *'parole'* in linguistics. There are systems and the articulations of systems in practice. The point is that there must be some degree of order by which symbols, norms and values are connected in cultures and religions (Leach 1976). However, the order of systems may not be accurately replicated at the level of practice: not all speakers of a language speak it in the same way, and not all religious individuals stick to all the practices all the time. This does not, however indicate that systems do not exist, only that some use them inadequately. Instead of talking about 'systems', which may convey the idea of something static and fixed, scholars tend to use such terms as 'clusters', 'networks' or 'patterns' depending on the object of study. Nonetheless, there must be *some* amount of order, some constraints, or it would all be incomprehensible, like a language without any grammar or games without rules. It is that amount of order or 'recurrent patterns' that interests not only scholars in the study of religion but also social scientists such as anthropologists, sociologists and political scientists. Then again, the genetic questions of how it has all come 'out of our minds' in human evolution is yet another realm to study.

Religion and evolution and religion in evolution

Renewed interest in human evolution and new inspirations from cognitive science are the latest additions to the study of religion over the past few decades. These two theoretical perspectives have merged in the research of a group of scientists. The question of whether there are valid explanations of the origin of religion has recently occupied both evolutionary psychologists and cognitive scientists (Boyer 2001; Jensen 2009a). The work of the anthropologist Pascal Boyer (see Chapter 1) has been particularly influential in this 'cognitive turn' in the study of religion where he has turned the idea of 'religion as explanation' on its head (Boyer 2001: 11–12). The intellectualist theory about religion is 'all false', according to Boyer: he explains that religion is simply the evolutionary outcome of the ways in which human cognition works. Religion is an epiphenomenon: a non-adaptive by-product of the evolution of large brains with too much imagination. Religious ideas are 'catchy', nothing more. They have spread among humans because they are 'counter-intuitive' and 'attention grabbing'. Here, Boyer builds on the anthropologist Dan Sperber's notion of an 'epidemiology of representations', that is, how ideas spread: when representations are distributed in a population and stabilise they form 'culture' (Sperber 1996). Not anything goes, however, and so some cultures and religions are more receptive or resistant to some ideas than others, and thus the idea of an 'immunology' of culture and religion is also applicable in the study of the spread of religious ideas (Sørensen 2004).

Many cognitive scientists of religion are critical of religion and consider it but a by-product of evolution, something that unfortunately happened as human brains grew more complex, imaginative and projective. There is almost a new echo of Feuerbach's critique of religion in the cognitive science of religion. Here is what Walter Capps wrote in 1995 (before the cognitive turn in the study of religion) on the 'essence question' among some earlier critical voices on religion:

> The new wave of Feuerbachian-inspired thinkers turned the paradigm in another direction. They considered the proposal that religion owns a *sine qua non*, but they were unwilling to assume that religion possesses an indubitable quality. In their view it is quite conceivable that religion has an essence, but it is possible, too, that the essence is unreal. What if religion is a mere projection? This is what Feuerbach called it, and Karl Marx as well, following his influence. What if it turns out to be mere illusion (as Sigmund Freud proposed)? What if it is produced out of the resources of the imagination? Or, instead of being a product of rationality, ethical awareness, or aesthetic sensitivity, what if it is elicited simply out of whatever mental apparatuses are responsible for creating fictions and figments?
>
> (Capps 1995: 37–8)

Religion is unlikely to have been designed or 'selected for' in human evolution. It is too complex a phenomenon (like music for instance) to have evolved as a 'unit'. 'It' may well be seen as a by-product, a 'spandrel' of human cognitive evolution, but still 'it' may have played a positive role in human social and cultural evolution (Powell and Clarke 2012). Below is a list proposed by the anthropologist Scott Atran and the psychologist Ara Norenzayan which clearly demonstrates how complex 'it' is and why it is, accordingly, unimaginable that there should be any singular explanation of religion:

> In every society, there are 1. Widespread counterfactual and counterintuitive beliefs in supernatural agents (gods, ghosts, goblins, etc.) 2. Hard-to-fake public expressions of costly material commitments to supernatural agents, that is, offering and sacrifice (offerings of goods, property, time, life) 3. Mastering by supernatural agents of people's existential anxieties (death, deception, disease, catastrophe, pain, loneliness, injustice, want, loss) 4.

Ritualized, rhythmic sensory coordination of (1), (2), and (3), that is, communion (congregation, intimate fellowship, etc.)

In all societies there is an evolutionary canalization and convergence of (1), (2), (3), and (4) that tends toward what we shall refer to as 'religion'; that is, passionate communal displays of costly commitments to counterintuitive worlds governed by supernatural agents. Although these facets of religion emerge in all known cultures and animate most individual human beings in the world, there are considerable individual and cultural differences in the degree of religious commitment. The question as to the origin and nature of these intriguing and important differences we leave open.

(Atran and Norenzayan 2004: 713–14)

The two authors present 'an evolutionary perspective that envisions religion as a converging by-product of several cognitive and emotional mechanisms that evolved for mundane adaptive tasks' (Atran and Norenzayan 2004: 714). Their description of the topics indicates the scope of the complexity of the question, but there can be little doubt that some other *non*-religious social behavioural patterns, 'communal practice', must have been in place before religion could evolve. Thinking alone did not do it (Sterelny 2018; Turner et al. 2017).

Humans need not have any special brain module or mechanism to be religious – it is all already there and evolved for other 'mundane' purposes: if you talk to your god you talk as if to another person. Commerce with the gods at many points resemble human interaction, only that it is mostly twisted and tweaked, sometimes invisible or at other times almost grotesquely inflated and proportioned, the Vatican 'house of god' is certainly not an ordinary house.

Human religiosity evolved out of yet other psychological dispositions, such as the human moral proclivities acquired through evolution. Thus, instead of traditionally seeing religion as providing morality it could be the other way around: that evolved human moral psychology could account, at least partially, for religion as a complex social phenomenon, one that rides piggy-back on evolved moral psychology. This has been suggested forcefully through recent work in moral psychology (Haidt 2012). It is conspicuous, at least to a scholar of religion, that the moral foundations registered by scientists working in experimental moral psychology are seemingly found in all the world's religions.

The question of the role of religion in human evolution (social and cultural) turns, not least, on the possibility and potential function of 'group selection': does religion – in all its complexity – support group survival, enhance a group's 'fitness' and provide a given population with means for cooperation and competition vis-à-vis other groups? Charles Darwin thought so, because a group with high morals would fare better than those with lower morals. This line of thought was pursued by biologist David Sloan Wilson in his 2002 work which opens with the illuminating quote from Darwin (in 1871):

There can be no doubt that a tribe including many members who, from possessing in a high degree the spirit of patriotism, fidelity, obedience, courage, and sympathy, were always ready to aid one another, and to sacrifice themselves for the common good would be victorious over most other tribes; and this would be natural selection.

(Wilson 2002: 5)

Although Darwin does not explicitly refer to religion here, many of these items come with religion as a 'unified system of beliefs and practices' (as was Durkheim's view of religion). To Wilson and others of a functionalist persuasion religion functions, once it is in place, as a 'unifying system' of social, moral and cognitive coordination. Other questions concern the origins of and status that these functions may have had in evolution, in both individuals and groups. It is reasonable to assume that a social invention as complex and enduring as religion must have brought some adaptive advantage or the underlying psychological mechanisms would have been selected out. This is the *cui bono?* (Latin: to the benefit of whom?) question of religion in evolutionary terms: is religion to the benefit of the individual, the group, society or culture? Darwin and, much later, Wilson agree on group selection' which has (otherwise) been anathema in most of biology for decades. However, recent theoretical revolutions in epigenetics on the roles that the environment, natural as well as social, play in the life of organisms demonstrate that they are not as genetically predetermined as commonly imagined. Genes for various behaviours can be turned on and off, so there is no immutable biological mechanism that prevents religious 'unifying systems' from influencing the behaviour of individuals and groups. Humans are exceptionally apt at responding to their social, cultural, emotional and cognitive environments and in most of human history (some kind of) religion has been part of these environments. Religion, and all that constitutes it, provides humans with something to 'act on' and 'think with', for example in terms of shared cognitive models in their world views and their emotional responses in activities such as rituals. In the theory of the psychologist Merlin Donald, humans have 'hybrid minds' that are created and function in *culture* as a distributed cognitive network. Hybrid minds have direct experience of the world as other animals but they are also embedded in cultural webs, such as those provided by religious traditions, be they of Japanese Shinto, African Nuer, Thai Mahayana, Iranian Shi'ism, American Calvinist or any other known religious tradition, because it is a basic feature of religious traditions that they function in this way. That also means that the individual mind is exposed to 'deep enculturation' (Donald 2001). In theories of social and cultural evolution such as Wilson's and Donald's, religion has played an important role (for better or worse) in the evolution of humankind. Theirs is yet another and more positive evolutionary view of the origins and functions of religion. Nevertheless, as their view is based on approximately the same evidence as the other views, it becomes apparent here that the 'subject matter and theoretical object' distinction is essential. Thus, to the question 'What is religion?' the answer will mostly be 'Who do you ask?' to finish this brief survey of the 'idea of religion', Table 2.3 summarises the various views and ideas of religion and who typically work or have worked with them.

Table 2.3 The problems in the study of religion and the kinds of scholars involved

Problem	Scholars (and audience)
Truth in religion versus criticism of religion	Theologians, philosophers
Romanticism and emotional religion	Philosophers, theologians, literati, artists
Science and the critique of religion	Philosophers, general public
Essence of religion vs. functions of religion	Theologians, philosophers
Intellectualism: religion as explanation	Anthropologists, general public
History of religions: origins, developments, texts	Historians of religion, philologists
Religion and the individual	Psychologists, theologians
Religion, collective and social	Anthropologists, sociologists
Religion and evolution and religion in evolution	Evolutionary psychologists, anthropologists

3   Types and elements of religion

The tautological definition: on the sacred and the profane

This chapter presents a number of exploratory tools for describing and classifying the many kinds of religion, in history and in today's world. It should thus help us further to understand and explain religions past and present. On the surface, the wide range of religions may appear so different that comparison and generalisation would seem impossible. It is also quite problematic, as we have already noticed, to talk about 'a religion' as if it were tangible thing, a neatly bounded object. It is not so.

On the other hand, the sheer fact that we do talk about 'religions' as belonging to some kind of class, using an abstract noun for a concept to denote that class, should make us realise that, as particular and different as these religions may appear, they nevertheless have some things in common as do games, music and pizzas (Jensen 2017). What they do have in common and how, where and why they differ are the subjects here below.

A very basic distinction in religion, probably the most fundamental one because it is used to discern religion in the first place, is that of the *sacred* and the *profane*, and so that is the place to begin. Although known as a common distinction since antiquity in Greece and in Rome, it was the French sociologist Émile Durkheim who clearly formulated it as an analytical distinction for the study of religion in 1912:

> All known religious beliefs, whether simple or complex, present a common quality: they presuppose a classification of things – the real or ideal things men represent for themselves – into two classes, two opposite kinds, generally designated by two distinct terms effectively translated by the words profane and sacred. The division of the world into two comprehensive domains, one sacred, the other profane, is the hallmark of religious thought.
>
> (2001: 36)

Durkheim continued to explain how all kinds of objects, persons and actions may be sacralised, that is, made sacred. The scope of things sacred varies greatly among religions and there is no fixed catalogue – there need not be gods to worship. And so, he affirmed that on this view even the oldest form of

Theravada Buddhism is also to be considered religion 'because in the absence of gods, it accepts the existence of sacred things, namely the Four Noble Truths and the practices derived from them' (Durkheim 2001: 37). Durkheim has a point, and so, in this book, all variations of Buddhism are among the religious traditions of this world. Not all religious traditions refer to superhuman beings in the same way or scope, but they do contain or refer to matters 'sacred'. This is, actually, why we call religions 'religion' – admittedly a somewhat circular way of defining, yes, but tautology is inescapable in this kind of definition: 'Only if there is a division of matters into the two categories sacred and profane do we talk about religion.' If there is a *sine qua non* ('that without which it is not') for the definition of religion, the 'sacred and profane' distinction is a most plausible candidate. Thus, in this case it is a *difference* between the ordinary and the special and not a substance or essence, which is the necessary condition of the definition. Following the Durkheimian tradition and adding dimensions from the more recent cognitive science of religion, Jesper Sørensen stipulates on the construction of the sacred domain: 'The sacred domain thus involves special beings violating ordinary ontological assumptions, special and privileged discursive repertoires, and special modes of interaction' (2007: 63). This makes good sense because not only beings but also many other 'objects' in religious traditions can be special and violate ordinary ontological assumptions: Words can be sacred and so can mountaintops.

The question of the 'essence' of religion has been a stubborn one in the study of religion. Not least, the influence of the philosopher G. W. F. Hegel (1770–1831) inspired earlier generations of scholars of religion to talk quite freely of the 'essence of religion' (Capps 1995: 1–52). Very often, by 'essence', they actually meant the *referents* of religious traditions, namely the superhuman or supernatural agents or other 'marks' of a transcendent, sacred realm. It is difficult to discern what the essence of religion is or possibly could be. There is, after all, a conspicuous difference between looking for an essence of a concept or an essence of a phenomenon. The quest for essence was a focal point in a metaphysical tradition that considered phenomena as manifestations of 'underlying essences', that is, of the real, unchanging core or 'nature of things'. Whenever the idea of a transcendent 'essence of religion' appears, there is normally a Hegelian, if not an implicit Platonic or religious inspiration behind the conception. Rudolf Otto, for instance, assumed that the divine was the essence behind the appearance of the holy. When humans have religious experiences, it is because there actually is something that prompts the experiences, says Otto. Schleiermacher stated that when humans feel a 'createdness' it is because there is a creator. When people believe in god, they will say that it is because there is a god, or 'how could you be in love if there is no loved one?'

In current philosophical and psychological terms, such subjective arguments are not valid; one's own first-person feeling of some cause or referent is no guarantee for the existence of that cause or referent (Jensen 2011a). In the perspectives of cognitive psychology, it is understandable that humans look for such essences as it is part of our most basic psychological make-up to assume the existence of essences and causes. Moreover, reporting a feeling of the 'numinous' is categorically different from talking about the feeling of a mosquito bite.

However, the preference of humans to divide their worlds into the two realms of the sacred and the profane is a psychological, anthropological, historical and sociological fact and thus a 'something' that is amenable to study. Science is regrettably unable to refer to anything transcendental or metaphysical as evidence or validation.

Since Durkheim, many scholars have used the sacred/profane distinction in defining, analysing and understanding religion. Among them, the historian of religions Mircea Eliade insistently promoted it in a large number of publications as that feature around which religions revolve (see, e.g., Eliade 1987). However, Eliade was quite elusive on the issue of the meaning of the 'sacred' and never offered a clear definition of religion. The closest is a statement to the effect that the sacred is a 'structure in human consciousness' and that would place it within the realm of psychology. In Eliade's view, humans cannot escape their propensity to categorise the world in this fundamental dichotomy: it is a way of setting up distinctions in amorphous space and time and so creating a sacred cosmology. Historical and anthropological records certainly attest to this, but there is a marked difference between looking for religion as a public and observable affair in society and history and looking for it in consciousness. It never became clear how Eliade connected these two realms, but his intuition was sound enough because religion *has* to come from somewhere and that somewhere can hardly be anything other than the human mind. This means that it is logical to begin to look for the source of religion in the mental make-up of humans, in their cognitive equipment. Devout people might venture that the human mind receives the impetus for religion from the sacred realm. But, as just noted, this would be beyond the reach of scholarly and scientific investigation. Most likely, humans get religion from other humans but they could not do so without having human minds in the first place. Later we shall look at how humans produce symbolic and cultural environments and how this then influences minds in return. Before that, here is a brief look at the place and role of the human mind and what it does in relation to religion in general.

E-religion and i-religion

The apparently great divide between scholars in the well-known research traditions of historical, sociological and philological studies and the recent cognitive science of religion proponents can be neatly solved by applying the distinction between *i-religion* and *e-religion* where 'i-' stands for 'internal' and 'e-' for 'external'. This distinction originates from linguistics, with the division between 'e-' and 'i-' language where e-language spoken, audible, public and externally recorded and i-language is the internal language in the mind-brain. though in a somewhat different form, a similar dichotomy is known from the history of philosophy in Hegel's distinction between the human 'Subjective Spirit' and 'Objectified Spirit', where Hegel saw social institutions such as law and government as arising out of the human subjective spirit. Then, when 'objectified', these products of the spirit become 'social facts' (in Durkheim's terminology) which subsequent generations will have to internalise to become competent members in society and culture. Language is one such obvious social fact that needs learning, in a context and as part of a way of life. This is how people learn religion in most societies: anthropological and historical records demonstrate that explicit instruction is the exception rather than the rule. Languages in traditional societies often have countless expressions that relate to myth, ritual and religion. The religion-related shares of vocabularies are substantial also in literate traditions. As all the world's societies and cultures are, or have been religious until recently, it is obvious that any understanding of their histories, arts, literatures and music demand an understanding of their religious dimensions. With no knowledge of the Bible, Qur'an, Mahabharata, or the writings of Confucius, to name but a few examples, the artistic traditions in and of their respective cultural spheres remain impenetrable. Period, and that is one of the major reasons for the study of the world's religious traditions.

Religion, language, culture and society consist of social acts and facts that any newcomer into the group will have to appropriate and (gradually) master. Somewhere down the line, social facts are made up of mental acts and facts (Searle 2010). Once objectified, mental facts become social facts, and when these are internalised they change their status from social facts into mental facts (see, e.g., Berger 1990). There does not seem to be any more to acquiring religion than that. We are left with social acts and facts (which are ultimately made of mental acts and facts), and so with religion in 'i-' or 'e-' versions. Without mental facts, there would probably not be any social facts and without social facts, mental facts would most likely just be individual solipsistic states of mind. The whole point of having hybrid minds is that *we* can use the stuff of *other* minds to think with. This is the most basic and most important cognitive function of language, of culture and of religion. Now, social facts are precisely the stuff that most historians, archaeologists, anthropologists and sociologists of religion have studied as observable e-religion. They have studied religion 'outside-the-head' in texts, in social practices such as rituals, purity systems, in monuments, in material culture, in all those forms that are symbolically available to newcomers in society. For about a century there has been a general consensus in the study of religion to focus on e-religion, and that history is well covered in most textbooks and introductions to the study of religion. Meanwhile, i-religion mostly remained the province of the psychology of religion. It was not that influential, as one may be convinced of by considering the limited number of journals and departments in that field. It has been deplorably marginal both in the general study of religion and in psychology as a whole. This is remarkable, and in contrast to the public interest in both psychology and religion, as any visit to a bookshop will demonstrate. There is an explanation for this: many psychologists shared Freud's dislike for religion or took no interest in it and, conversely, many religious people were anxious, as were many academics in the study of religion, about psychology and psychologists as trying not to explain, but to explain away, religion and reduce it to irrationality, wishful thinking or neurosis. Then again, scholars of religion, such as historians or anthropologists, often considered psychologists of religion to have (hidden) religious agendas and so judged them dubious scholars (Stausberg 2013).

Religion as a social fact, and between minds

This seems to be changing. Pascal Boyer's view of religion (see Chapters 1 and 2 above) is unquestionably critical but it also indicates how the recent cognitive study and science of religion has become a new psychology of religion that offers new insights and results to the established psychology of religion research (Farias and Barrett 2013). Adding to this new diversity, much of the cognitive research on religion is carried out by scholars with very diverse backgrounds: there are anthropologists, cognitive scientists, philosophers, psychologists, theologians and, of course, some historians of religion. Today, scholars are better equipped to move back and forth between e-religion and i-religion. To better understand this, we may take a closer look into the mental mechanisms that enable the modes of social constructionism that sociologist Peter L. Berger described in 1967 (Berger 1990). I shall outline this possibility here and note its philosophical implications as well.

Philosopher John R. Searle explored the basic structure of human civilisation in a theory of how humans construct institutional facts and social institutions (2010). One of Searle's prime examples is the invention and importance of money, but it might as well have been language, sport, culture or religion. The first and necessary condition for social invention is collective intentionality, the 'we intend' mode, so that the social group is able to agree on assigning status function to an item in the collective imagination and classification system. The second condition is the application of rules: 'constitutive rules' in Searle's terminology. The construction of institutional reality is primarily achieved in language, and especially through (1) speech acts and (2) written language. As Searle notes:

> Once a tribe gets written language, all sorts of other developments become possible. This stability of written language enables the creation and continued existence of status functions that do not require any physical existence beyond the linguistic representations themselves. Two striking examples of this are both fairly modern inventions, invented long after the creation of written language: modern forms of money that dispense with actual currency, especially electronic money, and limited liability corporations.
>
> (Searle 2010: 115)

When such social institutions as money, religion or politics are created they acquire power, political, financial or deontic, because they have status functions (*x* counts as *y*). The interesting point, as Searle underlines, is that:

> The status function doesn't really exist except insofar as it is represented as existing. In a sense, there is an element of imagination in the existence of private property, marriage, and government because in each case we have to treat something as something that it is not intrinsically.
>
> (Searle 2010: 121)

The Imagined World Made Real is the title of the 2003 book by psycho-biologist Henry Plotkin. He set out to investigate how the human sciences can work 'towards a natural science of culture' for, as he says on cultural imagination and theory of mind, 'what we can be absolutely certain about is that culture, as an expression of human intelligence, is the product of a specific and knowable set of psychological and neurological mechanisms' (Plotkin 2003: 211). Considering how stunning it is that even small children acquire the capacity to create and maintain institutional reality, Searle presents this example: 'Small children can say to each other, "Okay, I'll be Adam and you be Eve, and we'll let this block be the apple.". This, if one allows oneself to think about it, is a stunning intellectual feat' (2010: 121). Imagination certainly is the prerequisite for religion. Not only because religion, as we broadly conceive of it, is a social construction, consisting of ideas, intentions, norms, rules and roles, but because all of this would not be possible if humans were unable to *imagine* Krishna as an avatar of Vishnu, why the ancestors are angry, how to imitate a sacred person's life, how to reflect on the Buddha's teachings or follow the advice of the Delphic oracle.

Imagination really is the foundation of religion as well as of culture in general. Imagination is the foundation for the miracle that enabled humans to break out of their solipsistic animal mental state and share with others, not only food and care, but also knowledge and creativity. Creative, imaginative language is exemplified in myth where narratives provide cultural content for individuals and groups: myths offer the possibility of 'seeing *x* as *y*'. The evolutionary psychologist Merlin Donald reflects in the following way on the link between culture, narrative and mind:

> In Paleolithic cultures, and in aboriginal cultures in general, the entire scenario of human life gains its perceived importance from myth; decisions are influenced by myth; and the place of every object, animal, plant, and social custom is set in myth. Myth governs the collective mind.
>
> (Donald 1991: 268)

Language, myth and social institutions thus bridge the gap between i-religion and e-religion. Humans have 'hybrid minds' with the capacity for external memory storage in language and artefacts (such as in writing and in 'the cloud') with which they can form and use vast cognitive networks (Donald 2001). The philosophers Andy Clark, David Chalmers and Mark Rowlands jointly launched the hypothesis of 'externalism' concerning how mental content can be externalised in many ways as 'extended mind' (e.g., Rowlands 2010). This is possible because humans have language (again), symbols, instruments and books (such as this one!) where the contents and objects of cognitive processes can be stored in such manners that others may be able to use them (or, for example, you yourself, when you have forgotten something). Religious objects, such as icons or statues, have encoded, recorded or absorbed religious intentions and attitudes from the individuals who have made them according to their tradition. In a deeply important sense, such objects *speak*. Without 'extended mind' religion would not exist. Humans share their ideas about the world, including ideas about gods, ancestors, rituals and sacred institutions. Religions, as religious traditions observed by groups, form vast networks of shared knowledge, values and modes of practice.

The anthropologist Edwin Hutchins studied the navigation skills of Polynesian islanders and noticed how they used different tools (jointly in and outside minds) to keep track of their course over large distances in the Pacific Ocean. Later, he studied how navy personnel on a large ship navigate together and came up with the idea of 'distributed cognition', that is, how humans 'cognize' together in distributed cognition and so are able to perform tasks that no one single individual could master (Hutchins 1995). This also happens when humans are building canoes or houses because the participants are able to *share* a plan jointly. The same skills are necessary for a group to be able perform religious rituals – or play football. Now, these skills are so commonly human and ubiquitous that they have largely gone unnoticed, but without them social life as we know it would not be possible. The developmental psychologist Michael Tomasello has researched the (most likely) cultural origins of human cognition (Tomasello 1999). Of course, as Tomasello says, human basic cognition is the necessary condition for there being culture in the first place, but then he ingeniously demonstrates how distinctly human cognition also feeds on cultural evolution. Through cultural evolution humans have become 'smarter' because they are able to add continuously to cultural inventions, for instance in cognitive tools such as numerals, writing and literacy or in institutions such as systems of ritual purity and morality. Tomasello describes this phenomenon of continuous cultural 'adding on' as 'racheting' (1999: 36–41). This is of special importance for the study of religion, because it reminds us how religion has evolved culturally and socially and how it has probably been a very powerful tool in the evolution of humankind, as we know it (Rappaport 1999). The human capacity for 'being in' language, in culture and in religion has been decisive for the imaginative and normative behaviours of human groups. Humanity has only survived by beings in groups, in society and in culture and so religion, in all its diversity, may also have been an apt survival mechanism for groups (Wilson 2002). Religion may provide organising mechanisms for individual and social behaviour. Religion is part of what the neurologist Antonio Damasio terms 'extended consciousness' in his account of the 'moulding of a person by education and culture' to become a bearer of identity with autobiographical memory:

Extended consciousness allows human organisms to reach the very peak of their mental abilities. Consider some of these: the ability to create helpful artifacts; the ability to consider the mind of the other; the ability to suffer with pain as opposed to just feel pain and react to it; the ability to sense the possibility of death in the self and in the other; the ability to value life; the ability to construct a sense of good and evil distinct from pleasure and pain; the ability to take into account the interests of the other and of the collective.

(2000: 230)

Damasio points out how these features of consciousness lead to conscience as the pinnacle of human distinctiveness. These features are also found and used in all known religious traditions and so point to some universal psychological, cultural and social functions of religion. History offers no evidence on how religion and these features of consciousness are related causally. It seems a safe bet, however, that without those features there would not have been any religion. Again, all this points to the multidimensional character of that conglomerate of human activity that is commonly called religion.

Typologies of kinds and elements of religion

Now that we have some ideas of where religion comes from, typologising appears more feasible. Products of the human mind do seem to exhibit certain regularities; languages, myths, religions and all the other things that make up human culture display similarities in forms, functions, structures and meanings. As noted above, the psychic unity hypothesis was launched by Adolf Bastian and put to use by E. B. Tylor in his groundbreaking anthropological work in 1871. It reasonably claims that all humans have the same biological brain and largely use them in similar ways. However, as Damasio's example of consciousness demonstrated, differences arise in how brains are used, for what and why. The similar conditions apply to religion: as an amalgam of human thought and behaviour there are notable differences on the surface levels of religion, but there are also similarities and commonalities, and if there is to be a general study of religion at all, there must also be universals (Jensen 2001). Generally, there is a reasonable assumption that the basis of human universals is necessarily biological, innate and uniform and such conditions logically also pertain to religion as a human endeavour (Paden 2016). However, cultural variation is not solely responsible for the remaining differences. This view of culture as providing only variations and not similarities is wrong, however intuitively attractive. As Pascal Boyer explains on the evolution and development of intuitive (mental) learning systems, it is more complex:

It may be of help at this point to emphasize a number of characteristics of evolved intuitive systems ... Intuitive understandings are not necessarily 'innate', if this term means that they are present at birth and carry the same contents at different stages of development. That is, no-one needs to assume that infants' minds include, e.g., an 'animal' concept that is identical to the intuitive understanding of animals in adults. All that is implied here is the capacity to form such understandings, given normal environments. It would be very surprising if cognition emerged fully-formed, when so many other evolved capacities take a long time to unfold. Humans are not born equipped with teeth or a working system of sexual drives. Throughout an organism's lifetime, many genes are tuned on or off during development at appropriate stages ...

Intuitive systems are learning systems. Each domain-specific system is specialized in picking up particular kinds of information in the organism's environment. So, contrary to a widespread assumption in popular under-standings of genetic evolution, acquired information and genetically specified information are not a zero-sum system ...

Evolved cognitive systems result in contextually appropriate intuitions. This is because intuitive understandings are there to allow organisms to acquire information that is contextually appropriate, and to calibrate behaviour according to that behaviour ... Consider for instance the fact that, in some places, one tends to react aggressively even to minor insults, while in others people shrug off even major attacks ... Such cultural dif-ferences are to be expected. The whole point of evolved systems is that they are learning systems, which pick up specific appropriate information in the environments, and one should expect these to produce appropriate, that is, different results in different places. That is why it is certainly wrong to expect intuitive understandings to produce cultural universals. Conversely, it would be equally misguided to assume that reflective understandings are invariably culturally specific.

(Boyer 2010: 379–80)

Thus, there are differences that may be explained by biology and similarities that may be explained by culture and so universals in religion may be found on various levels. The uniformities in human nature *and* in culture warrant *typological* comparison and display how it makes sense to compare analogous religions or elements of religions such as ritual or prayer, even when the reli-gions or elements compared have nothing in common in historical terms. Religions and their constitutive elements are products of the human mind and of human social behaviour. As such they need to have features and functions that are recognisable to other human minds and across history and culture, that is, they are features of the human psychic unity hypothesis.

Typological comparison in the study of religion and culture is similar to lin-guists' comparison of, for example, modal verbs or genitive constructions in (unrelated) languages. Thus, typological comparison begins and ends in the scholar's curiosity; it is performed in the interest of scholarship and science. Such comparative analyses may inform us about aspects of human nature, of language or the fundamentals of 'making the social world'. Typological com-parison in the study of religion aims at constructing the scholars' understanding of religion in general and so helps us answer the question of 'What it this thing called religion?' The answers to that question are not found in specific historical and anthropological cases; instead they require systematic and generalising studies in a *typological phenomenology* of religion. Such an '-ology' of religious phenomena should provide an inventory, catalogue or a kind of periodic table of the elements of religion with the descriptions and classification of religious phenomena according to observable resemblances (Jensen 2003). The term 'phenomenology' may conjure up all kinds of misunderstanding (Wynn 2008; Tuckett 2016), but here it is simply used as the term for an '-ology' of all those items that make up religion. That actually was the earliest use of the term (Jensen 1993).

In contrast, in *genealogical* comparison actual historical relations secure the utility of the comparison, for example in the development of Latin into French, Spanish and Portuguese or proto-Semitic into Arabic and Hebrew. A very interesting example in the field of religion is how the linguistic genealogy permits comparison of ancient Indian (Vedic) mythology with the old Scandinavian and Icelandic because the languages involved (Sanskrit and Old Norse) are related as members of the Indo-European language family – a discovery made by the German linguist Franz Bopp (1781–1867). The cultures and religions of the Inuit and other circumpolar peoples also have commonalities that relate both to their languages and to their modes of subsistence as hunters primarily. Among North American native societies there are, conversely, social and cultural similarities in spite of great linguistic differences. Similar conditions appear on a larger scale in African culture areas, as between Bantu-speaking societies. Thus, genealogical comparison in the study of religion sets out to analyse and explain geographical, historical, technological (e.g., agriculture and ceramics) and linguistic similarities as the results of actual cultural contacts. It is methodologically important to differentiate between the two modes of comparison, as things that look alike are not always actually related, form and content may be very dissimilar. Earlier ethnographers overlooked this pitfall, for instance when they hypothesised how Central American peoples must have originated in Egypt because they built pyramid-like structures. In this context, it is apt to remember that the sciences of culture were almost obsessively historical until the 1920s and they were mainly looking for origins, historical connections, cultural diffusion, and origins. However, to think that one has explained something fully by knowing its origin goes by the name of the 'genetic fallacy'. More is required to present a more consistent picture of religion and religions.

Main types of religion

The criteria for distinguishing between various types and kinds of religion are a mixed bag, partly because many of these criteria have been invented ad hoc and partly because they reflect the interests of the various academic disciplines that have contributed to the study of religion. The matter has often been almost obscure and steeped in value judgements. Even the seemingly simple class of 'world religions' has turned out to be a matter of ambiguity and religious apologetics: what does 'world' mean and who is to decide? (Smith 2004). Here I shall try to present a relatively simple and practical view of the issue of classifying religions into types (cf. Box 3.1 below). The criteria for setting up a typology of religions may relate to such simple matters as the number of gods accepted in the tradition, or it may depend on the mode of subsistence: a pastoralist or nomadic society will typically have 'portable' gods and not a form of religion with large temples. Hunter and gatherer societies often have religions that focus on animals of prey.

The shape of a religious tradition may also relate to the sociological configuration of society: large-scale bureaucratic societies in history have had forms of religion involving 'Big Gods' and large amounts of personnel organised in hierarchies (Norenzayan 2013). This is consistent with general idea of many sociologists social anthropologists, as noted above as a symbolist theory, that the degree of religiosity in society correlates with the intensity of social organisation. The more hierarchy, the more subtribes, clans and other groups, such as guilds and specialists in a society, the more complex religious traditions tend to be (Bellah 2011).

We may also distinguish psychologically: some religions value insight and emotional control, others ecstasy and spirit possession. We may also differentiate between various kinds of dominant discourse and the values involved: is the religion positive towards this world or is it 'other-worldly' oriented? Does it value life on earth or does it focus on death and the afterlife? These are some of the salient points that go into the distinctions applied below. Space does not permit an extensive discussion of these factors, but it should be noted that the various disciplines involved in the study of religion also have different priorities, values and focus. Historians look towards politics, power, economy and technology. Social anthropologists analyse relations between social formations and types of religion. Sociologists are interested in modernity, secularisation and how various classes and groups 'have' religion. Psychologists wonder about the attachment styles that various religions prompt in the believers and whether religion may help them cope with life and death. Theologians care about dogmatics, the existential depth of religious belief systems and philosophers ponder the possible value of erroneous beliefs. We need to be aware that these differences and difficulties are there when reflecting on the different kinds and functions of religions. That is why a typological phenomenology of religion – like this one – unavoidably appears somewhat kaleidoscopic and eclectic.

Added to this, there is also the bare fact that many of these aspects and dimensions may be found side by side and in varying proportion. Some of the distinctions are very simple and some are very complex. There is no periodic table for elements of religion. However clumsy and preliminary the criteria for the current typologies may seem, it should be noted that some distinctions have become obsolete, mostly because of their inherent theological normativity. Consider the value judgements intrinsic in such pairs of opposites as 'revealed versus natural', 'miraculous versus reasonable' or, even more normative, 'faith versus superstition'. Thus, something more neutral should serve as a starting point.

Religions may be divided into two groups that share a seemingly simple analytic criterion: one versus many. If there are multiple gods, spirits or ancestors in a religious system, scholars speak of 'polytheism'. If there is only one sacralised superhuman agent as the object of worship then 'monotheism' is the conventional term. In the real world, however, there are multiple cases where this simple boundary breaks down. In various forms of Christianity, which is normally considered a monotheistic tradition, there is the problem of the Trinity and what the roles and functions of the Devil are. What is the status of the worship of Mother Mary, angels and saints? In various forms of Islam, there are saints or imams who are worshipped. As noted above, Durkheim included ancient Buddhism in the category of religion as there are 'things' worshipped, but these are not so much superhuman agents as sacralised entities of which there are myriads in the world of religion. The distinctions may also break down in traditions where elites represent the theologically correct interpretations of the tradition whereas most non-specialists have other and more varying views and practices. The distinction by number remains an ideal and analytic one.

The distinction between 'locative' and 'u-topic' is used to denote the difference between religions that are indigenous, autochthonous and with a cosmology that is tied to a particular area ('locus') and those that go beyond a specific locality. Most indigenous and ancient religions are (were) of the locative type that is normally tied to specific societies, cultures, languages and so to ethnicity. A locative tradition is of the land and the people: consider, for example, Japanese Shinto or Inuit religion in Greenland. The 'u-topic' are, as the term indicates, not tied to a specific *topos* (Greek: 'place') but express ideas, norms and values that are considered universal by the tradition itself. The current major religions Buddhism, Islam and Christianity are of this type. They are, and have been, universal, global and missionary in varying scope and intensity. Then again, even decidedly u-topic traditions may become local and markers of ethnicity, such as Islam in many places in Sub-Saharan Africa, Roman Catholicism in Northern Ireland or Vajrayana Buddhism for Tibetans. Universal religious traditions thus may become local. On the other hand, some locative and ethnic religions have become world religions, especially during the last few centuries, as the result of colonisation first and globalisation since. Judaism has its own complex history, Sikhism and various forms of Hinduism spread through parts of the former British Empire, from Fiji to Trinidad, and there are large congregations continuing locative Chinese religious traditions in North America.

In many religious traditions, the scriptures are read by and only known to the elites. When used in liturgy as the cultic language they may be incomprehensible to the ritual participants and the local people in general. Examples of such languages are Sanskrit, Arabic, Latin, Pali and others that are used in official and theologically correct liturgies. Around the globe, many devotees are more or less illiterate and cannot access and interpret the scriptures even when and where they are allowed to do so. Some traditions are esoteric and literary sources are only open to particular groups. Interestingly, higher rates of literacy today means that many more can read the sources and so have the means and skills to challenge the traditional orthodox hierarchies and authorities. Add to this the recent influences of new technologies such as the internet and satellite television, electronic qur'ans and bibles and the picture becomes very complex in terms of cultural, social, political and economic conditions. In most contemporary societies, it can be difficult to separate these factors that influence religious life. There are increasingly more interpretations and affiliations to choose from and participants in religious traditions may choose and change allegiance and adherence at a rate never seen before.

The sociologist Max Weber introduced the 'ideal type' distinction between 'church' and 'sect'. Weber's main interests centred on Christian religious history in Europe and the United States so his vocabulary is coloured by that emphasis. The difference is sociological (and not theological) and concerns membership (1) in a sect, which is voluntary, elective and may require tests, and (2) of a church, where members are (mostly) born into it. Note that this division is what Weber termed an 'ideal type' to think with and not a description of an actual fact. Most religious congregations tend to fall somewhere along this continuum. 'Sect' has now become a somewhat pejorative term and hardly any religious group would market itself as a sect.

Two more types of religion may be discerned by using an 'ideal type' division: that is between 'this-worldly' and 'other-worldly' religions. The first are mostly concerned with the 'blessings' of this world, for example with fertility, an abundance of food and social stability. They are 'risk-aversive' and typically function like insurance companies in the manner of 'Give the ancestors their due and they will look after us'. All ancient religious traditions were, and most native religions are, of this kind. The 'tit-for-tat' modes of exchange with the superhuman agents is basically moral and ethical as anthropologist have long known. Punishment administered from the superhuman realm will most likely have co-evolved with growing social complexity in a reinforcing dynamic as watchful agents would extend the range of social control (Purzycki et al. 2017).

The development of an expanded other-worldly orientation is mostly found among scriptural traditions. They often focus on rescue, redemption and salvation from this 'dysphoric' world and a sustained focus on the bliss to be attained in the next world or in some other 'euphoric' condition, be it in a kind of heaven or nirvana. With the other-worldly orientation often come moralistic and ethical outlooks on human life: rules are to follow and ideals to heed to qualify for the blessed fate in the afterlife. Ethical and moral considerations on how to treat people other than members of the tribe or 'in-group' also entered the history of religions – and there they have remained ever since.

This was a distinct historical development of 'other-worldly' ideas which can be followed in broad terms (although some crucial details are still missing). The invention of writing and recording 'external memory' is part of the story but not all. These 'other-worldly' oriented ideas seem to have emerged in the middle of the first millennium BCE, a period termed the 'Axial age' by the philosopher Karl Jaspers (1883–1969). These ideas were found almost simultaneously in China (Daoism), India (Buddhism and the *Upanishads*), Iran (Zoroastrianism), Greece

(Plato) and Palestine (the prophets of the Hebrew Bible) and they have recently re-emerged as a focal point of interest (Bellah 2011).

The 'karmic' religions are a set of South Asian traditions that account for the vicissitudes of human existence by through strong causality concerning not only ethics and morality but also concerning the very being of what there is (ontology) and how we can know about it (epistemology). The notion 'karmic' is as fundamental as, for example, monotheism, because the karma-ideas permeate the Indian as well as the Buddhist traditions as a cosmological and anthropological backbone, the *sine qua non* of these traditions. In very general terms, 'karma' stands for the idea of a close cause-and-effect relation of human thought and behaviour. For instance, in most Hindu traditions the ideas of karma are closely related to the notions of self and rebirth where the fate in one's coming existence depends on the 'karma score' obtained in this life according, of course, to the tradition's norms and rules. In large measure this justifies the individual's struggles and hopes to better his or her lot and ultimately escape this circle of rebirths (contrary to modern Western interpretations where rebirth is mostly considered a positive transformation). Thus, the individual can potentially, and to some extent, govern his or her own fate.

Some religious traditions operate with ideas of predestination, where everything is already 'written' or otherwise ordained as a basic anthropological and cosmological programme. This is quite the opposite of the karmic ideas, for with predestination the cause-and-effect relation is reversed: something outside the individual (e.g., a god) has already ordered the path of life and the fate after death. In the more austere versions there is then very little that can be done about that fate. Instead, it becomes imperative to know who one is and what one is then supposed to do. For that reason, traditions with notions of predestination abound in methods of knowledge procurement such as divination, oracles or scriptural interpretation that can provide reliable signs of whether one is damned or chosen. In psychological terms, this model of life and fate can provide much anxiety as well as much self-righteousness. The questions of why, how and what is predestined and who is lost, selected or saved have been persistent and pervasive in some traditions and especially so in various kinds of Islam and Christianity. Notions of predestinations and of fixed fates can be found in many traditions with ideas about an prearranged cosmos, in the ancient Mesopotamian but also non-literate ones such the Old Norse. Predestination ideology often conceals itself behind practices of divination – the attempts to find out what 'is hidden' about life, death and the universe. However, it is principally in monotheistic theologies that these ideas become philosophically troubling: 'If god is almighty, just and kind, why is there evil in the world?' As an analytical dichotomy, 'predestination-or-free will' is as much an ideal type as the others noted above. In real life, there are countless variations on these themes. The 'either/or' distinctions are analytic concepts, that is, they are tools for the scholars' analyses. In the scholars' actual empirical analyses, matters may prove much less clear-cut and utterly entangled, but if we did not have the analytic concepts, we would never now *what* was entangled in the first place.

Some religions abound in ritual and some do much less. Some focus intensely on human emotion, behaviour, the body, sexuality and ritual purity and others centre on scriptures, repetition and dogma. Based on his fieldwork in Papua New Guinea, the anthropologist Harvey Whitehouse developed an analytic distinction between 'imagistic' and 'doctrinal' *modes of religiosity*. The first involve religious traditions and rituals rich in 'sensory pageantry', that is, with rituals that are spectacular or memorable and so participants may still remember them even when seldom repeated. This will be especially important in non-literate societies based on oral tradition. If the rituals are forgotten, culture and society may fall apart, so it is better that the rituals are kept memorable, intense, perhaps dangerous and extreme so that they shall remain in the episodic 'flashbulb' memories of the various groups of participants – and here even a passive audience can be very important. The second mode refers to kinds of rituals and religions governed by doctrines and frequent repetition of dogma as habitually found in literate cultures (Whitehouse 2000). In ideal type terms and perhaps somewhat exaggerated, the distinction is between rare but emotionally arousing rituals in imagistic religious traditions and frequent but 'boring' rituals along with repetitions of semantic contents in doctrines and narratives. This latter mode is, however, good for the survival of the dogmatic teachings and so for the institutions at large.

Now, the modes of religiosity distinction principally concerns the role and function of kinds of emotion, the impact of memory on religiosity and how religious commitments are experienced, organised, transmitted and politicised. Accordingly, it is a functional view, not so much about religion as a social system as about the ways in which the human mental architecture and mechanisms enable humans to continue and uphold their religious traditions. Memory is the key here. The two modes distinction takes its departure in individual psychological processes (i-religion) that lead to certain kinds of religious and social formations (e-religion). Whitehouse's ideal type distinction between the two modes of religiosity is methodologically attractive and useful, not least because the two types are interwoven in practice in many traditions: 'Doctrinal and imagistic modes of religiosity are not types of religion but organizing principles for religious experience and action. It is very common for both modes of religiosity to be present within a single religious tradition' (Whitehouse 2002: 309). Historically, most of the large scriptural traditions such as Buddhism, Christianity, Hinduism or Islam have been dominant in populations that were illiterate, or uneducated in the ritual or liturgical language such as Pali, Greek, Latin, Sanskrit and Arabic. Most attendants and participants would have only scant knowledge of the doctrinal content, which might then not remain so *relevant* in their semantic memory. In those circumstances, other more imagistic elements of the tradition could be boosted and become cognitively and emotionally attractive. They could then attract attention and provide experience and involvement conceived as relevant for and by the 'lay' people, in what has been variously been termed 'folk', 'popular', and 'little' tradition, or in the more recent research manner: 'lived religion'. (e.g., Hall 1997; Rüpke 2016). The study of religion has all too often focused on doctrinal features and tended to forget that religions are *also* extremely oriented towards emotion, positively or negatively. There is no know religious tradition that does not concern, regulate, up-or-down scale human emotions. Religions *do* create, shape and regulate emotions and so the connections between emotions and religious ideology and practice, individually and collectively is a field of research that should not be overlooked (e.g., Corrigan 2008, 2017).

Returning to the inevitably tautological and circular nature of definitions of religion we can see that all religions consist of elements, or phenomena, that make up an 'other' or 'second' world thought of as superimposed on the material one. Such thought-of worlds are typically inhabited by superhuman agents: gods, saints, demons, spirits and/or ancestors. They may also contain elements that are sacralised because of their axiomatic value and function. This is why Durkheim considered even ancient Buddhism to be a religion: there are sacred things that are set apart and inviolable. The anthropologist Roy Rappaport followed the same idea with his emphasis on 'ultimate sacred postulates', which need not be anthropomorphic (human-like) superhuman agents, as the decisive criterion for distinguishing between religion and non-religion (Rappaport 1999). In many religious traditions these agents and elements operate in more or less ordered world views, as described and interpreted by the anthropologist Edmund Leach (1910–89) in his now classic structuralist analyses of religious cosmologies (1976). Many, if not most, religious traditions have notions of stability and inviolability as their ontological basis, that is, what they are 'really about'. In most indigenous or native traditions this inherent conservatism is predominantly taken for granted: it need not be expressed explicitly or directly. The world simply will be an ordered place – a 'cosmos' – for as long as humans play their part correctly. The very idea of playing 'correctly' presupposes a set of norms and values and these are (for the most part) sacred in the sense that they are 'ultimate'. As Pascal Boyer pointed out, should humans dare tamper with the correct order of the world there are superhuman 'policing' agents (gods, spirits or ancestors) with 'full strategic knowledge' ready to take action (2001: 164–7). It is a robust psychological finding that humans need to inhabit ordered space and that if they do not find it then they make it. And so, the order *wished for* is projected onto the universe to make it humanly meaningful, as the sociologist Peter L. Berger noted in 1967 (Berger 1990). In many literate religious traditions these ideas about the permanent world order are directly and explicitly expressed in such notions as the ancient Egyptian Ma'at, the Hindu Rta, the Buddhist Dhamma and the Chinese Dao – all embody the kind of ideas that (some) sociologists indicate by the Greek word *nomos*: law and order.

There is an interesting general difference between polytheistic and monotheistic traditions that follows from their social, cultural and cognitive organisation of how behaviour and belief interrelate. Polytheistic traditions tend to emphasise that the commands of law and order are best met in right practice, in 'orthopraxy', and the monotheistic traditions stress that the rightful way of life is determined in and by 'orthodoxy', with an emphasis primarily on belief as mental attitudes and behavioural dispositions. As a corollary, this division means that 'straying from the path' can be seen either as violations of rules of purity or as heresy.

It is easy for humans to stray, and even more so in scripturalist and doctrinal, monotheistic traditions. Humans have a propensity for theological incorrectness. When asked to consciously reflect on their representations of gods respondents tend to follow the orthodox doctrines of their tradition, but when quick responses are required, they lapse into intuitive reactions about the superhuman agents that are clearly not correct theologically but follow ordinary paths in social cognition, that is, how humans normally think about others and in relation to themselves (Boyer 2001: 281–5).

To round up this tentative classification, Box 3.1 summarises these characteristic dichotomies in an analytic typology of religions. Remember that we are talking about 'ideal types': they are 'labels'. These labels may be used in the characterisation of any tradition or expression of a tradition.

Box 3.1 Characteristic types of religion

polytheistic vs. monotheistic

locative vs. u-topic

ethnic vs. global

oral tradition vs. literate tradition

elite vs. 'folk'

church vs. sect

this-worldly/blessing vs. other-worldly

salvific missionary vs. non-missionary

karmic vs. non-karmic

imagistic vs. doctrinal

orthopractic vs. orthodox

Changes in types of religion

Why are there different kinds and types of religion? Notice that this question is a variation of the question of what caused religion in the first place: what are the generative, causal factors for there being religion at all? If religions were caused by the same, universal human mental factors, why are they different then? What are the selective mechanisms behind the diversity? What are the dependent and the independent variables? These are far from trivial questions and the answers are not simple.

However, from antiquity and on to the early days of the academic study of religion these questions were largely answered in a metaphysical and religious manner: different nations had different gods because the gods had revealed themselves to those nations. Later, Christian and Muslim theological explanations have focused on how various peoples behaved towards the revelations offered to them: some did it right, were pious and survived, while others did it wrong, were heretics and apostates that disappeared. History was a lesson in divine retribution: earthquakes, famines and the distribution of human nations were part of a divine order.

Then, much later, when the religious and metaphysical explanations lost credibility with the Enlightenment, the emergence of the scientific world view and the coming of evolutionary theory, other kinds of explanation emerged (see Chapter 2). A reasonable and plausible explanation of possible developments of types of religion was introduced, focusing on the correspondences between religious worlds and the kinds of societies to which they belong: humans would respect, worship and sacralise matters that were important to them; not least to their survival and well-being. Countless anthropological records could testify to this, as 'primitives' all over the world had myths, rituals and institutions aimed at preserving fertility, success in hunting and gathering, and survival. Correspondences between modes of subsistence, world views and religious formations seemed obvious: hunter-gatherers venerated superhuman agents that provided game, pastoral peoples sacrificed to gods who would secure the health of their herds, horticulturalists (that is, small-scale agriculturists in tropical climates) performed elaborate rituals to secure the growth of tuber plants, and agriculturalists respected goddesses of botanical abundance. This fundamentally economic view of the material modes of subsistence as causal and responsible for the shape of a religious tradition is quite obvious and relevant as long the focus is on primal, locative, societies. This view is also known from Marxist economic and political theory where the two levels of subsistence and religion are termed 'base' and 'superstructure'. Consequently, both parallel developments and differences in the histories of religions are commonly described (also by non-Marxists) as based on modes of subsistence that produce corresponding belief systems (Morris 1987: 5–50).

Anthropological correspondence theory holds a different explanatory model, one that ratchets up from the basic economic or material conditions to social structure or social formation as the independent variables that account for the shape of religion. Correspondence theory (see Chapter 2) drew on the inspiration of Durkheim (the French Sociological School), and it dominated in British social anthropology as the leading theoretical inspiration for the study of religion in small-scale societies during much of the twentieth century (Evans-Pritchard 1966: 48–77). Correspondence theory also has room for societies with increasing institutional complexity, that is, for societies with complicated political, hierarchical and cultural systems. Here, examples could be the Japanese Shinto imperial-mythological traditions that focused on order, purity and *nomos* with biannual purity rituals at the imperial court that symbolically cleanse the emperor's realm and so emulate the actual exercise of power to maintain law and order. From the Mediterranean world in antiquity, historical studies show how modes of petition to the gods follow changes in organisation from classical city states to large Hellenistic kingship political formations: the ways of addressing the gods changed with the ways of addressing the rulers. In religion, social changes lead to linguistic and ritual changes. In other circumstances, language is the variable that causes (at least some) religious change, especially when imported along with a new language, such as when (among many more) Buddhism and Pali were introduced in South East Asia, Islam and Arabic in Persia or Christianity and

Latin in Scandinavia. With different languages come different ways of talking and thinking about the world, and so both social and cognitive changes in society and culture may follow as well.

Similarly, psychological explanations of the origin and diversity of religion would describe how psychological formations can turn universal biological and, sometimes, cultural capacities into specific mentalities. Different shapes of religious traditions might look like different personality traits or attachment styles on a larger scale, as if religious traditions or cultures have their own collective personalities. The anthropologist Margaret Mead once characterised the anthropologist Ruth Benedict's view of culture as 'personality writ large' (Benedict 2005: xiii). Although necessarily a gross simplification and something that might lead to stereotyping, there could be some truth to the idea and a comparable picture might hold for religion. This is what the philosopher Lucien Lévy-Bruhl (1857–1939) attempted to investigate with an inspiration from Durkheim (Evans-Pritchard 1966: 78–99). Specific cultures and societies have their particular view of the world, and where some see gods in mountains and spirits in trees others care about souls of animals or matters unclean. These culturally specific modes of thought are 'collective representations' that the members of the culture or religion share; Lévy-Bruhl focused on these social and cultural conditions, that is, what is 'available for thought', rather than on individual psychology (Morris 1987: 182–6). Evidently, consistent patterns of child-rearing, cultural learning and emotional conditioning *do* provide templates for thought and behaviour that encourage preferred thought and behaviour, and so the group or religious tradition takes on a kind collective personality, mentality or may be seen as a 'thought collective'. Thus, the contents of 'cognitive universes' matter because they contain what individuals and groups are able to *think with* in terms of both causes and effects: 'Why were the ancestors angry and what can we do about it? Let's make the rituals more elaborate!' Collective psychology and mentality may thus provide both the causes and the effects of religious change: pietism, monasticism and fundamentalism (to name but a few) may be the consequences of prior situations, or they may bring about and cause other conditions. At least prophets and reformers know this. Changes in religion can be brought about by changes in religion. Someone gets a new idea and it may catch on. They are the ones we remember.

This means that the variables can be altered so that it is *religion* that causes changes in culture, society, economy and material conditions. Anthropological and historical evidence confirms this. Max Weber espoused this view in 1904 when he put forward the hypothesis of the Protestant and Puritan Christian origins of the capitalist mentality ('Spirit') in early modern Europe and North America. The very brief version runs: it was godly and a sign of predestination for salvation to be industrious and wealthy but ungodly to spend and splurge, and so capital accumulates (Weber 2001). There are countless examples of religion causing, shaping and regulating social, political and economic life in later developments of (mostly) literate cultures. The spread of Judaism, Christianity, Islam and Buddhism bear witness to this.

Religions have exerted mutual influences on each other throughout history. A large part of the work of historians of religion is devoted to the tracing, description, analysis and explanation of influences between religions: Where and when did the ideas of Heaven and Hell emerge? Who invented angels? Developments in the histories of religions have ranged from theories of cultural diffusion, such as the now extinct hypothesis of pan-Babylonianism, which claimed that all human culture, mythology and religion hailed from ancient Babylon, to modern historical analyses that provide economic explanations for the conditions of the emergence of early Islam (trade routes in Arabia) or Buddhism (growing wealth in the agricultural kingdoms of northern India). However, the development and spread of religious ideas, teachings and doctrines do not necessarily follow fixed patterns and rules. When it comes to humanity's inventions of its own mirror-images, almost anything is possible. The conclusion is that there is no single direction of causality with social phenomena as complex as religion. It all depends on the specific case.

Theoretically determined types of religion

In Chapters 1 and 2, we saw some examples of religion as 'produced by theory'. It became clear that religion takes on a wholly different shape when viewed according to one or the other theory: it can be almost anything from comfort and joy to repression and folly. Sometimes the differences are such that had it not been for the use of the (useful) term 'religion' the reader might think that the scholars and scientists were simply not talking about the same thing. It is, however, possible to summarise the four main types of theory about religion, as in Table 3.1.

The following three chapters will be concerned with classifying the inventories of religion, that is, the phenomena they consist of and how they may be classified: beliefs, representations and narratives in Chapter 4, then practices and modes of religious behaviour in Chapter 5 and finally religious institutions, such as the systems of norms and values in behaviour, morality and ethics in Chapter 6.

Table 3.1 The four main types of theory about religion

Name/type of theory	Description	Examples
Intellectualist	Religion as world views and explanation of social, cultural conditions and fate	Ancient Hindu myths, biblical creation story, divine origins of the tribe or nation, divination and oracle
Symbolist/ correspondence	Religion as expressing social structures, the result of economic and political forces	Animals as symbols of clans, divine origins of groups, the emperor as divine
Existentialist	Religion as providing emotional comfort and belonging, coping with the vicissitudes of the world	Prayers and healing rituals, group formations with emotional support
Cognitivist	Religion as emerging from 'mental machinery', counter-intuitive ontology, adaptive or non-adaptive in evolution	Non-existing, imagined beings considered casually effective in this world

4   Beliefs, ideas and representations

This chapter focuses on the issue of beliefs, ideas and representations, as they constitute religious cosmologies or 'world views' in their individual and collective appearances. This choice of presenting beliefs, ideas and representations before rituals and institutions may be seen as motivated by Christian theological and especially Protestant thought. That is, however, not the case, for it is a common and very valid anthropological insight that most religious traditions are *lived* more than dogmatically reflected. The religious practices and institutions are what matter in daily life (Vásquez 2011). The reason for placing beliefs first in this volume is that they are *logically* prior, although not necessarily chronologically prior. This demands a brief explanation. For there to be religion *at all* there must be religious beliefs, ideas and representations; these are expressed, propagated, codified and solidified in religious traditions. In the cultural reproduction as well as in the individual appropriation of religion this line of causality may well be different: it is the exposure to rituals and religion in ordinary practice that forms the basis of individual development, and in cultural transmission rituals and institutions are often the primary bases which are then attributed beliefs. The position of beliefs, ideas and representations as primary is thus a theoretically motivated choice.

Depending on the point of view, religious beliefs and convictions may be seen as anything from deeply true, pious and spiritually significant to matters of delusion, superstition and fantasy. Whatever relations religious beliefs and convictions have to the material world of matter, such beliefs and convictions are normally very strongly held. Psychological experiments demonstrate how sacred beliefs and values are actually increased when threatened or questioned – or compromised by offers of money for modified commitments. Offering cash to people for relinquishing a sacred value will most likely make them respond with resentment. The reason seems to be that convictions and beliefs are deeply normative and influence the ways in which humans perceive their worlds, and in this way are fundamental to the world view and ethos of individuals and groups.

Although all humans constantly have and act on beliefs, it is not easy to answer the question of 'What are beliefs really?' One reason is that the question is misguided because of the use of a single word (and associated concept) to denote a wide range of complex mental phenomena. There is so far no possibility whatever of demonstrating the existence of 'belief' by using, for example, brain-scanning techniques. This is because even the most simple of mental phenomena have very complex neurobiological substrates, that is, the neuro-chemical processes actually taking place in a 'belief-processing' brain. This is the 'map and territory' question again: ordinary language may prove seriously deficient when used in the pursuit of complex scientific knowledge. However, some salient features of the concept of belief can be found in mainstream philosophy of mind. Here is the generalised description offered by philosopher Eric Schwitzgebel in the *Stanford Encyclopedia of Philosophy*:

> Contemporary analytic philosophers of mind generally use the term 'belief' to refer to the attitude we have, roughly, whenever we take something to be the case or regard it as true. To believe something, in this sense, needn't involve actively reflecting on it: Of the vast number of things ordinary adults believe, only a few can be at the fore of the mind at any single time. Nor does the term 'belief', in standard philosophical usage, imply any uncertainty or any extended reflection about the matter in question (as it sometimes does in ordinary English usage). Many of the things we believe, in the relevant sense, are quite mundane: that we have heads, that it's the 21st century, that a coffee mug is on the desk. Forming beliefs is thus one of the most basic and important features of the mind, and the concept of belief plays a crucial role in both philosophy of mind and epistemology. The 'mind–body problem', for example, so central to philosophy of mind, is in part the question of whether and how a purely physical organism can have beliefs. Much of epistemology revolves around questions about when and how our beliefs are justified or qualify as knowledge.
>
> Most contemporary philosophers characterize belief as a 'propositional attitude' ... A propositional attitude, then, is the mental state of having some attitude, stance, take, or opinion about a proposition or about the potential state of affairs in which that proposition is true ... For example: Ahmed [the subject] hopes [the attitude] that Alpha Centauri hosts intelligent life [the proposition], or Yifeng [the subject] doubts [the attitude] that New York City will exist in four hundred years. What one person doubts or hopes, another might fear, or believe, or desire, or intend – different attitudes, all toward the same proposition. Contemporary discussions of belief are often embedded in more general discussions of the propositional attitudes; and treatments of the propositional attitudes often take belief as the first and foremost example.
>
> (Schwitzgebel 2010: 1)

The philosopher Kevin Schilbrack has taken up the problem of the place and role of religious beliefs in understanding and explaining religious behaviour critically and constructively (Schilbrack 2014). He notes that it has become almost fashionable over the past few decades to deny the role of religious beliefs (or call them attitudes, certainties, convictions, faiths, ideas, mindsets, representations, thoughts, or views according to the specific task) in understanding and explaining religious behaviour, and that for several reasons. First, this admittedly traditional view should perpetuate a Christian and especially Protestant bias in the perception of religion. Second, because it is a fact that most religious behaviour has become automatic; believers do what they do without explicitly referring to, or being driven by, their beliefs, at least not explicitly. Third, because beliefs are envisaged as inner, private mental states that others, such as scholarly 'outsiders', have no access to. Against these recent denials of the role of beliefs among 'belief eliminativists' and methodological scepticisms, Schilbrack notes how believing is something that a person, and not just a brain, does: 'Instead, to have a belief is to have a propensity or a tendency, or a set of them, typically shaped by one's social context, to interact with the world and with others according to a more or less specifiable pattern' (2014: 63). Believing is not just a mental activity – it is embedded in a form of life: 'A religious belief therefore cannot be separated from a religious pattern of behavior' (Schilbrack 2014: 64). Right here, Schilbrack ingeniously draws on the classic insights of the philosopher Gilbert Ryle: 'going on a pilgrimage is both a physical and a mental process, but it is not two processes'. Thus, the bodily and social aspects of belief are essential because, 'people learn their primary beliefs about the world in their interactions with others. Beliefs are then collective in the sense that in the first instance they are common to and shared by members of a discursive or interpretive community'.

(Schilbrack 2014: 68)

Consequently, it does not make sense to say that people hold religious beliefs and simultaneously claim that we can never figure out what they are: 'We live in a common shared world with Daoist alchemists, Christian crusaders, Lakota dancers, and so on' (Schilbrack 2014: 68). The best thing to do, then, is to view belief as 'an attitude of taking true that is a socially informed pattern of thinking, feeling, speaking and acting' and so beliefs are not 'mysterious inner objects' (Schilbrack 2014: 75). Consequently, we must regard beliefs, as set of representations, attitudes and propositions are the *logical* foundation of religious behavioural patterns and institutions no matter what caused them. Beliefs may have historical, social or psychological causes, but they are beliefs nevertheless and so, logically, the foundations of belief-related behaviour. It is also worth noting that at least some of what passes as belief either in the sense as dispositions or as holding something to be true is actually driven by intuitive cognitive processes. That is, there are some 'beliefs' that we simply cannot avoid having in virtue of being human. Then again, this only enlarges the inferential and interpretational potential of beliefs and actions.

It is of course true that the concept of belief as used in contemporary discourse is a recent Western invention and so should it be used with caution, but it is also true that people can have beliefs without knowing why they have them and act on them. The concept of 'belief' may be local, but the existence of belief – attitudes, certainties, convictions, faiths, ideas, mindsets, representa-tions, thoughts, or views – is global. Thus, we may forget the invitation to eliminate 'belief' in the study and philosophy of religion. Leaving aside other theoretical and methodological problems with the issue here, it appears that only humans can have propositional attitudes because language is essential for the formation of these, and it also evident that perceptions (sight, touch, etc.) as well as emotions (joy, fear, etc.) are involved in having beliefs in the way that beliefs are conceptualised here – as form of life. Because of the complex refer-ences of the concept of belief to brain activity, some consider the concept as unscientific and better avoided, but then again no useful replacement in within reach. So, with due consideration, it is maintained here as a useful and non-reified concept.

All humans in all societies, cultures and religions have beliefs, and many have religious beliefs. That is beyond doubt, but do all cultures also *know* that they have beliefs and, especially, religious beliefs? The answer, based on the evidence from history, anthropology and the history of religions is: no. Do they all have terms for beliefs, true or false? No. This indicates that it is not necessary to know consciously that one is having beliefs to *have* beliefs. Did the ancient Greeks believe in their myths and their god? Yes and no, they simply took them for granted (Eidinow 2019). It is worth noting here that 'belief' *in this context* does not necessarily mean a faith-like belief in a god-head or predestination, it simply means having 'propositional attitudes' towards the contents of one's world. Then again the limits of the world may be far-ranging and include, as in the case of religious traditions, many coun-ter-intuitive, metaphysical and transcendent elements that do not have actual referents in the material world. Religion thrives, as Ludwig Feuerbach saw, by making the other-worldly appear mundane; it is part of the religious world view. Beliefs can be very deep, or shallow, very steadfast or vague. Here, belief simply means that we take something to be the case or regard it as true. The reasons for, and the ways of the 'taking', also appeared in Clifford Geertz's definition (above in Chapter 1), where religious symbol systems were '(3) formulating conceptions of a general order of existence and (4) clothing these conceptions with such an aura of factuality that (5) the moods and motivations seem uniquely realistic' (Geertz 1973: 90).

Where does belief come from?

It takes a special kind of mind to have religious beliefs – not an especially reli-gious mind, but a human mind, which is very special in comparison with other animal minds. To understand just how special *ordinary* human minds are, it is beneficial to look back in deep evolutionary history. Historian of religions Armin W. Geertz presents a number of salient points in this regard in his edi-torial introduction to *Origins of Religion, Cognition and Culture* (2013). Geertz identifies the four most decisive 'key human features' of the human ability to develop religion as:

1   a finely honed social cognition;
2   a drive to communicate and cooperate;
3   a self-deceptive brain;
4   a superstitious brain prone to unusual mental and/or emotional experiences.

In unpacking these features, it became evident not only that we need to rethink how to understand religious thought and behaviour in terms of the kinds of brains we have, but we also need to incorporate these insights into our evolutionary scenarios. With these four features, it is possible to account for the hows and whys of religion and to relate them to some of the current evolutionary theories. Thus, I claim, we are intelligent apes that are highly emotional, easily spooked, very superstitious, extremely sensitive to social norms and virtual realities and equipped with nervous systems that are vulnerable to influence from conspecifics and their symbolic worlds. We and our brains are constantly predicting and constantly dwelling on the future in our attempts to navigate social and natural environments. Our brains fill in quite a bit, but our cultures are also in our brains and around them, filling in many more things.

These traits are prerequisites for religious behaviour. In looking through the archaeological records, with all the caveats and disagreements in mind, and yet, in accordance with an evolutionary theory of slowly emerging steps, I argue that the grand narrative of the cultural explosion of our own subspecies has blinded us to the fact that nothing emerges out of nothing. Or, to put it in more positive terms, our traits and functions and abilities and worlds are accumulations of prior ones. There can be no doubt, although there are many who have it, that symbolic behaviour is evident in the archaeological record before the appearance of *Homo sapiens*. Therefore, in our search for the origins of religion, cognition and culture, we will need to look beyond ourselves into the deep past, even before the rise of the hominins, to understand who we are and where we came from.

(Geertz 2013: 52)

Geertz's line of thought owes much to the hypotheses of neuropsychologist Merlin Donald in *Origins of the Modern Mind* (1991) and *A Mind So Rare* (2001). Donald points out that there is one striking, yet very simple, feature of human behaviour which no other species manages to do consciously and voluntarily. That is mimesis, or imitation, which again requires voluntary imagination and recall from memory. In a very deep sense, imagination is the basis of it all: belief, behaviour, culture, society and religion. In Donald's exposition, mimesis – the ability to imitate others and also oneself in relation to an imagined ideal – requires the ability to recall an ideal from memory. Karl Marx stated that the worst of architects is better than the best of bees, because the architect (and so the builder) has an idea *in the mind* before building. It is this very special ability to *first* build in the mind that is the very basic and decisive factor in the making of human culture. The role of the imagination in ontogenesis, that is, the development of children into adult members of society and culture, is immense because imagination is part of the scaffolding that provides support for narrative comprehension, active role-playing, social competence and *religious* imagination (Harris 2000: 42–5). Without imagination, children would simply not be able to learn religion (and religion would not have existed in the first place). They need to be able to imagine how the ancestors built the world, Krishna as avatar of Vishnu, the prophet Muhammad's journey to the heavens, or the mythological history of Japan. In religion, belief and imagination come together and are represented in visual art or narrative form.

What are beliefs, ideas, representations made of?

Beliefs, ideas and representations are made of brain states, of course, but we cannot (yet) see those and, thus, there is more than grey matter to the story; beliefs, ideas and representations are as much collective, social and symbolic as they are individual, mental entities. Cultural products and tools such as language, myth and art are essential for the ability of actual human minds to live both in this material world and in 'possible worlds'. The psychologist Jerome Bruner emphasised that possible worlds are made of all that which humans can imagine and *talk about*: things experienced, remembered, imagined, and even things impossible (Bruner 1986). Humans are able to narratively synthesise all such things in the mind with the support of symbols and metaphors which have flexible meanings (Jensen 2016).

To better understand (1) the different kinds of religious signs and signification; (2) the making of meaning; and (3) the interpretation of meaning by individuals and communities, it is essential to divide the variety of signs into the three main kinds of *icon*, *index* and *symbol* (see, e.g., Leach 1976). This is a common distinction in the field of semiotics, which is the scientific study of signs, their production, organisation, meaning and interpretation. Broadly conceived, the study of religion is also a study of signs, and the semiotic study of religion is therefore an obvious subfield in the study of religion (Yelle 2013). The three categories of *icon*, *index* and *symbol* are distinguished as follows:

- An *icon* is a sign that looks like, or mimics, its referent (from Greek *eikon*: image). Signs, maps and portraits are icons when they resemble that which they refer to: a road sign with a '+' on it means a road crossing, and that is just what it looks like.
- An *index* points to something (*index* is the 'pointing finger' in Latin), like a waving flag is an index of wind or smoke is an index of fire. The relation of index and reference is called *metonymic* because they cohere and have an intrinsic relationship.
- A *symbol* is a sign that has its meaning by convention. Some symbols are exceptionally arbitrary and abstract, as when a white bird is a symbol of peace or a snake of evil, whereas some others are motivated by their use or quality, for example when water is used as a symbol of life or purity.

The relation between symbols and their referents is called *metaphoric* as they depend on conventions of asserted relations between signs and referents, which come from different contexts, for example birds and peace or snakes and evil (the Greek word *metaphor* means transfer or transport). In reality, a sign may be all three. Take an example from the Christian traditions: a cross at the altar in a church is an icon, a replica of the cross of crucifixion; on a road map a cross is an index that points to the location of a church; and finally, a cross can be a symbol of Christianity as a whole or of Christ's sufferings. Readers may substitute with examples from other religious traditions most familiar to them.

Signs and symbols in religion can be material and conceptual; they can be linguistic (words, terms, sentences) as well as visual and graphic. Anything from single words ('Trinity') to giant temple complexes (Borobudur in Java) can be symbols. Although some higher mammals may be trained to respond to some signs, humans seem to be the only animals that operate with symbols *as* symbols (Deacon 1997). The cognitive operations with signs and symbols in human minds are complex, but humans do them amazingly effortlessly, as explained by the anthropologist Edmund Leach:

> The essence of the matter is, that with *symbolism* [metaphor] ... we use our human imagination to associate together two entities or sets of entities, either material or abstract, which ordinarily belong to quite different contexts. Thus:
> 1 'the lion is a beast' is a statement to a normal non-human context 'in Nature';
> 2 'the king is the most powerful man in the state' is a statement referring to a normal context 'in Society';
> 3 'the lion is the king of the beasts' is a symbolic (metaphoric) statement. It acquires meaning by mixing the two contexts 'in the mind'.
>
> (Leach 1976: 39)

Metaphors are fundamental in the cognitive and emotional operations of human minds and not just for use in stylistic embellishment as classic literary theory would have it. Humans 'live by metaphors' and language and thought are full of them (Lakoff and Johnson 1980). Metaphors represent a large and important part of religious thought and signification. The competence for metaphors depends on cognitive decoupling, the human ability to think about things out of their proper contexts, for example, when rituals or dramas are made to resemble and represent hunting and killing. Rituals are to a large degree 'as if' metaphorical actions because they are both like and unlike ordinary actions. Furthermore, the cognitive decoupling ability is as important in belief formation as in ritual; it is also in use when, for example, a god is referred to as 'Mother' or 'Father'.

Metaphorical conceptual 'mixing' is ubiquitous in religious thoughts, actions and institutions. Consequently, after the lion example, Leach adds that 'A metaphoric mixing of contexts of this general sort is characteristic of all material forms of religious expression' (Leach 1976: 39). Leach calls this way of symbolically representing something sacred in material form a *condensation*. Here is an example from the Hindu traditions:

1 'The God Siva is a source of divine potency' is a statement in a
   metaphysical context.
2 'The penis is a source of animal potency' is a statement in the context
   of functional biology.
3 'The *lingam* is a carved object shaped like a penis' is a statement in
   the context of material physics, which involves an iconic relationship
   between *lingam* and penis.
4 The familiar Hindu assertion 'the *lingam* is the god Siva' then acquires
   meaning by mixing together the contexts of (1), (2) and (3) 'in the mind'.

(Leach 1976: 39)

The study of the use of metaphors and their cognitive and linguistic prerequisites
has since emerged more fully in 'cognitive blending' and mental space theory
(Turner 1996; Fauconnier 1997, 2003). It turns out that the ideas behind magic
and *all other* religious thought are based upon such cognitive blending (Sørensen
2007; Slingerland 2008). Religious traditions abound with blends of the human
and the divine, or superhuman: heroes, ancestors, gods and many other beings
are composed of and by cognitive blending with a basic recipe that reads somewhat like: 'something ordinary, something special and something impossible'.
The complex claims from the history of Christian theology about the double
nature of Jesus Christ as a cognitive blend of human and divine illustrate this
(examples below on the counter-intuitive properties of many religious concepts
will further demonstrate the ubiquity of cognitive blending in religion).

Religious belief formations and functions are fundamentally characterised by (1)
the distinction between sacred and profane; and (2) the ensuing strong authority
when they become tied to 'ultimate sacred postulates', as the anthropologist Roy
Rappaport termed the class of metaphysical axioms that constitute the bedrock of
religious universes (Rappaport 1999: 287). In a religious cosmology or world view
(two terms used interchangeably by most scholars), the two worlds are tied
together by the use of symbols, metaphors and blending. Without the use of such
linguistics and semiotic devices, it would not be possible for humans in this world
to imagine the 'other world' nor to communicate with it. It is because humans can
imagine gods, ancestors and other sacred beings and objects in the 'other world'
that they can uphold the conceived existence of it. The ideas about the 'other
world' do in many ways resemble ideas in and about the material world. Especially
noticeable are the ideas of anthropomorphism: that much of the 'other world' is
inhabited with human-like beings. To this we now turn.

Religious beliefs: anthropomorphism and dualism

Religious beliefs presume the existence of gods, spirits or ancestors that are imagined as in many ways anthropomorphic (human-shaped). Anthropomorphism is a
fundamental condition of human projection, as the anthropologist Stewart Guthrie
has shown (1993). Edward B. Tylor had already pointed out in 1871 how animism – 'the belief in spiritual beings' – is the root of religion. Recent research has

demonstrated why and how humans are natural animists: the developmental psychologist Paul Bloom has shown how a general human propensity for soul-and-body beliefs and how religious thought and belief are moulded on such 'natural dualism' (Bloom 2004). On this issue, developmental psychology now offers a window into the human mind that should be of great interest to the humanities and the social sciences alike. As Bloom states in a later argument specifically concerning religious beliefs:

> There is a more specific reason why developmental psychologists should be interested in religious belief. Much of the research in cognitive development concerns aspects of understanding that are plainly true of the world, and that are manifest in the input – such as how children come to know that objects are solid, or people have beliefs, or languages have nouns. Religion is unusual because it is about entities and processes and events that are not evident in the senses ... All languages have a word that refers to hands, for instance, but this is probably because it is important for people everywhere to talk about hands, not because of a specific innate propensity toward hand-naming. Similarly, beliefs in Gods, the afterlife, and so on may be universal, not because they are innate, but because such beliefs emerge in all societies, perhaps as solutions to some problems that all human groups face. From this perspective, universals of religious belief are cultural inventions, created by adults. A complete developmental account of the growth of religious belief, then, would be one of cultural learning.
>
> (Bloom 2007: 147–9)

Bloom's own work amply shows this and also why it is that all known cultures are dualist (2004). As with the concept of belief, very few cultures and religions have the words and concepts of 'dualism' and 'animism', but in fact they *do* have both dualism and animism: no dualism and no animism would mean no religion. If there is religion, then there is dualism and animism. Some cultures may claim that they are not dualist because they consider, for instance, their ancestral spirits to be as real and alive as the next-door neighbour, but that only proves how dualist they really are. These features of the human mind tie in well with another religious universal: beliefs about an afterlife. Developmental psychologist Jesse Bering (2006) studied children's imaginative abilities to investigate the developmental psychological bases for the belief in souls and afterlife. In Bering's own summary, the task was to examine:

> how people's belief in an afterlife, as well as closely related supernatural beliefs, may open an empirical backdoor to our understanding of the evolution of human social cognition ... Many of the predominant questions of existential psychology strike at the heart of cognitive science. They involve: causal attribution (why is mortal behavior represented as being causally related to one's after-life? how are dead agents envisaged as communicating messages to the living?), moral judgment (why are certain social behaviors,

i.e., transgressions, believed to have ultimate repercussions after death or to reap the punishment of disgruntled ancestors?), theory of mind (how can we know what it is 'like' to be dead? what social-cognitive strategies do people use to reason about the minds of the dead?), concept acquisition (how does a common-sense dualism interact with a formalized socio-religious indoctrination in childhood? how are supernatural properties of the dead conceptualized by young minds?), and teleological reasoning (why do people so often see their lives as being designed for a purpose that must be accomplished before they perish? how do various life events affect people's interpretation of this purpose?), among others.

(Bering 2006: 453)

Humans have a propensity to hold beliefs, that is, to believe in what they experience, imagine or are told; they could not survive without having and holding on to their ordinary beliefs. However, the belief in gods and other superhuman agents is a more complex affair, one that also involves moral imagination and the pressures of the social world (see, e.g., Boyer 2001: Chapter 5; Bering 2012; Bloom 2012). Altogether, these psychological and social mechanisms seem to explain why it is that religions do not 'go away' (Hinde 1999). In the modern world, where individuality is highly valued, there is a tendency to see religion and religious belief and behaviour as matters of individual preference. However, it has not always been so, nor is this the case in many places. The social and cultural forces that lead to religiosity are strong and determine whether and how individuals become religious or not. Durkheim was right on this issue: if people around you are religious – in a culture where religion is valued – you are more likely to become religious yourself (Diener and Myers 2011). Social forces matter for belief.

Beliefs: intuitive and reflective

Humans are prone to believe what others believe and to believe what they hear from others. A very limited share of our total sum of beliefs about the world comes from our own first-hand experience. Some may say that they have met Jesus, but very few humans (if any) would have met Jesus *before* having heard about him (and if they had, they would probably not have known who they met). So, religious beliefs *are* context-dependent and there will be (statistically) more believers in places where there were more believers in the past. Religious beliefs may be 'contagious', as Pascal Boyer stated (see Chapter 1), or spread in an 'epidemiology of representations', as suggested by the anthropologist Dan Sperber (1996). Sperber also introduced a very useful distinction between two ideal types of beliefs: *intuitive* and *reflective*. The first are the kinds of beliefs that humans have based on their own experience. As Sperber notes, 'Intuitive beliefs are derived, or derivable from perception ... on the whole concrete and reliable in ordinary circumstances' (1996: 89). On the other hand, reflective beliefs are beliefs that we acquire from others, from tradition, and so on: 'They cause belief behaviors because, one way or another, the beliefs in which they are embedded validate them' (Sperber 1996: 89). For instance, a population believes in ancestors and so they act on those beliefs, which may range 'from loosely held assumptions to fundamental creeds' (Sperber 1996: 89–90). Although such beliefs may seem mysterious (to the outsider), 'that does not make these beliefs irrational: they are rationally held if there are rational grounds to trust the source of belief (e.g., the parent, the teacher, or the scientist)' (Sperber 1996: 91). Sperber's conclusion is worth quoting:

> there are two classes of beliefs and they achieve rationality in different ways. Intuitive beliefs owe their rationality to essentially innate, hence universal, perceptual and inferential mechanisms; as a result they do not vary dramatically, and are essentially mutually consistent across culture. Those beliefs which vary across cultures to the extent of seeming irrational from another culture's point of view are typically reflective beliefs with a content that is partly mysterious to the believers themselves. Such beliefs are rationally held, not in virtue of their content, but in virtue of their source.
>
> (Sperber 1996: 92)

Beliefs as representations: a catalogue

Further, religious beliefs and representations are characterised by their fairly uniform and consistent variations of non-religious beliefs and representations. Therefore, as Pascal Boyer argues, it is possible to make a catalogue of the limited number of possible types of religious beliefs and representations of superhuman agents. As Boyer says, 'In other words, there are not that many ways of 'tweaking' intuitive ontology so as to produce supernatural concepts, so that a 'general catalogue of the supernatural' should be rather short' (2000: 198–9). The catalogue is shown in Table 4.1. As an illustration of how this works, Boyer gives the following example:

> For instance, this is the template for the concepts of 'spirit' that we find in so many cultures: (1) an ontological category: PERSON; (2) a violation of intuitive physics, for example, spirits are invisible; (3) activation of non-violated expectations: being persons, spirits have a mind, they can perceive events, forms beliefs, have intentions, etc.; (4) place-holder for additional (local) detail.
>
> (Boyer 2000: 198)

Religious beliefs and representations are the basic building blocks in the formation of religious ethos and world-making in cosmologies, ethics and moral systems (Paden 1994). The contents of religious worlds make up various kinds of religious (sometimes esoteric) knowledge, and these are continually being reproduced, especially so in non-literate religious traditions (Barth 1990). However, even in literate and dogmatic traditions beliefs do change, perhaps not literally (that is, the

Table 4.1 The 'general catalogue' of the supernatural (after Boyer 2000: 198–9)

Agent		Tweaking	Examples
1	Person	Breach of physical expectations	Ghost have no bodies
2	Person	Breach of biological expectations	Angels live forever
3	Person	Breach of psychological expectations	Zombies have no minds
4	Animal	Breach of physical expectations	Horses that fly
5	Animal	Breach of biological expectations	Unicorns have no offspring
6	Animal	Breach of psychological expectations	Snakes that read minds
7	Plant	Breach of physical expectations	Plant that is invisible
8	Plant	Breach of biological expectations	Plant that never dies
9	Plant	Transfer of psychological expectations	A tree that remembers, a cactus that has god-like power
10	Natural object	Breach of physical expectations	A stone that flies
11	Natural object	Transfer of biological expectations	A mountain that is alive
12	Natural object	Transfer of psychological expectations	A river that reads minds
13	Artefact	Breach of physical expectations	Statue that appears in more than one place
14	Artefact	Transfer of biological expectations	Statue that is alive
15	Artefact	Transfer of psychological expectations	Relic that remembers

basic text remains the same) but on the level of interpretation: beliefs are the property of interpretive communities and when communities interpret differently, that may lead to the formation of different communities. The histories of the major literate religious traditions bear ample witness to this. If people change their beliefs and interpretations, they often also change their behaviours. This is how new religious groups are born. Why they change beliefs is a different and often complicated matter (see below).

Interactive hierarchies: from ghosts to gods

'Religion is about gods.' This would be the intuitive assumption in many parts of the world. But how central and important are gods? Do 'gods', great and small, represent a useful general and comparative *category*? Is it functional for the study of religion? Or is it too tradition-laden, permeated with colonialist and missionary discourse and apologetics? The suspicion is there: 'The comparison of different religious traditions has shown that an ontological assumption of a general concept of god all too often implies a projection of European, Jewish-Christian categories onto very different symbol systems without respecting the unique structures of such systems' (Pezzoli-Olgiati 2016: 1). Not so long ago, most generalisations and comparisons of matters pertaining to 'other' religions were made out of context and in relation to how matters compared to notions known to the comparers. In fact, that is a common condition of translation, but here the outcomes were not innocent as they were involved in politics and economical dominance. For the academic endeavours, it is now obvious that *theological* biases were involved in the assumption that religions 'are about gods'. The same idea also shows up in the opposite and familiar claim that Buddhism is not a religion because there is no godhead to be worshipped.

Upon closer methodological consideration, it turns out that 'god' is an imprecise category. Anyone who wishes for an essential definition that goes beyond the conventional will be disappointed. The 'essence' of gods derives straight from that of other counter-intuitive superhuman agents as outline by Pascal Boyer above and in accordance with E. B. Tylor's famous idea of religion arising from the 'belief in spiritual beings' (1871: 10). No scholarly sophisticated theory of gods exists, so the present model of a continuum, or hierarchy, ranging from ghosts and ancestors to demons and gods is the best there is. As already noted, some other superhuman agents do not resemble humans at all, such as mountains, trees of streams, but they may equally be objects of veneration, ritual observance and sacred communication. Here, the focus is on those agents that are habitually taken as gods, those that more or less resemble humans, act like humans and who are important for human affairs. Admittedly not a very precise categorisation, but enough for the present task.

A functional definition of gods works more adequately, especially when theory-laden rather than governed by tradition and religious outlook, such as this attempt: 'Gods, of all sizes, are imagined agents who use superhuman powers and abilities and who are able to communicate and symbolically exchange with humans.' The emphasis on communication and reciprocity is important and so it resembles a structural definition with a focus on the immanence-transcendence relation: Gods et al. are mostly located in an 'other world', but they may be reached there or they may appear in this world. Their existence and qualities are transmitted in myth, legend and dogma; in some places and at some times directly in visions and in possessions. For the most part they can be reached, in return, by ritual means. Versions of gods with power and boundless extensions are found in 'pantheism', the idea that everything is in and encompassed by the godhead. The sheer size of such a being evidences counter-intuitivity which may also be expressed either as this world being transported to the other-worldly realm or that this latter is being covered by it.

Many imagined agents can be counter-intuitive – Mickey Mouse, for instance. However, cognitive attraction and entertainment value are not enough. The fictive mouse lacks *social relevance* such as ghosts, demons, saints and gods have because they *matter* in and to human lives (Atran 2002: 13–14).

The apparitions and appearances of other-worldly beings may be expressed as and in anything that humans can imagine: from the stylised, iconic representations of Shive in stone lingams (above, Chapter 3) to names and formulae, visual representations of all kinds to the extremely anthropomorphic ('human-like') – only with the exception that the size may differ, such as in a recently built 88-metres-tall (!) Chinese Buddha statue. The statue of the goddess Athene in Athens in antiquity measured some 11 metres – a manifestation of the importance of the goddess but certainly also a demonstration of the city's influence and wealth. Other religious traditions barely allows the name of the god(s) to be mentioned or an image to be drawn. Non-literal traditions with little visual plastic art may use natural phenomena to indicate a god's presence, such as when the Nuer of southern Sudan say 'e Kwoth' ('it is Spirit') about a range of objects and events in nature (Evans-Pritchard 1966: 123–43). The potential range of representations is vast but always a dependent variable upon something other, be it, for instance, dogma, ritual or politics. Displays of all kinds exhibit the functions of the gods. For instance, the Hindu goddess Durga is depicted with eight arms holding a myriad of weapons to show that she is always protecting mankind in every direction of the world. The diplays have emotional and cognitive functions: they intensify emotions and function as cognitive anchors that help secure abstract thought. Almost anything may go as a condensed symbol with a range of connotations that are brought into play: from a crucifix or a peyote cactus to sacred cows in India or bear cubs that are central symbols of the gods in the religious tradition of the Ainu ethnos ('nation') in Japan.

Similarly, the powers of gods, demons, ancestors and ghosts may vary immensely, but without exception they are extra-human. Even the smallest ghosts or the nastiest little demons have particular powers that far exceed those of the ordinary mortals. Most likely they are manifestations of Ludwig Feuerbach's idea of projections of the human psyche and so instances of wishful thinking: 'if only we could...' Loss of control may leave humans helpless, so *imagined* control is better than none. Ghosts, ancestors et al. provide that. They are superhuman agents that should be placated and pleased and reciprocal action in the form of 'do-ut-des' (Latin: 'I-give-so-that-you give') usually works. As already noted on the main types of religion (Chapter 3), polytheistic and locative religious traditions may boast a multitude of superhuman agents in a 'pantheon' (Greek: 'all gods'). Great and small gods are organised in genealogies and hierarchies with functional distinctions and relevant division of labour. There may be gods that take care of just anything – in any imaginable way.

The Old Norse religious tradition was (as far as the sources can be trusted) a loose composition of local variants of gods. There was no ordered theology but a mass of myths and legends where the most prominent gods, Thor, Odinn and Freyr took care of weather, war and fertility. The status, function and power of the individual god depended on local cultic tradition. The gods of the Norsemen were clearly functional gods as is normally the case in polytheistic traditions – there was a degree of systematicity, a kind of network logic but no elaborate theology. The Maori ethnos of New Zealand traditionally related to a large family of gods, descended from the Earth Mother and the Sky Father. Many of their functions and importance are commonsensical, but for others it is really necessary to know the traditional lore, the mythical reasoning behind their attributes – for instance why the god of forests and birds, Tanemahuta, has a daughter, Hinenui-tepo, who is the goddess of death.

The gods are often important signifiers in the cultural webs of meaning – they are semantic attractors around which various symbolic references coalesce. The Hindu tradition consists of an extremely complex polytheistic pantheon along with multifaceted interpretative practices. Fortunately, the Hindu tradition is quite liberal on the side of dogma, and most practitioners select a single god(dess) as their ritual focus. 'Henotheism' is the term for this selection of one object of devotion among many. Monotheistic thought emanated from polytheistic traditions, but there does seems to be any logical underlying schema or reason for these changes other than historical contingency. The 'axial age' changes in ideology and morality did contribute to the monotheistic impetus in for example, in ancient Iran, where the teachings of Zoroaster merged earlier individual gods into aspects of the single godhead Ahura Mazda. But there was no similar drive in India or China. However, monotheism presents a specific problem, namely that of *theodicy*: If the only God is almighty, just and good, why is there injustice and suffering in the world? Who is to blame? Countless theologians of the monotheistic traditions have occupied themselves with these problems – so far to no avail. There is no single answer to that question. However, such logical problems do arise when religiosity turns into theology; that is when philosophy and logic become important as competing modes of discourse (Wiebe 1991). When monotheistic thought insists on *one* way as right and reject others as wrong, this may ultimately foster exclusion, persecution and violence (Assmann 2009).

Some gods are *higher* than others, and in many polytheistic schemes there are hierarchies and genealogies of gods, as mothers and fathers, daughters and sons. The classical Indian, Greek and Roman are well known historical examples, but complex polytheistic traditions there have been, and are, in other parts of the world, from West African Yoruba religion to Japanese Shinto (Swanson 1960; Paper 2005). Many of them reflect patriarchal society, and most have a 'High god' as ruler. Thus, they frequently mirror tiers in social hierarchy and division of labour in society. As a general rule for polytheistic religious traditions, more complex societies have more complex pantheons and elaborate cultic administrations. In some places, the apex of the hierarchy is occupied by a *Deus Otiosus* (Latin: 'resting god'), a non-interfering god who left the work to others after having created the universe. Lesser beings will take care of the mundane task of caring for humans, with various chores according to, for example, age, gender, social rank and occupation. In addition to greater and lesser gods, these lesser beings may be angels and saints and as such they function as mediators between this and the 'other world'. In monotheistic traditions, such tasks may be delegated to local saints who have special powers and who may heal and save in their specific locality (Thomas 2003: 27–8). Bakers, butchers and beer brewers also had their own in medieval Christianity. Anthropomorphic beings with special powers abound in just about *any* tradition the world has seen and also where the official forms of religions do *not* want them. That is because they are very human and generally, they function precisely as extensions and amplifications of ordinary human capabilities: What humans cannot do, know or handle – *they* can. In other places these 'minor agents' proliferate alongside or are part of the larger cosmology and in crowded companies of local gods, demons, spirits, fairies and ancestors – just to name the most prevalent. As the historical and ethnographic records demonstrate, various forms of elite and monastic Buddhism exist along with complex spirit worship (e.g., Spiro 2017). Often, the popular 'substratum' of minor agents remain from earlier forms of religion and so they are translated or transformed into shapes and functions that can merge with the dominant tradition. The most important feature of the inhabitants of the interactive hierarchies, from ghosts to gods, lies in the powers that they have and may administer to best support human life in this world – and perhaps the next. Rudolf Otto's notion of the *numinous* inspiring awe and wonder were just one side of this human response to the gods that humans have dealt with for a very long time. Then, dealing with other-worldly beings, from ghost to gods is no lowly task, requires skills. Religion certainly is about gods, but it *really* is about humans.

Religiosity: holding beliefs, and acting on them

Religiosity is the common term for individual interior aspects of religious belief and behaviour, and so it is definable as the 'holding of beliefs and acting on them'. As mental phenomena, religious beliefs belong to the domain of i-religion. However, beliefs are not just interior mental activities. It is a category mistake to think of the mind as a kind of container and belief as some object inside the container. Instead, following Schilbrack and viewing beliefs as *dispositions* means that they are not just invisible mental activities because 'to have a belief is to have a propensity or a tendency, or a set of them, typically shaped by one's social context to interact with the world and with others according to a more or less specifiable pattern' (Schilbrack 2014: 63). In that sense, beliefs are also social facts as they come to be held by individuals when the contents of beliefs and the propositional attitudes to them are being distributed and reproduced in society and culture. If beliefs were entirely and only in minds, they would truly be difficult to study but fortunately (also for the study of them) they circulate in culture and society, just as, for example, songs, ideas and stories do. Thus, they can be picked up by individuals and groups who internalise the contents of the beliefs. Just like learning that the name for a specific colour is 'red' in English and that is what the word means, so the beliefs that Buddha was enlightened, Muhammad is the messenger of God, and many other propositions mean just what they generally mean *among* a group of people, an interpretive community.

Consequently, beliefs exist in culture and as such they may be appropriated, cultivated, criticised or redefined in their distribution and transmission. Beliefs are ideas, concepts, templates and patterns that *exist* in culture, which are then internalised in cognition and emotion. In this manner, they become the constituents of behaviour and then again objectivised and externalised for others (Berger 1990). This is basically how religious ideas propagate and circulate. For these same reasons, they are also not as private as they might seem at a first glance; insiders may privilege or hide their ideas, but that does not mean that these ideas are *in principle* inaccessible to outsiders (Jensen 2011a). Private beliefs are versions of public beliefs, just as private language (talking to myself) is a version of public language, and private money (what I have in my pocket) is a version of ordinary public money. Genuinely private money would not function as *currency*.

Beliefs in the mind in i-religion are thus also an integral part of e-religion, and so *religiosity* as a general term refers to modes of behaviour that are regulated by commitment to a religious perspective that is (ultimately) governed by the 'ultimate sacred postulates'. The term 'religiosity' may then be used to cover all modes of behaviour that refer to the accepted system or network of beliefs. Clifford Geertz (see Chapter 1) pointed out how human experience is shaped by religion: how the 'religious perspective' provides cognitive governance through a conviction of what is 'really real' and by the 'imbuing of a certain specific complex of symbols – of the metaphysic they formulate and the style of life they recommend – with a persuasive authority which, from an analytic point of view, is the essence of religious action' (Geertz 1973: 112). The degree to which religiosity acts as cognitive governance in human existence varies, of course, all the way from an insignificant dash of spirituality to a complete immersion in Jewish orthodox religious practice, in Buddhist monastic life, or where the existential dimension of religiosity is the ultimately meaningful as in the thought of Paul Tillich (see Chapter 1). In some traditional societies, life in general is so wholly intertwined with religious beliefs and practices that it is difficult to see what is not (e.g., Zuesse 1992).

Beliefs modulating beliefs: unconscious and conscious acting

Beliefs do not stand alone: they are, as propositional attitudes in language, always enmeshed in networks of other beliefs and attitudes that mutually influence each other in the minds of humans, consciously or unconsciously, individually or collectively. How and why people hold, change or give up beliefs always depends on the (mostly unconscious) relations to other mental processes. For centuries, philosophers who were attracted to these problems only had introspection and their own reasoning to try to work out how minds work. But, as Pascal Boyer points out, 'When psychologists replaced all these with experimental studies, they found a whole menagerie of mental processes that apparently conspire to lead us away from clear and supported beliefs' (Boyer 2001: 300). In a condensed form, here is his record of various unconscious effects on beliefs: 'consensus effect', where people adjust their perception impressions to those of others; 'false consensus effect', when someone believes that others think like herself; 'generation effect', where self-generated information is believed more strongly that perceptions of others ('*I* did see it'); 'memory illusions' such as in false memories, for instance imagining a particular action often enough will give an illusion that it was actually performed; 'source monitoring defects' set in when people become unsure of whether they heard or read something first, second or third hand; 'confirmation bias' is very common: when people have particular ideas they better recall instances that confirm, rather than refute, their own bias; 'cognitive dissonance reduction' is where 'People tend to readjust memories of previous beliefs and impressions in light of new experience. If some information leads them to form a particular impression of some people, they will tend to think that they had that impression all along, even if their previous judgement were in fact the opposite' (Boyer 2001: 300–1). Far from being trivial psychological themes, such mental processes are very frequent and important in religious life, both when people consider their own beliefs and actions and when they consider those of others, in the same group or among outsiders.

A remarkable example of the influence of religious beliefs, values and expectations comes from a recent study of the influence of perceived charisma of Christian healers among members of a charismatic movement in Denmark. Assumptions about the divine powers of the healers influence how praying practitioners perceive the efficacy of intercessory prayers. When believers were engaged in prayer and perceived the influence of the charismatic healers, brain-scanning showed that the cognitive activity in the executive systems of their brains decreased, that is, they became less alert and more trusting. This means that the belief in the charismatic powers of a healer modulated participants' beliefs, and the study demonstrates how humans 'hand over' some of their cognitive functions to others with perceived authority: this is thus an effect of the perceived authority of religious leadership (Schjødt et al. 2011).

Examples such as this one demonstrate how important and how powerful prior expectations are to the interpretation of events. All humans interpret their world in relation to experience and memory, to intuitive as well as reflective beliefs, and according to the norms and values of their culture. Therefore, we may say that there are *constitutive* beliefs, directly following from the ultimate sacred postulates, and *regulative* beliefs that are involved in the governance of behaviour, thought and emotion. For instance, if a religious tradition stipulates directly in its ritual prescriptions that pork is unclean food then this will have a regulative effect on the experiences and behaviours of the followers of the tradition. Human cognition is both biological *and* cultural and so it functions in relation to social, cultural and religious values and norms. Humans boast 'dual process' cognition where the biological (intuitive beliefs) and the socio-cultural (reflective beliefs) merge and mesh (Kahneman 2011). As a result, human cognition is *special* in the sense that it is regulated by social, cultural and religious norms. Humans have normative cognition that is tightly connected with religious rituals and institutions (Jensen 2013; see also Chapters 5 and 6).

Religious experience

In 1902, the psychologist William James defined religious experience as 'the feelings, acts, and experiences of individual men in their solitude, so far as they apprehend themselves to stand in relation to whatever they may consider divine' (James 1985: 34). In spite of this reasonably distinct definition, the concept of religious experience has been a vexed one. It has a long and complicated history in theology, philosophy, psychology and other scholarship on religion. For instance, in the copious work of Mircea Eliade, the experiential dimension became both the premise for and the conclusion about religion in general (Pals 2006: 193–228). In most of these fields, there has been a marked tendency for religious experience to be associated with ideas mainly from Christian Protestant theology with its distinct focus on individual faith. Religious experience was conceptualised theologically and taken to prove its own referent, the 'reality of the sacred' as an ontologically existing entity. Religious traditions approve of this mode of interpretation: just as the experience of heat depends on the presence of heat, so the religious experience depends on the presence of something superhuman that prompts the experience. As the philosopher Friedrich Schleiermacher (1768–1834) explained it: the feeling of being God's creature flows from the fact of having being created by God (e.g., Capps 1995: 13–18). This is clearly a theological interpretation – as seen also in the work of Rudolf Otto (above).

For the agnostic outsider, this mode of interpretation neither validates nor proves the existence of any superhuman cause; it only proves that the experiencer claims to have an experience that is given an interpretation that is in accordance with the given religious tradition. Consequently, in the ways that the category of religious experience has mostly been presented by its advocates, it has seemed to be of limited use in studies of other traditions than Christian (Needham 1973). The use of the category often generates more trouble than elucidation, and it certainly is not a self-evident, nor a theoretically innocent one. As Ann Taves notes in the first introductory paragraph of a monograph on the topic:

> The idea of 'religious experience' is deeply embedded in the study of religion and religions as it (religion) and they (religions) have come to be understood in the modern West. In the nineteenth and twentieth centuries, many modernizers in the West and elsewhere advanced the idea that a certain kind of experience, whether characterized as religious, mystical, or spiritual, constituted the essence of 'religion' and the common core of the world's 'religions'. This understanding of religion and the religions dominated the academic study of religion during the last century.
>
> (Taves 2011: 1)

As Taves further explains, many scholars (especially theologians and historians of religions) saw religious experience as the very essence of religion. This view has been criticised over the past half century and later largely abandoned. It was a understanding that took religious experience to be a *sui generis* category, and scholars argued that the views of believers (first person or subjective) should be privileged and not attempted to be explained 'in biological, psychological, or sociological terms for fear of 'reducing' it to something else' (Taves 2011: 1). Therefore, as for example, Rudolf Otto believed, the study of religion should also be *sui generis*, and conducted with a certain religious sensitivity. That theoretical premise has since been shown to be a liberal theological bias (e.g., Wiebe 1999; McCutcheon 2003).

The introduction to an encyclopedia entry on the experiential phenomenology of religion indicates how the category of religious experience continues to be a complex and opaque one. The theologian Mark Wynn notes that:

> Commentators on religious experience disagree on the role of phenomen-ological considerations. Is there a phenomenology that is distinctive of religious experience? And if there is, do we have a reliable vocabulary to describe it? Is there a phenomenology of mystical experience which crosses faith boundaries? Or are such experiences saturated with tradition-specific doctrinal assumptions? Are reports of religious experiences in central cases best read as doctrine-inspired interpretations of the subjective character of the experience, rather than as accounts of their phenomenology? And does the affective phenomenology of religious experience do any epistemic work? Let's consider some of these issues.
>
> (Wynn 2008: 1)

In this connection the complexities of talking about 'belief' and 'experience' are further increased by introducing the notion of the phenomenology of religion. In many academic disciplines (e.g., philosophy, sociology or anthropology) 'phenomenology' indicates an interest in the dimensions of subjective experience of the matters studied. In philosophy a typical definition is that phenomenology is the study of structures of consciousness as experienced from the first-person point of view. In (for example) sociological analyses such studies might concern the experience of being unemployed or belonging to a minority. In the study of religion, then, from around 1930, 'phenomenology' became the attempt to study subjective religious experience (Cox 2010). This has proven to be notoriously difficult, if not impossible. It also added to the disciplinary confusion that 'phenomenology of religion' was already in use as a label for the comparative study of religions and of elements of religion. That earlier kind of classificatory phenomenology of religion had other problems, namely those of comparison and generalisation, but these problems are not unmanageable (Jensen 2003: chapter 2). In fact, the present book is an attempt to produce an up-to-date version of such classificatory phenomenologies of religion.

Until very recently, phenomenological research has been based solely on subjects' self-reports (as used in psychology) without the possibility of external correlations or controls. However, there are new methods such as brain-scanning technologies that increasingly allow for complementary research practices. These are, however, also theoretically challenging and not easy to manage conceptually (Hinde 1999: 185–205). They may also introduce other complications that need conceptual clarification concerning how and how much experiences have neural correlates (Schjødt 2011). As the historian of religion Ann Taves notices on current attempts to bridge the gap between the humanities and the sciences:

> Finally, in the last decade and a half (since 1990), there has been a dramatic increase in studies examining the neurological, cognitive, and evolutionary underpinnings of religion in light of the rapid advances in the study of the brain and consciousness. Scholars who identify with the growing subfield of the cognitive science of religion are drawn from disparate disciplines including psychology, anthropology, religious studies, and philosophy. Though most of them are well versed in the study of religion, they have focused on belief and practice (ritual) and with a few exceptions ... have ignored experience ... In addition, scholars and researchers, including a number of self-identified neurotheologians, most of whom lack training in theology or religious studies ... have enthusiastically embraced the challenges of identifying the neural correlates of religious experience without engaging the critiques of the concept that led many scholars of religion to abandon it.
>
> (Taves 2011: 8)

Thus, on the issue of religious experience some confusion remains: there is no way to brain scan muddled concepts and get clear answers. However, some results of the research on experience are remarkable, such as when experiments demonstrate how 'out-of-body' experiences can be replicated experimentally. Such experiences have often been given more or less religious, transcendental or spiritual interpretations and so taken as evidence of the reality of 'something beyond'. Recent research shows how such experiences are produced as results of electrical stimulation of the right angular gyrus in the brain (Metzinger 2009: 75–114). This is a clear example of what a 'natural explanation' means.

In the present theoretical outlook, religious experience may be straightforwardly defined (from an analytic point of view) as 'experience with an added component of religious belief'. This definition rejects the idea that religious experience should be *sui generis* and irreducible. Therefore, a religious experience is an experience to which the concept 'religious' is attributed (consciously or unconsciously). It may well be that it is an experience that is difficult for the experiencing subject to convey to others, but that is not special or something that only concerns religious experience. Instead of privileging religious experience as an inexplicable category of human understanding that defies scrutiny, Ann Taves advocates a 'building block approach' to 'experiences deemed religious':

> Rather than abandon the study of experience, we should disaggregate the concept of 'religious experience' and study the wide range of experiences to which religious significance has been attributed. If we want to understand

how anything at all, including experience, *becomes* religious, we need to turn our attention to the processes whereby people sometimes ascribe the special characteristics to things that we (as scholars) associate with terms such as 'religious,' 'magical', 'mystical,' 'spiritual,' et cetera. Disaggregating 'religious experience' in this way will allow us to focus on the interaction between psychobiological, social, and cultural-linguistic processes in relation to carefully specified types of experiences sometimes considered religious and to build methodological bridges across the divide between the humanities and the sciences.

(Taves 2011: 7)

Taves' appeal to a better understanding and use of the concept (instead of throwing it onto the heap of discarded notions) includes careful analyses of the concepts and objects of study. That is needed. The same goes, and perhaps even more so, for the kinds of religious experience connected with the notion of 'mysticism'. As mysticism belongs to practice in the present theoretical perspective, it will be among the topics of Chapter 5.

What to believe and how to think: divination and oracles as special knowledge

Religious beliefs and experiences are also often applied in highly conscious and intentional manners: that is, with special attention and emphasis on the procurement of information to act on or to organise other beliefs on. If such information is not already at hand, in scriptures, memory or other media, there are the ancient, ubiquitous and pervasive practices of *divination* (from Latin *divinare*: to foresee) and oracles (from Latin *orare*: to speak). Both are usually rendered as prophecy, foretelling or prediction, that is, with an emphasis on information about the future, but they may as well aim at finding explanations for past events or present conditions. The practices of divination and oracles are clearly modes of ritual (discussed in Chapter 5) and they articulate religious institutions (discussed in Chapter 6), so here the focus is on divination and oracles as normative systems of beliefs and representations. Divination and oracles are ways of getting to know about all that which humans do not ordinarily know through their senses: for example, the secrets of nature or the secrets of the superhuman agents. In some cases information is requested from the latter, as many of them have 'full strategic knowledge': they know what humans do *not* know. In other cases, various practices are employed to elicit information that is otherwise hidden about the course of nature. Divination and oracle institutions and practices are conceived of as networks of systematic relations, correlations and causations between this and the 'other world': things in this world are signs of necessity, knowledge and intentionality. Mircea Eliade (1987) pointed this out in his notion of 'hierophany', that is, signs by which the sacred is revealed.

In either case, oracles, divination rituals and the quest for special knowledge have social and psychological functions as they help to modify doubts, satisfy curiosity, alleviate fears and calm anger. On closer inspection, divination is far from mysterious; it is a rational solution when there is nothing obvious to make sense from. Humans just do not like chance and contingency: 'No meaning' is cognitively dreadful so humans build their own intentionality into everything. There is a certain naturalness in divination as a way of making the universe speak because humans are naturally inclined to attribute intentionality to their surroundings. It is better to 'be on the look-out', and unusual 'things' attract more attention than do ordinary ones. Counter-intuitive 'things' attract even more attention, and so have 'cognitive salience'. Boyer's list in Table 4.1 can be useful in analyses of divination (Lisdorf 2004).

The ensuing cognitive and emotional functions of divination are examples of classical psychological functionalism: strategic knowledge acquisition helps explain contingency ('Why does this happen to me/us?') and so reduces anxiety and assists in coping at individual and collective levels. Divination assists in creating joint intentionality and enables distributed and joint action programmes, and so it supports humans in working together at the social, institutional and political levels. Obeying the declaration of the oracle, for instance, will provide confidence in prediction and reduce complexity. Such divinatory practices also deter violence, as they enable participants to blame other agents (human or superhuman) if things go wrong: either the divinatory ritual was faulty and must be repeated or other powers were stronger. However, when individuals or groups compete, there can be all kinds of rivalry, fraud and deception and so other *humans* might be to blame. In such instances, divination may hit back and *produce* anxiety. The number of things that humans can worry about is indefinite.

Divination may also entail a sacrifice of free will and in some sense (in the outsider's view) is the apotheosis of coincidence and contingency: probability and chance are converted into divine or natural necessities. Predestination may look like the lazy solution, but in traditions oriented towards predestination, devotees soon begin to look for signs. Divination is above all a clear case of religious semiosis (sign-making) and semiotics (sign organisation and interpretation). If religion is about beliefs and faith, which Western traditions have traditionally emphasised, then, in most places, it is about the beliefs and faith *in knowledge*.

The diviners and the diviners' audience believe that divination reveals the way the world truly is. It is a special case of wishful thinking to hold such beliefs, and the wishful thinking consists not only in what is believed but also in the manner in which it is believed. Divination is driven by the human cognitive propensity to be able to predict: the human brain is above all a prediction machine. When groups of religious people agree on how to solve prediction problems, divination is often the outcome. There are two basic strategies underlying the many modes of divination practice: (a) *omens*, the spontaneous occurrences of strange events and (b) *augury*, which operates within a determined range of probability. Table 4.2 lists some divinatory practices. These practices are all concerned with what individuals or groups should know about past and present situations, and what to do about future situations. They are, in a sense, time-travel tools.

To present an idea of how divination works, here is the example of hepatoscopy: archaeological excavations at Mari in Syria have produced thirty-two model livers from the nineteenth-century BCE palace. Liver models were used to train diviners in divination, and they functioned as memory props, that is, they were 'exograms' of what diviners should have in mind when operating with actual livers from the sacrificial animals. The relation between clay model livers and the rule of the land may seem far-fetched to the modern mind, but this was the intention behind the divinatory practice: to be able to weigh political decisions in high uncertainty conditions. In ancient Mesopotamia, the liver was very important as it was considered the organ of feeling and thinking. Anomalies of past divination livers referred to known events, and both liver signs and events had been meticulously recorded. Then, in a new divination ritual, livers were compared with the records to predict future events. As a mode of religious belief, discourse and practice, these forms of divination show how the distinctions between domains in the world are collapsed: what happens to a sheep liver depends on divine providence and political decisions. Such religiously validated (agreeing with tradition) knowledge can be obtained in the traditions' scriptures. The power of reflective beliefs is well illustrated by divination practices. Many of them have highly elaborate techniques, such as the Chinese I Ching system. Oral cultures may also have elaborate techniques for divination *without* the aid of written sources, such as the Yoruba Ifa divination system in West Africa where extensive learning and memorisation were required of the practitioners. A tentative definition of divination could run

Table 4.2 Some divinatory practices

Name	Technique	Examples
Astrology	Observing and calculating motion of celestial objects	Ancient Chinese astrology, modern (and computerised) astrology
Cleromancy	Casting or drawing lots: stones, beads, seeds, etc.	The Ifa divination system of the Yoruba
Hepatoscopy	Observing irregularities in animal livers	The ancient Syrian and Mesopotamian reading of livers from sacrificial animals
Cheiromantics	Palm of hand reading	In antiquity as well as in more occult and popular practice today
Rhapsodomantics	Using random parts of sacred scripture	Christian practice of placing a finger into the Bible at random and explaining/predicting based on the verse(s) selected

like this: 'Divination and oracle institutions and practices are networks of systematic relation, correlation and causation between this and the other world so that things in this world are signs of necessity, knowledge and intentionality'.

Religious language and discourse

The characteristic genres and particular features of religious language, symbolism and narrative have attracted attention from philosophers, theologians and other scholars since antiquity. It is obvious that different discourses, or 'modes of speaking', may present very different impressions of their objects – the things they talk 'about'. Religious discourses are a case in point. They speak about the world in manners that are clearly different from modern common-sense or scientific discourse. This is not surprising, as religious discourse is commonly expressed in what has come to be labelled 'religious language'. Religious language and discourse display some peculiarities over against ordinary language. The discussion about the status, function and validity of religious statements in language and discourse is complex and should be reflected upon with diligence and care. The matter is not quite as simple as it may be imagined in a common-sense empiricist manner: 'religion is nonsense, whereas science speaks the truth'.

Modes of discourse, manners of speaking or 'language games', are often very complex in the sense that even the most innocent-looking forms of descriptive language actually contain and employ many normative and prescriptive models and metaphors. As the philosopher Ludwig Wittgenstein noted: 'An entire mythology is stored within our language' (1993:133). Scientists' language about the human genome may be less mythological, but poets could not write poetry if there was no mythology in language. Forms of language and discourse serve different purposes. Table 4.3 gives a very simplified summary of the differences in an 'ideal type' fashion.

Religious language is permeated with transcendental and unassailable authority, which is derived from its relations to the ultimate sacred postulates.

Table 4.3 Ordinary and religious language: notable differences

Language	Ordinary language	Religious language
Meaning made	by reference to/correspondence with the ordinary world/epistemic limits set by science	by reference to/correspondence with the 'other world'/internal coherence in 'web of meaning'/epistemic limits set by tradition
Reference to	material world and common-sense conventions	transcendental/traditional truths or 'ultimate sacred postulates'/coherence with holistic web of signification
Cognitive functions	perceiving the world 'as it is' – including social conventions	conceptualising the 'thought-of-world'/creating salient moral and emotional coherence

In that sense, religious language is a circular and self-authenticating kind of language. Discourses, texts and narratives depend on hierophanies (revelations of the sacred) that proclaim their own truth-value along this model: 'What is written in this scripture is true because this scripture is true'. Thus,

> a universe founded in and by myth cannot be measured by rational standards of truth, at least not from the internal view of the tradition, as the mythical discourse is the very standard by which *other* forms of language have to be measured.
>
> (Jensen 2009a: 15)

In a similar manner, the value of religious language hinges on its internal coherence and consistency, not with a direct correspondence to the material world. Religious language has *social* correspondence: religious myth and discourse correspond to how the world is lived and seen *from inside* the perspectives of the mythically founded universe. By so doing, it reinforces its own truth-value by being an image of the image it has itself constructed. Religious language is not 'non-sense'; it may contain and express much sense, all in spite of having 'special' references:

> As the religious conception of the world has its special characteristics, the same applies to religious language as a general category. Certainly, there are various kinds of religious language: dogmas, moral and ethical teachings, sermons, dietary rules, etc. This could lead to the conclusion that the language of religion is quite ordinary; there are prescriptions, imperatives and prohibitions and other grammatical and syntactical forms known from ordinary language. In general, religious language is thus normative but that is not all there is to it. The most important feature of the religious linguistic universe is that, although it uses ordinary everyday language as its basis, it is also foundational. Religious language is related to the foundation of the cosmos it refers to, and this foundation is mostly encountered in myths.
>
> (Jensen 2009a: 15)

Summing up, Table 4.4 displays typical relations and differences between ordinary and religious beliefs, discourse and narrative.

Discourse, authority and dogma

When religious traditions change from oral to literate, new possibilities emerge for the storing of semantic knowledge in narratives and discourses as instruments for the conservation of collective, external memory. The same possibilities of external memory storage also generate means for reflection, scrutiny, criticism, denial, debate and dissent, and so literacy can be a mixed blessing for religious traditions as well as for their guardians and interpreters. Literate religious traditions can be stored in many different formats and with the aid of very different technologies.

Table 4.4 Ordinary and religious beliefs, modes of discourse, and narratives

	Ordinary (examples)	Religious (examples)
Beliefs	intuitive: own perception reflective: others' information	reflective: based on others' information / authority backed / 'ultimate sacred postulates' / unquestionable
Modes of discourse	scientific / political / public / media / ethical / moral (secular)	religious / sacred / axiomatic / dogmatic mythical / ethical / moral (sacred)
Narratives	ordinary talk / news / folk tales / fiction (novels, etc.)	canons / dogma / myths / legends: normative / edifying / entertaining ('attention-grabbing')

Consider the difference in accessibility between ancient Egyptian hieroglyphs and electronic Qur'an apps. The first required extensive training and were a privilege only for the few; the latter enables its user to become an instant independent religious scholar and criticise the traditional authorities. In between these two extremes, all kinds of combinations and variations are possible. In the more striking cases of variations and blendings of traditions and their elements, such as traditional West African religions and Christianity, the resulting new tradition is often called *syncretism* in the study of religion (Leopold and Jensen 2004). In fact, many religious traditions are more or less syncretistic, as they are composed of ingredients and influences from different sources. However, the same religious traditions will typically deny this and insist on being original, pristine and pure and of divine original and special inspiration, from voodoo to Scientology. Such denial is a typical feature of religious discourse and an integral component in the construction of authority. Very few religious traditions have been known to express that they are not the best, the most trustworthy and insightful, and so on. Religious discourse has as one of its main characteristics the declaration of its own infallibility.

In literate traditions, some collections of scriptures are attributed special authority and truth-value, in some cases because the speaking subject of the text is considered the supreme godhead itself, or because the text contains special revelations, apocalypses or other knowledge considered very valuable. Most literate traditions have operated with many different sources and versions. During long historical processes, and often with considerable disagreement in the interpretive communities, certain versions have been chosen or designated as the most correct, insightful or inspired. They become approved as *canon* (Greek: 'measuring stick'), as the standard. Canonical texts are called 'closed' when they are no longer allowed to be edited. The standard canonised texts are often termed *textus receptus* (the received text) and as such they have the maximum authority – also because the traces of editing have been elided, removed or disguised. Students in the study of religion are surprised when they begin reading scholarly and critical versions of the sacred text compilations from many of the literate religious traditions. Many of the students are (as most people) used to think of the Bible as one book, and then they discover all the notes in the *critical apparatus* that disclose the different sources, datings and commentary. The Qur'an also has a traditional history of compilation, though short, during the reign of the caliph Uthman (644–56 CE): one version was established as the original and other versions that had begun to circulate were destroyed. In Judaism, Christianity and Islam, as well as in other and later traditions, there have been many and severe disagreements between various groups and their versions and interpretations of their sacred scriptures. In Christianity, there were debates about the double nature (man and god) of Jesus as Christ ('the anointed one') and about which scriptures should be included in the Bible and still, the Bible versions in the main Christian churches are not identical. Some of the scriptures held by the churches to be of uncertain status were called *apocrypha* (Greek: 'things hidden') and excluded from the canonised versions. Originally, 'apocryphal' was a positive term referring to writings only for the initiated. Later, the word would mean dubious, false or heretical. An interesting example that has caused much controversy in scholarship is the Gospel of Thomas, discovered in Egypt in 1945. It is not a narrative like the other gospels but a collection containing 114 *logia* ('sayings') of Jesus (Pagels 2003). Some of these sayings are familiar and consistent with the standard gospels while others have a more Gnostic character. Gnostic texts and ideas (from the early centuries CE) are examples of the kinds of discourse that were not included in the canonised Christian Bible. Gnostics, whoever they were (see below), claimed a certain special and *esoteric* ('for the initiated') sacred insight or *gnosis* (Greek: 'knowledge') into self-knowledge, the spiritual nature of the cosmos and the mystical enlightenment leading to deliverance from the material existence. Some promoted the idea that humans really are godly. Obviously, such ideas and practices questioned the authority of Catholic teachings as well as the institution and organisation of the emerging church. Gnosticism, the common term for these esoteric movements, also demonstrates how a body of thought and learning may be known as *discourse* and not as belonging to a distinct social formation because it is simply not known *who* the Gnostics were. However, 'gnostic' is also an example of how a derogative or depreciative term comes into circulation.

In the Islamic traditions, stories have circulated about verses that were edited out of the Qur'an or about extra chapters added in Shi'a Muslim versions. (By the way, just as the number of *logia* in the Gospel of Thomas was 114, there are 114 *suras* in the Qur'an.) In the Buddhist and other Asian traditions, countless manuscripts go into the formation of the various interpretive traditions, with appropriate control of who counts as 'true master' or what counts as 'true insight'. Generally, however, the Asian traditions are more lenient towards variations in interpretation than the monotheistic traditions. Often, they are more concerned with *orthopraxy*, that is, doing matters in the right way, than about *orthodoxy*, that is, holding the right beliefs.

In conclusion, it appears that discrepancies and discussions have not always been driven just by piety. Agreement and disagreement are caused as much by authority, hierarchy, control, power as by resources and wealth. The formations

Table 4.5 Levels of discourse hierarchy

Discourse hierarchy	Examples
transcendent (source of unquestionable authority)	The sanctified origins of ultimate sacred postulates, axioms, gods, ancestors, etc. ('What goes without saying')
Interpretant (conveys information)	'Signs of the sacred': incarnations, sacred narratives, divination, prophets, reformers, saints, monks, teachers, organisations, institutions, etc.
Participant	Groups of believers, congregations, organisations, institutions, etc.

of canons as the authorised collections of discourses mostly correlate with political and other pressures. Here, the Chinese classical religious and philosophical traditions provide clear examples, as they are as much concerned with divining the right kind of political rule as with spiritual exercise and familial piety (Allen 1991).

Almost everywhere, the modes of interpretation are, and have been, associated with and related to exercise of power. The formations of canons, the appropriate patterns of interpretation, and the corps of approved interpreters are habitually linked to mundane matters too. To illustrate and simplify, Table 4.5 gives a 'discourse theoretical' diagram indicating how religious communication, discourse and narrative are sanctified and organised in a three-tier architecture (Jensen 2009a: 16).

Typically, sacred discourses provide many and very good reasons for why humans should pay attention to them: they supply knowledge. Many are the scriptural narratives with *apocalypse* (Greek: 'uncovering'), the disclosure of information, and so the texts in and of themselves become 'superhuman agents with full strategic knowledge'. Of ultimate moral consequence is the special genre *eschatology* (Greek: knowledge of the last things), because the ideas about fate after death, judgement, and Heaven and Hell are admonitions and warnings to the members of the community *here* and *now*. The following example is from the Islamic tradition, from the Qur'an. It is *Sura* (chapter) 78, called *An-Nabaa* (Arabic: the tidings), where Allah speaks as 'We' about the fate of those who did not listen and heed the warnings:

> Verily the day of sorting out is a thing appointed, the day that the trumpet shall be sounded and ye shall come forth in crowds; and the heavens shall be opened as if it were doors, and the mountains shall vanish, as if it were a mirage. Truly Hell is a place of ambush, for the transgressors a place of destination: they will dwell therein for ages. Nothing cool shall they taste therein, nor any drink, save a boiling fluid, and a fluid, dark, murky, intensely cold – a fitting recompense. For that they used not to fear any account, but they treated Our signs as false. And all things have We preserved on record: 'So taste ye.

For no increase shall We grant you, except in punishment'. Verily, for the righteous there will be a fulfilment of desires; gardens enclosed, and grape-vines; companions of equal age; and a cup full. No vanity shall they hear, nor untruth; recompense from thy Lord, a gift sufficient.

(Sura 78:17–36)

The moral lesson is unmistakable: the visions of things to come are presented in the service of the righteous and as a defence against moral decay. It is a warning and an example of how moralising discourses function as apocalypses and eschatologies. For the righteous there is recompense, but the interpretation of just how that is to be understood is not always obvious. For instance, the nature the 'companions of equal age' mentioned requires additional commentary such as that provided by the later Muslim tradition, the *Hadith*, which is composed of reports on the sayings and doings of the prophet Muhammad. Nothing in the Qur'an suggests seventy-two virgins. However, in a collection by at-Tirmidhi (d. 892 CE) it is stated that someone had heard Muhammad saying that 'The smallest reward for the people of Heaven is an abode where there are eighty thousand servants and seventy-two *houris*, over which stands a dome decorated with pearls, aquamarine and ruby, as wide as the distance from al-Jabiyyah to Sanaa.' This is evidently legendary (reported more than 250 years after the death of Muhammad), if not outright mythological (the subject matter being vividly imaginary). The nature of the *houris* has been widely debated, as they might have been angels, virgins or just young maidens symbolising the purity and beauty of Heaven. In short and as so often before: the nature of the message changes with the means of interpretation.

Myth, in particular

Just as eschatological narratives that speak about the 'last things' are genuinely concerned with what humans should do in the here and now, the kinds of narrative commonly called *myths* – stories about wondrous and inexplicable things, even from the beginning of the world – are really about the lives of humans and the worlds in which they unfold now. Many myths are narrative cosmologies, stories about the worlds and what is in them, and as such they are also fundamentally, and indirectly, stories about humans: they are 'anthropologies'. many are the myths that explain where humans come from, how their relations to ancestors, gods and animals came about and how they are consequently destined to act. In this sense of placing humans in the world through narrative, there is very little difference between the myths of non-literate peoples and the tracts of the literate traditions. Mythical narratives are central to how humans understand themselves in a given religious tradition. The subjects of myths may really be anything, but they are always important subjects such as gods, spirits, mind, body, purity, gender, sexuality, family or the entire systems of classification (Jensen 2016). Paraphrasing the linguist Ferdinand de Saussure (see Chapter 2), the systems of classification are like the language system (*langue*) and the mythical narratives and their elements (*mythemes*) are expressions of the systems – like speech and articulation (*parole*).

There are and have been countless myths and many different approaches to myth (Jensen 2009a). Here is a now classic interpretive generalisation of scholars' view of the contents and functions of myth as offered by a historian of religions (who was a specialist in Native North American traditions):

> The *myth* is an epic narrative dealing with figures belonging to the supernatural sphere: cosmic beings, gods and spirits. The action of the narrative takes place in a remote prehistoric period, but in principle the once consummated course of events is still of topical interest: timeless and eternal as the course of the planets. The scene of the drama is as a rule (but not always) another world than our own: heaven, the underworld or an unknown country. The myth gives instruction concerning the world of the gods, and therewith concerning the cosmic order; it confirms the social order and the cultural values obtaining in it and it is itself sacred. It is therefore self-evident that it is to be embraced with belief and reverence.
>
> (Hultkrantz 1957: 12–13)

The folklorist William Bascom supplied the differences between genres in another classical typology

> *Myths* are those narratives which, in the society in which they are told, are considered to be truthful accounts of what happened in the remote past. *Legends* are prose narratives which, like myths, are regarded as true by the narrator and his audience, but they are set in a period considered less remote, when the world was much as it is today. *Folktales* are prose narratives which are regarded as fiction.
>
> (Bascom 1965: 4)

Table 4.6 highlights the differences between these three genres as 'ideal types'. The division of genres is tentative rather than conclusive because the distinctive criteria concern matters as different as time, historicity, purpose, function, content and reference. It is thus only indicative and the different traits may be combined in actual narratives and discourses.

Being ideal types, these are *models* of genres as scholars understand them and as models, they direct our attention to the various features they highlight.

Table 4.6 Genres: contents and functions

Function/temporality	Historical	Non-historical
Pious/edifying	Legend	Myth
Aetiological	Legend	Myth
Entertaining	Folk tales	Fairy tale

Myths can be interesting from a number of perspectives, whether philosophical, psychological, sociological, semiotic and cognitive, and these perspectives may well be combined in the analyses of the narratives (Jensen 2009a).

There are many kinds of myths. In the literature about them, a certain amount of definitorial individualism is discernible. The more traditional catalogue of myths looks somewhat like this: *cosmogonic* myths about the creation of the world, *anthropogonic* myths about the origin of humankind, *theogonic* myths about the origin of the god(s), myths about animals, fire, agriculture, cooking, sexual and gender relations, song and dance, sacred kingship and social hierarchy, myths of floods and droughts, ancestors and demons, rituals and special religious, social and professional roles. In short, anything that can be or has been of importance to humans in this world may become the subject of myth. Other criteria of distinction besides form, contents and referents could be the functions and contexts of myths. After some consideration, I have arrived at this definition or, perhaps better, 'generalised interpretation': 'Myths are traditional, authoritative narratives referring to transcendent referents, and which fuse the lived-in world with the thought-of-world in such a manner that this present world seems the only plausible version' (Jensen 2009a: 10). The literary theorist and semiotician Roland Barthes once stated that myth is 'what-goes-without-saying', because myth does more than refer to what is perceived as the natural order; myth actually *creates* the natural order (Barthes 2000: 11). Myths and classification systems, along with rituals and institutions, play the fundamental role in upholding religious world views. However, the functions of myth may also be social and political, so that myths come to create, then mirror and sustain the order of the world.

As to the ideological functions of myth, there are two peculiarities. The first is that even though myths narrate forwards, from the beginnings until later (often to the present human condition), they are 'scripted' backwards, because they are narrated by humans from *the perspective of* the present condition. That present condition is not necessarily the present time: the story about the disobedience of Adam and Eve informs us about the origin of the human condition as seen in the Abrahamic monotheistic traditions, what then happened and the consequences thereof. A somewhat different fate resulted from this original 'crime' in each of the traditions, Judaism, Christianity and Islam, because the basic story is told in different versions and contexts. The second peculiarity is that myths *hide* the fact that humans produce them, mostly pretending to have superhuman origins. The world is made by myth and the myth tells how the world is. This is evidently circular, but that is a formal characteristic of both myth and religious language. Thus myth, and religious language as an extension of myth, sets up a world. 'Our' world is always a world mediated by language, and we would not know the world as *our* world if not through language. It is for this reason that myth and religious language, as perceived from within the traditional universe, lay the foundations for all that follows. This also means that a universe founded in and by myth cannot be measured by rational standards of truth. From inside the tradition, however, it *is* the truth, because the mythical discourse is the very standard by which *other* forms and expressions of language are measured. They set their own rationality, for it is also a characteristic of myths and the cosmologies expressed in religious language and world views that they are not just randomly non-rational; they have their own sets of rules of compositions and regulations, otherwise they would be impossible for humans to operate in and from. They must make sense.

The myths of classical antiquity were no uniform collection of stories. Homer and Hesiod were the two largest collections of narrative tradition, dating back approximately to the sixth century BCE. In written form, they became the general cultural property of the Greek-speaking world in classical times (sixth to fourth century BCE). Later, in Hellenistic and Roman times, they became the models for other editors and compilers, 'mythographers' as they were called. Classical authors and playwrights used the mythological material. The stock of mythological motifs was enormous, and it was a widely known universe of imaginations that writers, orators, politicians and philosophers could refer to. In current idiom, one could say that the mythological inventory was a web of significations from which it was possible to download materials for many kinds of communication. Among the 'consumers' of myth, the philosophers went their own way and from the time of Xenophanes (570–480 BCE), the Greek term *muthos* ('myth') became increasingly applied to stories about gods, heroes, demons, fairies and so on, that is, to stories that were not to be *trusted* in the ordinary sense. Before that philosophical critique, the word *muthos* simply referred to the spoken word, belonging to the general category of *logos* ('what is said'). Now, with the philosophical critique, *logos* became the word for rational speech that referred to arguments and truths. Thus, myth, as the opposite, became a term for untrue and irrational stories.

Thus, already in antiquity, there was scepticism concerning the validity of myths. As it was realised that they could not be understood literally, many attempts were presented so as to explain what myths could then *really* be about. How can they make sense? How can they be interpreted? The general idea was (and still is) that there *had* to be some kind of explanation for the creation and existence of myth. The historian of religions Lauri Honko compiled a concise catalogue of these modes of explanation and interpretation in antiquity (Honko 1984). The catalogue is also interesting because it demonstrates how ideas that are more than two thousand years old are still used in common discourse. Honko (1984) lists the following ten forms of myth-interpretation in antiquity:

1 mythographic interpretations used by poets and others who believed in and transmitted the myths in their works;
2 philosophical rational criticisms of various kinds, where the rejection of myth was often quite harsh;
3 the pre-scientific explanations and interpretations where the mythical lived on along with early scientific speculation;
4 allegorical 'nature'-interpretation where Apollo is fire, Poseidon water, Artemis the moon, and so on;

5   allegorical interpretation based on spiritual qualities where Aphrodite is desire, Athena wisdom, Hermes the intellect, and so on;

6   etymological interpretations trying to make sense of the names of the gods by tracing an original meaning: 'the secret of the gods lay in their names and epithets';

7   historical interpretation, amply found in Herodotus, where gods are borrowed from other cultures or the idea that myths 'really' refer to historical events;

8   euhemeristic interpretations as a variation on this: the gods were originally remarkable humans who had then been deified;

9   'sociological' interpretations as in, for example, the author Critias (460–403 BCE) who 'taught that the gods had been invented to maintain social order';

10   psychological interpretations where the belief in gods and so on is seen as the outcome of fear and anxiety.

Most of these ways of interpreting and making sense of myths and mythologies are still common today and abound in popular literature on myth. However, current advances in other fields might allow for novel and more explanatory approaches to myth. There seems to be obvious promise for new scholarship on myth in recent theorising in narratology (the science of narrative), in the cognitive sciences, in blending theory and in metaphor theory (Jensen 2009a). The myths may be old but the study of myth it still in its infancy.

5   Religious practices and behaviours, also known as 'ritual'

What comes first in religion: ritual behaviour or religious belief? There is probably no way of knowing and so it may seem odd that there has been an enduring discussion in the study of religion on whether ritual or belief is primary (Bell 1997: 3–21). The outcomes of this debate were, however, not quite irrespective of who conducted it. As guardians of literate monotheistic traditions with a focus on faith and belief, Christian theologians will logically tend to view ritual as subordinate, but many historians of religion and philosophers growing out of Christian cultural traditions have also stressed the primacy of faith and therefore also belief as primary and necessary for the significance of ritual. To them, belief was primary, providing meaning to ritual as well as being the very cause of ritual: belief comes first – ritual follows, and is what it is because of belief.

Contrary to that view, scholars of a more social-science orientation such as sociologists and anthropologists have emphasised the social cohesive nature and functions of ritual and therefore a probable priority of ritual over belief. Historical and archaeological evidence shows how ritual spaces and buildings have served first one and since another belief system: many early churches were built on ancient polytheistic ritual places. Recently, evolutionary and cognitive theorists have also offered explanations that favour the primacy of ritual, partly because ritual seems to be older in evolutionary terms and partly because similar ritual forms apparently may have different meanings attributed to them, and similar rituals can be associated with varying beliefs. Whatever the case may be, the stance of the investigator is important because it determines the selection of data, the direction of analysis and the bases for interpretation, explanation and understanding (Jensen 2009d).

When religion appeared as an object of study in the late seventeenth century, there was still a noticeable Christian Protestant bias in the attitude towards rituals and in the study of them. This bias had its background in theological conceptions against the idea of 'justification by works', that is, the dogmatic position that humans cannot 'save themselves' – because only God administers grace. The Protestant disregard of ritual was later carried on in the early phase of history of religions research in the late nineteenth century as this was predominantly modelled on the template of Christian dogmatic and clerical history. The most important issues were to trace the origins and developments of doctrines and so ritual partly fell out of the picture.

The attitude towards Christmas celebrations among the Puritan Fathers in seventeenth-century New England is an example of that Protestant bias against ritual: Christmas celebrations were censored and largely absent because the Puritans associated Christmas with idolatry and paganism. In 1647, the English Parliament passed a law (enforced until 1660) that made Christmas illegal, and those celebrating it might be arrested. In the United States, Christmas became a federal holiday only in 1870. The rest, as they say, is history. On the other hand, rituals are important whether they are mentioned in the scripture (be it of whatever religion) or not. The Puritan awareness of the heathen origin of Christmas also attests to the apparent longevity of a ritual tradition and its continuous reconceptualisation. What began (most likely) as an ancient Germanic Yuletide celebration at winter solstice, then a Christian commemoration ritual, has now become a commercial spectacle – the annual celebration of consumer society and market economy – and family ritual in many parts of the world. So, is this really the same ritual in different interpretations? No, only the date (with Orthodox exceptions) suggests that these rituals are somehow genealogically related, and so the hypothesis of ritual continuity merits constant checking against whatever evidence is available. Ritual content is underdetermined by ritual form: things that look alike need not have similar functions or similar meanings.

A brief sketch of some views of ritual

Theories about ritual may have very different emphases: at one end of the spectrum, some focus on piety as a means for believers to relate to their god and at the other, some focus on ritual as a means of social control in the exercise of power (Bell 1992, 1997). In spite of such theoretical differences, it can be stated that all forms of religious practice and behaviour are related, in one way or another, to matters considered sacred in the tradition or, as Durkheim noted, 'practices relative to sacred things' (2001: 46). This takes shape either by ritually changing profane materials and matters into sacred ones or by maintaining established sacrality (and authority) of the religious tradition in various modes of human individual and social practice. Ritual communication with the 'other world' ensures that ideas, behaviours, values and norms endure in relation to what any given tradition considers sacred. This is visibly what ritual does – but how does it do it? Rituals puzzle scholars today and so they also did in the late nineteenth century when the non-confessional academic study of religion was pioneered (Kreinath et al. 2008). When seen from the outside, religious rituals began to appear strange and problematic instead of being pious and self-evident modes of action as seen from the inside. What is the good of ritual actions that do not have an instrumental goal or a perceptible result? Are there hidden causes, functions and benefits? A large number of scholars have offered, if not solutions, then at least hypotheses and suggestions. Here is a brief review.

Early evolutionary theorists of religion Edward Burnett Tylor (1832–1917) and James George Frazer (1854–1951) essentially saw rituals as leftovers, 'survivals', from earlier stages of primitive religion. Their view was based on the doctrine of animism: that 'primitives' and 'early humans' considered not only humans, but also animals, plants and even inanimate objects to have souls. For these early evolutionary theorists, ritual demonstrated the existence of primitive 'survivals' into later stages of culture and even in contemporary religion. Typical of their time, their interpretations of ritual practice were intellectualist and literalist: intellectualist in the sense that rituals reflect a way of understanding the world and literalist because rituals were believed (by the practitioners) to actually work on the world. Both assumptions were deemed erroneous, the primitives made mistakes – and that was considered enough of an explanation in those days.

In the slightly younger myth and ritual school, the hypothesised endurance of ritual forms was used in attempts to unlock the riddles of myths. If a corresponding ritual could be traced back in time, then the original meaning of the myth could likewise be discovered (Segal 1999: 37–47). This approach was influential for some decades in the early half of the twentieth century in classical, biblical and Near Eastern studies but it did not contribute much to a solution of the 'problem of ritual'. As it turned out, it was mostly very difficult, if not impossible, to find the corresponding rituals and so the interest in the myth and ritual school faded.

A new type of answer to the problem concerned the social functions of rituals as means to increase social cohesion in religious groups. This was the suggestion of the Old Testament scholar William Robertson Smith (1846–94). He studied ancient forms of sacrifice and discovered that the function of sacrifice was more than giving gifts to the gods. Sacrifice is also a 'communion' which consists of 'communication between the god and his worshippers by joint participation in the flesh and blood of a sacred victim' (Smith 2005: 345). Durkheim took Smith's notion of the primacy of ritual in religion and further elaborated it by emphasising how rituals function to sanction the obligations of the group. Rituals exert social force because they refer to the authority of superhuman agents and bind communities together in common attitudes. So again, and like myths, rituals are really not so much about gods as they are about humans: 'In fact, if religious ceremonies have any importance, it is because they set the collectivity in motion – groups gather to celebrate them' (Durkheim 2001: 258). This was a novel way of conceiving of ritual and it made sense to a new generation of scholars, primarily in British and French anthropology. The ideas of the social nature of ritual were later propagated by the French anthropologist Marcel Mauss (1872–1950). He considered ritual a mode of communication, a form of symbolic exchange through which humans and superhumans could be engaged together in the maintenance of the world. Thus, his model of sacrifice included the superhuman realm as important: 'One of the first groups of beings with which men had to enter into contract, and who, by definition, were there to make a contract with them, were above all both the spirits of the dead and of the gods' (Mauss 1990: 21). The Covenant of the Hebrew Bible is a very well-known example of this, but upon closer inspection all religions operate on this principle, whether humans sacrifice oxen or flowers representing themselves or mutter prayers. That is, the main condition is that humans live in accordance with rules related to the ultimate sacred postulates.

The anthropologist Bronislaw Malinowski (1884–1942) emphasised what such relations mean to the ritual participants. In his fieldwork among the Trobriand Islanders in Melanesia he focused on the psychological functions and effects of rituals. In agreement with his ideas of 'modern anthropology', he wished to emphasise that magic and religion were more than 'false doctrine' and 'crude philosophy' as the earlier evolutionist anthropologist had taught. Instead, rituals are 'a special mode of behaviour, a pragmatic attitude built up of reason, feeling and will alike'. Thus, rituals are pragmatic; they have functions and effects, in magic as well as in religion:

> Both magic and religion arise and function in situations of emotional stress: crises of life, lacunae in important pursuits, death and initiation into tribal mysteries, unhappy love and unsatisfied hate ... religious faith establishes, fixes, and enhances all valuable mental attitudes, such as reverence for tradition, harmony with environment, courage and confidence in the struggle with difficulties and at the prospect of death.
>
> (Malinowski 1992: 80–3)

This is a functionalist and instrumentalist view of rituals and religion as 'ways of working on the world' (as we might call it). Ritual participants believe that rituals have causal effects on the state of the world on various levels: not only on the material but also on the mental, the social and even the supernatural world. In the research literature, these multilevel effects of ritual – as they are imagined, expected and perceived by the insiders – are commonly called 'ritual efficacy'. As we shall see, the category of ritual has many dimensions, among which 'symbolic work' and its imagined efficacy are important. By performing such symbolic work, humans assume that they can achieve results on matters (e.g., metaphysical) that are otherwise outside the range of their practical or instrumental capabilities. The following sections provide examples of this and further elaborate on the notion of symbolic work.

Rituals also have distinctive forms and structures. One of the first to recognise this was the anthropologist Arnold van Gennep (1873–1957) who found (in 1909) that rituals, especially those he called 'rites of passage' (which actually constitute a majority of rituals), have a common tripartite sequential structure with a phase (1) of separation, (2) of transition and (3) of reintegration. This model can be refined into a five-phase model where the transition phase is now commonly termed 'liminal' (*limen* is Latin for 'threshold'): see Table 5.1.

Indeed, it is a simple model, but it paved the way for later and more sophisticated studies of ritual form and structure (Turner 2008). Following the tradition of van Gennep, scholars divide rituals of transition into three categories: 'crisis', 'initiation' and 'calendrical' rites. In Table 5.2, they are presented with more explicit emphasis on the symbolism of the phases and their associated valences (i.e. their social or emotional value).

Table 5.1 The structural five-phase model of rites of passage

Initial phase	Separation phase	Liminal phase	Integration phase	Final phase
Preparations/ leaving home	Getting ready/ becoming dressed in a special way	The actual transition	Becoming a member of the group	Returning home

Table 5.2 The structural five-phase model with valences

Type of ritual	Initial phase	Separation phase	Liminal phase	Integration phase	Final phase
Crisis/healing	Negative value/lack	Removal symbolism	Ritual control	Protection symbolism	Positive valence
Transition – initiation	Negative value/lack	Discarding symbolism	Ritual control/'com-munitas'	Integrative symbolism	Positive valence
Transition – calendrical	Neutral value/status quo	Protection symbolism	Ritual control	Conserva-tion symbolism	Positive valence

Looking at the valence progression in the ritual sequences, it is clear that the general drift of ritual action is to make things better, to liquidate possible lack and to move from dysphoric ('bad/sad') to euphoric ('good') situations and conditions. In an analysis of ritual, the question arises: Who is it for? What is it for? What does the performance aim to achieve? What is the 'ritual concern'?

Meaning in and of ritual(s)

The *meaning* of ritual is a complex and much debated issue. Ritual as such and in general (as a category) does not have any intrinsic meaning, but specific rituals certainly have meanings, perhaps even of immense proportions. It all depends on what we are looking for. Although it may be possible to find some rituals that seem meaningless the observer may be uninformed or the partici-pants oblivious of reason and purpose – most rituals are meaningful and have purposes. We may just consider evidently meaningful rituals such as marriages or sacrifices to ancestral spirits. The question of meaning simply depends on whether we are looking for a semantic content, a social significance or a psy-chological intention – to name but a few instances of the complex notion of 'meaning'. Rituals may have a point in themselves, for instance to join two individuals together as husband and wife, and humans may have a point in performing them (to get married), or the superhuman inhabitants of the 'other world' may have a point (as believers see it) in making humans perform rituals (marriage pleases the gods). This also indicates that traditions, cultures or societies may have a point in making some people perform certain actions to comply with the established norms and practices.

Ritual meaning comes in many shapes and shades, and it has been the subject of much research on ritual and religion during the past century (e.g., Kreinath et al. 2008). The search for meaning is often referred to as 'thick description', a term that originated with the philosopher Gilbert Ryle (1900–76) and later introduced in cultural anthropology by Clifford Geertz to denote the range of interpretative description of intentions invested in human action and communication (Geertz 1973). Such a 'thick interpretation' programme for the study of ritual where the meaning of the ritual comes into focus was distinctly articulated by the anthropologist James Peacock:

> Native expression is not thin. It is manufactured, not to answer some restricted question or test some narrow hypothesis, but to express the native's being. Ceremonies and rituals, myths and legends, ethnic politics – all are 'thick' with meanings; they distil into form a plethora of values, ideas, and experiences. Encounter with such forms is inevitably confusing, but the confusing richness of meaning leads to deeper understanding, provided we sort out the patterns and principles behind the meaning. This effort we call interpretation.
>
> (Peacock 2001: 90–1)

Now, if there are 'patterns and principles', then rituals are most likely not constructed at random, but often it takes some detective work to sort them out. It is also remarkable how often rituals hide their 'authors', and, typically, scholars are unable to disclose who the 'constructors' are. Only rarely can they pinpoint (with historical precision) named persons, such as a guru, a mystic or a prophet, who have established a specific practice. Most religious traditions will simply state that the originators of rituals are the gods, the ancestors or other superhuman agents known in the tradition. The responsible agent is then customarily imagined to be one of antiquity, authority and power whereby the behaviour prescribed gains in prestige and necessity. What is old or original is better. This is a common stipulation in pre-modern traditional society. The ancient Greek historian Herodotus (484–425 BCE) provides a good example when he wrote about Egyptian culture and religion with the greatest admiration because the Greeks considered the Egyptian to have the oldest and thus noblest of civilisations. All religions are in this sense conservative because rituals function as programmes for behaviour, and these programmes must not be changed if the right results are to be achieved. Ritual 'symbolic work' has 'efficacy' when and because it is performed the way it *ought* to be performed. Change in ritual performance therefore often amounts to creating new religious groups.

Ritual behaviour consequently consists of prescribed patterns of behaviour that are authoritative and beyond the intentions of the participants. The roles and patterns in a ritual performance are not encoded by the participants themselves but they are delivered by sacred agents and with absolute authority. The anthropologist Roy A. Rappaport stated: 'I take ritual to be a form or structure, defining it as the performance of more or less invariant sequences of formal acts and utterances not encoded by the performers.' He continues: 'no single feature of ritual is peculiar to it. It is in the conjunction of its features that it is unique' (Rappaport 1999: 31). The intentions of and in a ritual are part of the programme, and whoever wants to benefit from the efficacy of the ritual must take on the roles and obligations; this is independent of the individual participants' own intentions or state of mind. When two persons participate in a wedding ritual as bride and groom then they come out of the ritual as husband and wife irrespective of their own moods or motivations. The ritual *contains a programme* with the intention of making just this specific goal possible and that is then the *meaning* of that specific ritual: a sequence of actions that express intentions and achieve an intended state of affairs. Thus, the prescribed sequence of ritual actions carries intentionality and the intentions of the participants are irrelevant as long as they behave according to the plan of the ritual.

Rituals are manifestations of collective intentionality in the group because they express how the group collectively wishes to handle a specific situation, be it a ritual of crisis, of celebration or of supplication. From an outside scholarly and scientific perspective, rituals may obviously change the mental attitudes and physical conditions of the participants and their social contexts. However, to the insiders of a tradition there is much more than that at stake because rituals can also change both natural and supernatural affairs: some rituals will bring rain or hunters' prey, or they may placate the wrath of a god or secure the blessings of the ancestors. In ancient Egypt, temple priests assisted the sun in rising every morning: an example of ritual efficacy of cosmic proportions.

The ritual stance means that participants delegate the source of their actions to ritual prescription. In this sense, rituals become 'archetypal actions' (Humphrey and Laidlaw 1994). Rituals do not stand alone, for, as most other human socio-cultural products they are part of larger ritual cycles, for example annual for societies or lifelong for individuals or groups. Many societies have complex arrangements of rituals that unfold over longer timespans and geographical areas. In some societies, it is also clearly visible how ritual cycles interact within spheres of social activity, from economy, through politics, to ecology (Rappaport 1999).

As anthropological and historical data show, ritualising attributes special qualities to many kinds of actions and agents, but what exactly does this quality consist of and how is it produced? How are mundane everyday actions elevated to a ritualised level of special quality and importance? Below, I shall present a range of ritual elements, concepts and categories that provide us with some evidence of how this elevation of the everyday and common sense to the special, the sacralised and the inviolable is accomplished – because that is what happens in religious ritual. After that, a few boxes and tables will illustrate how the elements, concepts and categories are employed in complex arrangements in actual rituals. However, before that, here is a look at one of the more thorny issues in the study of religion.

Magic: a special problem in the study of religion and ritual

'Magic' has conventionally been a contested term in the study of religion. For a long time it was used to distinguish true religion from false superstition, proper theology from folk tradition. In the emerging study of religion, it was likewise often used as a pejorative term. Magic was looked upon as a degraded form of religion or as a 'bastard sister of science', as James G. Frazer termed it (1993: 50). Many scholars found it difficult to use the term without negative connotations, and others found it difficult to distinguish clearly between religion and magic (Dubuisson 2016). To Frazer it was easy: religion 'involves, first, a belief in superhuman beings who rule the world and, second, an attempt to win their favour', and so the course of nature must be 'elastic or variable'. This is 'directly opposed to the principles of magic as well as of science, both of which assume that the processes of nature are rigid and invariable in their operation' (Frazer 1993: 51).

Durkheim suggested a sociological distinction according to which the magician is a ritual specialist who has paying clients but is not in charge of a congregation: 'There is no church of magic. Between the magician and the individuals, there are no durable ties that make them members of a single moral body ... The magician has a clientele not a church' (Durkheim 2001: 43). The utility of these distinctions is obvious. However, there are also many commonalities between religion and magic, both of which are, it must be remembered, abstract and theory-dependent concepts and models with which we capture aspects of human activity: religion and magic use mental operations and forms of ritual practices that are fundamentally similar.

As an example of the ritual side of magical practice, here is a condensed example of instructions in some magical texts from antiquity. The uses and the presumed powers, the efficacy, of second-century CE magical Christian texts written in Coptic are aptly paraphrased by the theologians Marvin Meyer and Richard Smith:

> They direct the user to engage in activities that are marked off from normal activity by framing behavior through rules, repetitions, and other formalities. Ritual instructions pervade these texts. Stand over there, hold a pebble, tie seven threads in seven knots, say the names seven times, draw the figure in the bottom of the cup, write the spell with the finger of a mummy, write it with bat's blood, with menstrual blood, on papyrus, on clay, on lead, on tin, on a rib bone, on a parchment shaped like a sword, fold it, burn it, tie it to your arm, your thumb, drive a nail in it, bury it with a mummy, bury it under someone's doorstep, mix this recipe, drink. Or simply 'do the usual'.
>
> (Meyer and Smith 1994: 4)

In an attempt to cut through the complex and prolix discussions about the nature and functions of magic, cognitive scientist of religion Jesper Sørensen took up the problem in a new perspective using metaphor theory and cognitive blending theory (Sørensen 2007). Briefly stated, the general idea of magic is to change something in the world according to one's own wish. The means applied and the goals to be achieved by them may often seem unrelated in 'causally opaque mediation' (Sørensen 2007), that is, the means applied would not normally be considered the obvious tools outside the magical ritual settings. For example, how can a pin stuck into a doll cause the death of a person? In ancient Rome, a person's name and a curse could be written on a sheet of lead that was rolled up, tied and buried. That is a clear example of causally opaque relations, but we are actually able to interpret it by using the same mental mechanism as the ritual agent. More than a century ago, Frazer discovered the two main principles of magic thinking that are still valid: one is the mental association based on similarity ('metaphoric') and the other is mental association based on contiguity ('metonymy'). In Frazer's own words:

> If we analyse the principles of thought on which magic is based, they will probably be found to resolve themselves into two: first, that like produced like, or that an effect resembles its cause; and, second, that things that have once been in contact with each other continue to act on each other at a distance after the physical contact has been severed. The former principle maybe called the Law of Similarity, the latter the Law of Contact or Contagion.
>
> (Frazer 1993: 11)

Thus, the doll that stands for the black (evil) magic victim is even more vulnerable if the doll is equipped with a lock of hair from the target person. In many places around the world, people are very cautious with hair and nail clippings. However, magical practices are mostly used as beneficial and useful actions. Malinowski noticed how the Trobrianders never used magic when fishing inside the lagoon where waters were safe but always when fishing outside the lagoon. Magic is thus a kind of technology, also used by the Trobrianders in horticulture as the 'belly of my garden' example shows (see Box 5.1).

Box 5.1 Magic

'Magic is about changing the state or essence of persons, objects, acts and events through certain special and non-trivial kinds of actions with causally opaque mediation' (Sørensen 2007: 32).

The 'belly of my garden' example was described by Bronislaw Malinowski in 1935: the Yowota ritual is the inaugural ritual of the agricultural calendar and in that context the Vatuvi spell is important. It enhances ('efficacy') the fertility of the yam garden: 'The belly of my garden, ... leavens, ... rises, ... reclines, ... grows to the size of the bush-hen's nest, ... grows like an anthill, ... rises and is bowed down, ... rises like the iron-wood palm, ... lies down, ... swells as if with a child.' This 'belly of my garden' is a familiar conventional metaphor because for Trobrianders there is a direct relation between humans, the land and the soil of their garden. They are truly autochthonous: 'A given sub-clan, dominating a village politically and owning the garden magic, is believed to have originated out of a hole in the soil cultivated by this particular village.' Yams are called 'children of the garden', the land is owned by women through matrilineal descent but cultivated by men. 'So, like yams, humans originate from the soil, and like human children, yams are born.' The garden soil is conceptualised as female. As a result, the magical spells conceptually blend ideas about soil, planting, growth, nests and anthills on the 'nature side' and femininity, fertility, pregnancy, procreation and child-birth on the 'humanity side'. What is wished for, the desired development and future condition of the yam garden, is expressed in the 'belly of my garden' metaphor. This cultural model is used in the magical spells of the horticultural rituals. (After Sørensen 2007: 116–20.)

Sørensen concludes his resourceful analyses of magical thought and practice by stating that:

> Instead of understanding magic and religion as two equal systems opposing each other, I propose a more dynamic explanation. Magic is a general mode of ritual behaviour that, when appearing outside established, authorised and institutionalised religious rituals, prompts the creation of either new systems of beliefs and religious institutions, or provoke a re-evaluation, reflection and possibly change of already established ritual structures.
>
> (Sørensen 2007: 191)

As an interim conclusion, we may see how ritual, magical or religious, is part and parcel of the traditional human 'work on the world'. It is noteworthy, too, that Frazer's two principles hold not only for magical thinking: they are the basic cognitive operations underlying *all* religious thinking.

Ritual: working on a world 'wished for'

Humans live in a world of medium-sized objects, and there are many limits to what they actually can see and do. Stars and bacteria only emerged in human awareness after the adequate instruments appeared. Humans have, however, the unique ability of being able to imagine the world as they would want it. For instance, the philosopher Ludwig Feuerbach (1804–72) pointed out how humans' longing for a better world is displayed in religion, and the anthropologist Claude Lévi-Strauss (1908–2009) coined the structuralist binary distinction between *monde vécu* and *monde conçu*, the lived-in world and the thought-of world, that is such a common trait of mythologies. Only humans make this distinction in-the-mind, produce narratives about it and imagine how they might actually be able to 'work on' the world and attempt to control it to their own best purpose. To be able to do so, then matters that are either very tiny, vast in size or invisible must be converted into 'medium-sized' objects so that humans can see them, hold them and, perhaps, change them. It is here that ritual proves its worth: ritual is a *workshop* for maintaining, controlling, changing and repairing those things in the world that are outside the ordinary practical and instrumental reach of humans.

To control hunting, secure crops and avert disease rituals can solve the problem, and they can be magical or religious (sometimes both) and involve the relevant superhuman beings. However, to be able to do so, the agents, the means and actions of rituals need to be so designed and ordered that humans can handle them: everything has to become *scaled*, up or down, so that humans can manipulate the states of affairs. This is an important but often overlooked feature and function of ritual: it transforms affairs that depend on and relate to the 'other world' in such a manner that they look as if they are within the reach of humans. In this way humans become co-responsible for such affairs as the rising of the sun, the growth of plants, the weather, and – not least – the fate of individuals and groups (even after death). There are rituals for all these 'things' in many if not all cultures in human history.

Here below is a closer look at how this becomes possible. The main reason is the extreme cognitive fluidity that evolution has offered humans. The human gift for cognitive fluidity has the remarkable effect of convincing the agent involved that it is the world and not their own mental apparatus that changes, and so 'ontological fluidity' follows: ritual is special in the grammatical and syntactical sense that ordinary objects may become special sacred agents and ordinary persons may become special sacred instruments. The relations between subject, object, instrument and action may be reordered according to the purposes and workings of rituals (Lawson and McCauley 1990). In ritual, almost anything is possible, and language can be used in the most creative, constructive and performative ways. Religious ritual and language both follow and do not follow the rules of ordinary action and language.

Rituals, even the apparently dullest ones, can be highly expressive, and even the smallest gesture may signify complex and condensed symbolic meanings. The analogy between language and ritual becomes more perceptible when working on a large body of rituals in a specific cultural area, such as the south Asian one, where a multitude of ritual practices interact as in a complex web (Michaels 2015). Narratives speak, but action speaks louder than words as is well known.

Consider rituals to consist of acts with actors acting and the single acts as analogous to a sentence in language, e.g., 'Paul hits the ball.' Rituals would then be more like narratives as they consist of a complex of sequences of such sentences. Rituals follow the rules of ordinary action and language well enough for the language analogy to be theoretically viable. Rituals mediate between this and the other world, and they take their departure from what is known in this lived-in world to remain convincing as they simultaneously (may) reorganise the perception and conceptualisation of that world on the basis of the order of the thought-of world (see, e.g., Leach 1976). The examples in Table 5.3 demonstrate how ordinary categories of time, space, actions, persons, objects, instruments, status (which is an institutional 'thing') and

Table 5.3 Ordinary versus sacralised/sacred categories in ritual

Ordinary	Sacralised/sacred	Examples
Time	Time collapses	Present = past in ritual, e.g., when repeating a primeval act
Space	Space distinctions suspended/merged	Local space ritual may at the same time become a sacred ritual *other* space
Actions	Blending of actual action with metaphysical action/transfer of properties	Imitating deeds of superhuman agents (gods, etc.) or of sacred persons (e.g., prophets, saints)
Persons	Identity change/transfer of properties/violation of properties	Impersonating/possessed by superhuman agent (e.g., god)/sacred persons
Objects in nature	Quality and property change/transfer of properties	Stones that may magically bring rain/sacred mountains/sacred animals
Instruments	Quality and property change of artefacts/transfer of properties	Bread and wine as body and blood of god, sacred medicine bundles in traditional African curative rites
Status/office/role	Transforms agent property	Property (of office) transfer to shaman/priest/prophet/diviner/ritual healer
Meaning	Metaphysical/denotative meaning becomes connotative or metaphorical	Ritual language performative/creates other meaning/symbols as signs that transform (e.g., baptism)

meaning are re-recreated as sacred and employed in ritual to transform virtual worlds into tangible worlds that humans are then able to work on.

An elementary typology of ritual

These categorical transformations (Table 5.3) form the backbone of all ritual thought, symbolism and practice. The metaphorical qualities of symbolism and the capacity for cognitive blending allow humans to transform the matters of ordinary categories into special and sacralised matters and categories. Humans then use these constructs of the mind to maintain, transform, repair and sanctify all kinds of objects in their life-worlds. I present below a brief, formal (original and not yet conclusive) typology of ritual forms, functions, structures and meanings based on current research on ritual in a range of fields, ranging from anthropology to psychiatry. Ideally, the typology should comprise the totality of possible elements of thought and behaviour that combine in the symbolic exchange with the 'other world' and the superhuman agents (including 'non-agentive powers') that belong to it. Note that the notion of 'element' is used here in the broadest possible sense: an 'element' can be anything from a wooden stick to the notion of counter-intuitivity. An element is, in short, anything that goes into, has a place and a function the formation of ritual. Religious ritual is an integral component of human social life and culture, and as both of these are inextricably based on language and communication, the typology begins with 'special communication and signification', which in turn enable 'special action' performed by 'special agents' that produce, transmit or receive 'special cognition and emotion'. The last section of the typology concerns 'special functions in i-religion and e-religion' for individuals and groups in culture and society and their role in the maintenance of ordered human life in an ordered cosmos.

Ritual as special communication and signification

In many religious traditions, the language used in ritual is recognisably different from ordinary spoken language. Often an entirely different language is used in ritual settings, for example Arabic recitation of the Qur'an for speakers of Turkish, Hebrew for Americans, Sanskrit for speakers of contemporary Indian languages, Latin for Polish speakers and so forth. For those accustomed to participating in rituals in their own ordinary language it may be difficult to fully grasp the significance of participants' *lack* of understanding of what is being linguistically communicated. However, this directs attention to the dimensions or aspects of ritual that do not depend on participants' understanding of verbal communication or semantic knowledge. In a number of traditions, there is also a social dimension if the tradition requires special training, initiation, status or office that enables the worshipper to use the ritual language legitimately.

Sometimes, a different *kind* of the same language is used, for instance to invoke the Inuit Shaman's helping spirits or to communicate with the ancestors. Frequently, such 'spirit-talk' is meant to be powerful and in excessive variations, it can be purely nonsensical, as in the example of magical formulae. Very often, the ordinary language is used with different intonations and prosody (tone and rhythm) so that it is obvious to participants that something *special* is going on. Furthermore, special vocabulary, terminology and phrasing are included in forms of ritual language, especially terms of adoration, courtesy and respect. In this manner, the sacred–profane distinction can be expressed in countless ways, but they do not seem to be absolutely arbitrary. Rather, these forms of language in ritual conduct appear to follow universal distinctions in human social behaviour: a solemn prayer is rarely shouted from the rooftop.

There are many good reasons to think about religion as signification, for without signs (aural, visual or tactile) or signification there would not be any religion(s). There are many instances of remarkable signs, modes of signification, and sign interpretation in religion, from the manifestations of a god as a talking burning bush to a penis-shaped stone pillar. Signs and significations abound in all spheres of religion: in myth, hagiography (narratives about saints), in dogma, in ritual objects and in actions and in religious institutions. It is, to be more precise, by the appearance of *special* kinds of signs and significations that religion becomes discernible in the first place: by signs that are recognisable as signs but with special reference and meaning and used in special contexts. Humans have an almost uncanny ability to detect things *special*, things that are 'cognitively salient' and ritual systems commonly and widely exploit that ability.

Here again, the semiotic distinction between icon, index and symbol (see Leach 1976; and this volume, Chapter 4) will be important in the analyses of ritual forms and functions. As noted, the three types of signs are (1) *icon*: a sign that looks like its referent (X like a crossroad), (2) *index*: a sign that points to something (smoke as an index of fire) and (3) *symbol*: a sign with meaning attributed by convention (snake as a symbol of evil). Most symbols are arbitrary, as their attributed meanings depend on cultural conventions. However, some are universally motivated through their use or quality – water, for example, as a symbol of purity or blood of life. Remember that the relation between symbols and their referents is metaphoric because they blend different contexts: 'The lion is the king of the beasts' is a metaphoric statement that blends animals and royalty. Then again, an icon of a lion may become a symbol of kingship (lions appear in many royal heraldic coats of arms). A *signal* is a different kind of sign, characterised not by reference but by function: signals function as switches; they cause things to happen in a kind of trigger response.

These distinctions are not trivial. For an understanding of ritual, it is crucial to note how these three kinds of signs may all convert into signals that causally trigger actions of, for example, status, emotion or collective actions. This is the whole trick of ritual use of signs: they can be freely exchanged in the ritual space of meaning. If this sounds abstract, consider a few examples: in the Islamic Wudu' ritual of ablution, the washing of body parts is not just hygienic, it has a causal power that *transforms* the status of the actor from ritually unclean to clean and thus now able to perform the prayer. The transubstantiation of bread into a sacralised host in many Christian traditions has similar traits: the bread becomes special, sacralised and transformed into the body of Christ and turns into a causal signal of redemption with strong powers (efficacy) for the participants. The marvel of ritual space is that the ontology of 'things' becomes so flexible that almost anything can become something other: small bundles of twigs may become powerful medicine in healing rituals when the right spells have been said. A telling example of the power of ritual healing is given by the anthropologist Victor Turner on how the:

> Ndembu feel that by bringing certain objects into a ring of consecrated space they bring with these the powers and virtues they seem empirically to possess, and that by manipulating them in prescribed ways they can arrange and concentrate these powers, rather like laser beams, to destroy malignant forces.
>
> (Turner 1977: 43)

In ritual, almost anything goes as far as the elements are concerned. With what, how, when or why they are connected depends, in turn, both on the tradition in question and the grammar of symbols. That is, they are connected according to rules, or chaos might arise (Leach 1976).

The main basis for the ontological and semantic flexibility of ritual action is the multi-vocal nature of ritual symbols. When they are rich in meaning, they may point in many directions and join different domains. This enables the ritual manipulations of actions, actors, objects and other ingredients of the ritual so as to be able to perform the desired 'work-on-the-world' (Turner 1977). Ritual practice is often built on what Lévi-Strauss called *bricolage*, a French term for the handyman's practice of using the bits and pieces available for some other purpose. In rituals this happens all the time; many ordinary things are being used in special ways for very different purposes. It all hinges on the human capacities for imagination and projection and they are endlessly flexible. Humans can attribute meaning(s) to just about anything. It is the most remarkable aspect of meaning attribution in ritual, and in culture in general, that it unconsciously follows rules, as when speakers of a language talk without ever thinking of grammar. Rules and meanings are connected (Douglas 1973). The rules and meanings do not depend on reference to the material world because they are equally important in the imagination of the 'thought-of' world. That world is deeply involved in the construction of ritual practice and institutions to work on the world as 'wished for' through the relations and exchanges with the powers and agents of the 'other' or 'second' world. These are characterised by counter-intuitivity as token of their 'otherness' (cf. Boyer in Chapter 4 above).

It is precisely by virtue of the malleability of the signification processes that the contacts and exchanges with the 'other world' become possible: what seems to be one thing can be thought of as something entirely different, as in this case study example in Box 5.2 from the Ainu tradition.

Box 5.2 Ritual reciprocity

Ritual reciprocity is when human individuals and groups symbolically exchange goods and deeds with their superhuman agents in actions that reinforce the bonds or covenants between this and the 'other world'.

The Ainu people in Hokkaido, northern Japan, have a traditional ritual where a god, self-disguised as a cub bear, is sent back home to the gods' abode. The gods favour rice wine and wooden *Inaw* sticks which are precious to them and are used for celebrating in the other world, but which they are unfortunately unable to make themselves. Therefore, occasionally they decide to visit Humanland disguised as a young bear, which is then caught by hunters. It is fenced in and fed for a while and then at a specific time, at the *Iomante* (sending home) festival, it is killed by strangling, so as not to spill any blood, in an elaborate communal ritual. It is a *communion* sacrifice, where not only participants but also the dead bear is offered some of its own meat and soup. As the Ainu are dualists (most people in this world are), the killing is necessary to free the soul of the bear so that it may return home with the sacrificial gifts (rice wine, etc.). The point of reciprocity is that the cub shall return and tell the other gods that it was well looked after and entice the other gods to come and visit, and so contribute to the extended and hopefully permanent relations between humans and their gods.

All religious traditions seem to have (had) elaborate rules for maintaining the contract with the gods (or whatever is sacred) so that the stream of benefits may continue to flow. In anthropological theory, the 'trade' with superhuman agents (e.g., gods) is termed 'reciprocity' or 'symbolic exchange'. Most frequently, the superhuman agents bestow goods of all kinds (including immaterial spiritual ones) on humans who must do something in return to uphold the contract: they communicate by way of objects, gifts, praise or displays of orderly conduct to show that they are willing to follow their part of the agreement. Gifts are not just gifts: they carry obligations, on both the giver and the receiver (Mauss 1990). These forms of symbolic behaviour are communicative, and most often they 'go between', that is, they are mediators that fulfil the task of 'mediation' between the two worlds. In many contemporary post-axial religious traditions, the godhead does not require the sacrifice of sheep, beer or grain or so the official theologies say. On closer inspection, it is the *whole person* who should sacrifice herself by surrendering to god's will, the rules of a sacred book or fuse with the group identity (Jensen 2016a). Most religious traditions are built around the ideas, as often portrayed in myths, of the superhuman agents as creators of the entire cosmos. The ritual behaviours employed are often spectacular, rich in symbolism, and come as dramas and performances, for example re-enacting the fate of special, sacred or heroic beings: avatars, founders, incarnations, prophets, reformers, saints, and so on. Chinese New Year's rituals are worth attention not only for their elaborate displays but no less for their rich ritual semantics.

Ritual communication usually has a special dimension: it is *performative*. That is, it *does* something, such as uniting husband and wife in a wedding, giving children their names in name-giving ceremonies, healing patients in curative rites, changing the deceased into an ancestor. Ritual may change the nature of something by 'simply' by calling it something other than what it is. Rituals all over the world and in history really are full of transubstantiations in the genuine sense of the word. (These functions of language relate to speech act theory, to be explained in detail in Chapter 6.) Consequently, when ritual language appears to be descriptive and constative and talk about things in a matter of fact way it may actually be performative and creating the very matter-of-factness as part of the ritual context. What may seem mere labelling may in a reality be a *declaration* – to the effect that something has a special status or nature. Rituals may make things something other than they are: Wine as the blood of Christ, for example. Most likely, *any* ritual seems to make some use of this function.

Frequently, ritual communication appears as a kind of redundant 'auto-communication' that communicates something already well known to a community of interpreters: they already know the story, the procedure, the roles and the message. Why? Because this mode of communicative behaviour has social and cultural value: it (re-)circulates the ideas, values, codes and modes of practice that are relevant for cooperation and solidarity in the group, community, society or religious tradition (see, e.g., Rappaport 1999). Consequently, a good deal of ritual behaviour is about belonging and demonstrating in-group allegiance. Because some ritual and religious behaviour can be quite elaborate, expensive and cumbersome, ritual theorists use the term 'costly signalling' to characterise this kind of communicative behaviour (Bulbulia and Sosis 2011).

Ritual as special action

In ritual action, the malleability of ontology (i.e. things can have more than one nature), the fluidity of cognition (i.e. counter-intuitive notions as 'natural') and the substitutability of signs (i.e. metaphors functioning as icons or signals) may make for intriguing combinations of remarkable and attention-grabbing special actions with very complex symbolism (e.g., Turner 1977: Chapter 1). Rituals are performed at (1) special occasions, such as in times of crisis or according to a calendar and (2) in special locations. These may be large and permanent, such as the Grand Mosque in Mecca, or small and transient, such as the sand paintings in Navaho healing rituals. A ritual space can have any size and shape: the important thing is that it is *marked off* from the rest of the world. Hence, at special times and in special places, sacralising activities may take place (Smith 1987). Rituals are *special* actions, but many ritual actions are also almost like ordinary actions: feeding the gods in a morning ritual is done by offering food with hands, praying is done by talking, and processions consist in walking. However, ritual actions have a number of characteristics that must be noted here, as they are frequent, salient and demarcate rituals in contrast to ordinary actions (see Box 5.3). Time and space does not permit a more comprehensive discussion, so the points below are offered primarily as a set of topics and characteristics of ritual as 'special action' to be employed as inspirations for descriptions and analyses of rituals.

Box 5.3 Characteristics of ritual as 'special action'

Tweaking the ordinary: In contrast to ordinary, instrumental action, ritual action often comes as stereotyped, stylised or as a caricature of ordinary action. Ritual action seems non-functional, with 'opaque causality' where the cause–effect relation is concealed: it is difficult to see what it leads to (also called 'goal demotion' or 'displacement'; see below).

Efficacy: Ritual 'effect'. Differs from cause–effect relations in ordinary action as it is the *imagined* and *presumed* effect of the ritual action, depending on essence transfers and violations that transform time, space, actions, actors, objects into special ritual powerful categories (cf. Chapter 4).

The efficacy of a special chant is that it (supposedly) forces the spirits to bring rain. Rituals also have other effects, such as social or psychological effects, but 'efficacy' is the imagined metaphysical effect of ritual.

Inverted intentionality: Intentionality about how the world *ought* to be, the world as wished for, contrary to ordinary intentionality where mind adjusts to world as it is. Inverted intentionality contains programmes of constitutive and regulative rules by which rituals and related institutions are set up and maintained. Ritual contains intentionality programmes to cope with and change the world (for more on this issue, see Chapter 6).

Up- and down-scaling: Time and space dissolution, for example when rituals are re-articulating the primeval situations or actions. Matters invisible or of cosmic scale are transformed into manageable ritual elements. Time and space are collapsed, as past and present as well as here and there are identical/parallel in ritual ('ritual re-actualisation'), for example by 'doing the same thing' as significant superhuman agents first did.

Ritual control: Often rigorously monitored and executed along conventional schemata, patterns and roles for participants. Behaviour is 'not encoded by the performers' but by the programmes of intentionality of the ritual (its purpose or meaning).

Reversed grammar: Grammar where aspect, modus, time and subject–action–object relations are reversed or reordered so that unusual action and communication become possible (e.g., a stone with special power as subject/agent curing a person as patient/object).

Substitution of structure: Proximate and ultimate structures are substituted or reversed in ritual. What is done in this world has effects in another. Claims of the *ultimate* efficacy: initiation with 'promise of salvation' or ritual for 'placating the ancestors' have *proximate* effects: becoming members of a congregation and/or subjects of social control.

Special agents in ritual

The presentation above demonstrates that ritual communications and actions are to a large degree both ordinary and 'extra-ordinary', they are trivial *and* special and so are also the categories of ritual agents. In light of the foregoing, it follows that the categories of ritual agents are wide-ranging. Ritual agents can be persons, groups, institutions, objects, artefacts, dead agents, imagined agents, counter-intuitive agents, language, words, and songs: almost anything can be a ritual agent. Whether ritual agents are of one or another of these kinds, the remarkable thing is that they be can be substituted and so they violate the ordinary human sense of action grammar. As such, they have one thing in common: they are special and, typically, they have powers surpassing the ordinary, in one or several ways depending on their manner of relationship with the 'other world'.

First, ritual agents can be *human*: active subjects that have special, and often counter-intuitive, perception and cognition so that they may see things otherwise hidden. They may (be considered to) have direct experience of and communication with the 'other world' and this may again provide them with special status, authority and power, and offer legitimation of special roles and offices in the social hierarchy (see Table 5.4).

Second, special ritual agents can also be *instruments*, that is, objects or artefacts with special and typically counter-intuitive capacities: mountains, statues, relics or other special ritual objects and artefacts can be active subjects (in the grammatical sense) that have perception and cognition of human thought and will, and may act intentionally, for instance by bringing bliss or disaster. Obviously, such ritual objects and artefacts derive their role, status, authority and power, their ritual efficacy, from their close relation to the 'other world' because that is where their potency originates. In terms of size and matter, they may be anything from a small piece of bread to a holy mountain such as Wirikuta in the native Huichol tradition in Mexico (see Box 5.4).

Third, ritual agents also appear as *passive subjects*, often in the form of a patient in a healing ritual or an initiand (the person to be initiated in an initiation ritual). The passivity or object character of the patient role should not be underestimated, as the transformation of such objects may well be the purpose of the entire ritual order. The ritual leaders or instructors are important, as can often be perceived from their role and status (habitually 'costly signalled'), and the instruments are important as well, but the passive subjects are mostly what it is all about: transforming the ontological or social status of someone by treating the subject as an object, as a something. Thus, in ritual analysis the classical legal question *cui bono?* may be very appropriately asked. Who benefits? How? Why?

Ritual is pre-eminently social; it is a 'group thing' that unites individuals and groups: institutions and organisations such as monasteries, initiation groups, fraternities and bodies of professionals are all examples of this. Religious rituals commonly confirm pro-social group membership, emotional solidarity and in-group coordination and cooperation (Collins 2004). However, in other contexts, many rituals function as assortative, that is, they *exclude* others (Martin and Wiebe 2014). Thus, the pro-social nature of rituals in group formation and maintenance

Table 5.4 A typology of human ritual agents/specialists

Type	Characteristics
Medium	Channel *for* 'other world', more or less voluntary, receives special knowledge
Shaman	Channel *to* 'other world', seeks special knowledge
Prophet	Channel *of* 'other world', receives special knowledge
Priest	Distributes special knowledge of or from 'other world'
Sacraliser	Contacts 'other world' on behalf of client (individual/group)
Healer	Uses special powers from 'other world' in restorative practice

should be balanced with anthropological and historical analyses of the larger contexts of the groups. In large-scale societies, inter-group competition may display the 'dark side' of ritual practices (Boyns and Luery 2015). Table 5.6 is an attempt to classify main types of ritual groups (very broadly). It may not catch all possible combinations because it is not an exhaustive empirical labelling but rather an ideal typology. On closer examination, some ritual and tradition groups would turn out to be combinations of the types. For instance, the past Hindu caste system in India would appear to have contained combinations of the ethnic, congregation and guild types.

It should be remembered that not only are individuals and groups, institutions and traditions definable in *social* terms, typically through recognised membership of a specific collective. The boundaries of collectives may also be demarcated as 'interpretive communities' that inhabit 'spaces' of meaning. Interpretive communities are of a *cultural* nature because interpretation belongs to and operates in 'semantic universes', in cultures as systems of symbols. Such cultural boundaries also hold if or when participants disagree: the limits of a tradition are not to be drawn around those who agree – it should rather be drawn so as to delimit the 'space' of *meaningful disagreement*. For example, when Sunni and Shi'a Muslims

Table 5.5 Special instruments: two types

Instrument	Material object	Artefact (human made)
Ordinary	Part of nature	Made for practical/functional purposes
Sacralised	Sacred: transfer of counter-intuitive properties for metaphysical goals	Sacred: transfer of counter-intuitive properties for metaphysical goals

Table 5.6 Ritual groups: an ideal type classification

Type	Characteristics	Examples
Initiation group	Initiation required/ status group	Sororities/fraternities, special cult groups in, for example, Native North American traditions
Monastic group	World rejecting/ ascetic	Buddhist *sangha*, Greek Orthodox monasteries
Congregation/church group	Member by birth /family relation	In most indigenous/ethnic religion groups (e.g., Shinto) and in scriptural traditions: Vaishnavite Hindu, Sikh, Jewish, Christian, Islamic or Parsi
Sect/movement group	Voluntary membership	For example Brazilian Candomblé, Scientology
Guild group	Member by occupation/training	Catholic medieval masons, bakers, brewers and so on had specific patron saints

disagree on the authority of the first imams in the Islamic tradition, that question would be meaningless to a Japanese Shinto. Debating differing Buddhist Theravada and Mahayana notions of Nirvana does not make much difference to the celebration of Native American Hopi puppet ceremonies. The limits or borders of traditions that span various ethnic groups are thus often drawn by way of the different systems of symbols, languages and modes of interpretation and configurations of ritual action.

Special cognition and emotion

Rituals often seem odd and remarkable due to their peculiar forms – for instance by costly signalling. In that sense, rituals are cognitively salient: they attract attention and are therefore (often) memorable. They are different from ordinary instrumental or functional actions. Thus, they are *special* actions: but are the cognitive functions or emotions involved also special? The answer is no. Rituals draw on ordinary human cognitive and emotional systems and their functions. Again, it is the 'tweaking' that does it. Famous examples from the history of anthropological research demonstrate how early scholars had genuine difficulties in understanding ritual action (Tambiah 1990). The 'natives' or 'primitives' were supposed to be able to master only literal 'concrete thought' where the perceptual equals the conceptual. As an example, when the Nuer people (in southern Sudan) stated that a cucumber 'is' an ox in a sacrificial ritual they must be confused. The anthropologist E. E. Evans-Pritchard demonstrated that the Nuer were not confused because they do *not* confuse the perceptual, 'what is apparent to the senses' with the conceptual, how the object 'may be thought of' because it is only in certain ritual situations that the cucumber may substitute and play the role of the ox (Evans-Pritchard 1956). In ritual cognition, many special things may happen: pieces of bread (perceptual) may be sacralised and become (conceptual) the body of a god, but only in special ritual situations, at special places and times and with special agents. In rituals, the essences of things (what they are) may be twisted, tweaked, substituted or changed in almost any imaginable way.

Here again, the distinction between icon, index and metaphor becomes analytically useful in the study of religious and ritual signification and cognition (Leach 1976). Iconic illustrations are understood (by devotees) to look just like and have the same properties as that which they resemble and so icons and their references have similar essences. The little icon of Saint Anthony *is* Saint Anthony and has the characteristics of Saint Anthony (e.g., it/he might help you find things). Indices (plural of *index*) point to the presence or existence of references. Metaphors are juxtapositions of entities that have dissimilar essences, but these are moulded by social convention to merge and appear as similar or united as in the example of bread and body. An explanatory example: the Hindu god Shiva is displayed in phallic form as a lingam statue. The phallic form is iconic and at the same time it points indexically to Shiva's metaphysical presence and metaphorically displays Shiva's complex divine qualities.

It is precisely the capability of symbols to connect various semantic domains, relating them to narratives and other cultural information with emotional and cognitive functions that is played out in ritual. Rituals and the symbols involved in them do work on the human psychological functions: perception, cognition, memory and, not least, feelings and emotions. Rituals are emotion-regulation mechanisms, and any emotion may come into play in relation to rituals, anything from boredom to extreme experiences, from monotonous listening to walking on burning coals (Xygalatas 2012). Rituals have, as Victor Turner emphasised, an 'orectic pole' that concerns what is desired in and with ritual behaviour. On the Ndembu Isoma ritual, Turner notes:

> The symbols and their relations as found in the Isoma are not only a set of cognitive classification for ordering the Ndembu Universe. They are also, and perhaps more importantly, a set of evocative devices for rousing, channelling, and domesticating powerful emotion, such as hate, fear, affection and grief. They are also informed with purposiveness and have a 'conative' aspect. In brief, the whole person, not just the Ndembu 'mind', is existentially involved in the life or death issues with which Isoma is concerned.
>
> (Turner 1977: 42–3)

Ritual performances are articulations of traditions and world views, and, along with their associated norms and values, they are powerful in emotion regulation and so an important feature in the governance of social interaction. In ritual performances, the programmes of events to be performed will be combined with cultural ascriptions (what the tradition says) and the participants' actions, mental and physical. The participants' (active performers as well as audience) emotional and cognitive functions are enmeshed in contexts that may range from the religious universe, across bodily movement to innermost feelings and emotions, united in doing something that others also do, have done or will do. A century ago, Durkheim wrote on ritual effervescence (the intensifying of emotions in ritual) in communal rituals and hypothesised that such emotionality was the very cradle of religious life:

> Indeed, we have seen that when collective life reaches a certain degree of intensity it awakens religious thought because it determines a state of effervescence that changes the conditions of psychic activity. Vital energies become overstimulated, passions more powerful; there are even some that are only produced at this moment. Man does not recognize himself; he feels he is transformed, and so he transforms his surroundings.
>
> (Durkheim 2001: 317)

Durkheim's speculation is impossible to prove as there is no way of emotionally arousing actions and concomitant collective cognitive functions. The theoretical analyses of these matters are complex, as demonstrated by Robert N. McCauley and E. Thomas Lawson (2002: 89–123). Even more, anthropological research and cognitive experiments demonstrate that both performers and audience share emotional arousal (Konvalinka et al. 2011). Being in the same location and exposed to many of the same events and forces may create a sense of sharing experiences.

Box 5.4 Ritual learning as cultural reproduction

Ritual learning. How ritual is used to teach coming generations what is valuable and important in tradition. This example concerns the spirit journey of Huichol children in Mexico conducted by a ritual specialist who has typical shamanistic traits.

Each year, many among the Huichol people in Mexico go on a month-long pilgrimage to the sacred mountain of Wirikuta, more than 200 miles east of their ordinary home in the mountains of western Mexico. For the participants, who must be adults, the rituals on the way involve penitence, praying, feasting and the consumption of the hallucinogenic peyote cacti. Children are not allowed on the actual pilgrimage, but they are trained in an annual ritual called 'Our Mother's Ceremony'. It is celebrated at home in the village where the ritual specialist, called the 'Singer' (*mara'akame*), takes the children on a day-long 'spirit journey' while they are attending the ritual with their parents. The Singer chants and repeats hundreds of verses (four times!) referring to all the special places that they pass in the imagined flight over the land to Wirikuta, and he recalls all the special and mythological beings and actions that they must learn to associate with the pilgrimage. They learn about and greet deities on the way as well as learning to identify the dangerous and difficult passages. Part of the ritual involves confessions by parents to the goddesses and their hopes that sins can be atoned and diseases avoided by sacrificing and participating in the actual pilgrimage. Through attending this ritual annually, the children will come to know, almost by rote learning, what is at stake in the pilgrimage as well as the whole mythology and cosmology involved. The children are not explicitly taught and examined; they simply learn by being exposed to all that is said, shown and done in the ritual. The ritual for the children is practically as important in the social ontology of the Huichol as the adult pilgrimage itself. It is an example of how both semantic and episodic memory are involved in ritual training and cultural learning. These public manifestations of representations and beliefs are pedagogical and have reduplicate purposes in the maintenance of a religious tradition.

In many ways, ritual actions cut across both space and time, and so rituals are deeply involved in making humans do the *same* things and achieving social, cultural and religious 'synchronisation'. Even the most particular or singular agent who is the only one to do something as a special agent in a ritual is doing the same as other agents of the same kind. The role-taking aspect of ritual is crucial as it creates a sameness that allows the individual performer to (symbolically) transcend self, space and time and, not least, individual intentionality (Jensen 2016a).

Here is the key, it seems, to why it is that humans instinctively notice rituals. There is something in ritual stylised performance that triggers the human sensitivity to synchronicity and over-imitation, but there is also something about the 'non-functionality' of many ritual acts (Nielbo et al. 2013). Some bodily ritual acts, for instance, are straightforwardly understandable, such as when kneeling or prostration is used to signify respect, but other acts are without such inherent intention and they only become meaningful when given a cultural interpretation. Psychological investigations into this topic suggest that when humans look at events that are not immediately recognisable as practical, functional or intentional, then they will have problems with 'event segmentation' (figuring out what is going on), and this, in connection with an overload of sensory stimulation, may occasion cognitive depletion ('tiring' the brain). Subsequently, when there is no obvious instrumental or functional meaning to the non-functional (in cognitive terms), ritual action then cultural information and religious traditions are able to saturate the minds of participants with collective representations and emotions that fill out the 'empty slots' in action perception. This indicates how rituals 'work' with minds and bodies depends on cultural information and learning to become meaningful.

Functions of ritual in connecting i-religion and e-religion

Ritual signalling (in icons, indices and symbols) spans and connects this world and the 'other world' while it also allows collective representations and social institutions to merge with individual cognition and emotion, and so noticeably join i- and e-religion. Ritual participants' use of symbols unites prescribed collective emotions and cognition with those of the individuals; mourning ceremonies deploy other emotions than weddings. Ritual signalling is thus a powerful tool that enables the maintenance of the relations with the 'other world', individual as well as collective. Ritual symbols are (1) made of matters from the material and social world (objects, language, etc.) that (2) signify meaning about or from the 'other world' in (3) formats that are collective and social (4) to be internalised in individual cognition and emotion. Ritual significations that link individual, group, this and the 'other world' are thus to be seen as cognitive, emotional and social technologies that are able to cut across and dissolve distances in time and space. Ostensibly, in rituals, there are 'cosmological contracts' with exchanges and negotiations with agents from the 'other world', and, more imperceptibly, there are the concomitant social, cognitive and emotional effects. Furthermore, rituals may also regulate human relations to the environment and ecology, from hunting and fishing rights to regulations of large-scale irrigation systems. In fact, it seems that human cultural evolution has been highly dependent on religion and ritual as both may provide shared networks of practice and coordinate cognition and motivation (Rappaport 1999).

To the tempting question 'Is ritual good or bad?' the answer is either that the question is impossible to answer or 'that depends'. In the traditional literature on ritual, there has been a certain emphasis on the pro-social functions of ritual, such as when participants benefit from expressions of collective identity and common morality (Bell 1997: 23–60). In many cases, rituals *do* have positive social functions (integrating, coping, supportive), but this is mostly in pro-'in-group' functions more than anything else. In fact, rituals may create as much conflict as concord; just think of the rivalries between Christian Protestant groups, Sunni and Shi'ite Muslim communities or a limitless number of splinter groups in other traditions. Splinter groups were often formed over ritual conflicts. Rituals may be *assortative* (separating into groups) and the causes of conflict as well as the effects of conflict (Morris 1987: 246–52). Thus, the issue of whether ritual causes harmony or conflict largely depends on the historical and social contexts. For instance, an inclusive ritual is *exclusive* for those who are not allowed to be included, and the initiation into a special position means subordinating others, be it of another gender or group. Thus, nothing general can be said other than pointing to these mechanisms. It all depends on the context of the ritual and the level of analysis (Martin and Wiebe 2014).

In any specific case, the first task to ask '*Cui bono?*' That is, who or what benefits? Is it the performer(s) or the audience, or is it the institution that provides the ritual? Are there resources exchanged in the ritual under scrutiny? Who offers what? Money? Body? Flowers? What is the purpose beyond the programme of the ritual itself? Does it benefit an institution or an organisation? What do, for instance, mosques, monasteries or churches provide or gain through ritual more than the offers professed at the doctrinal level? Do they offer sacred protection, salvation or redemption – and is that all? And, not least, what are the costs? Obviously, there may be inclusion and membership at the individual and social levels, but there is also the ultimate continuation and growth of the institutions and organisations at the institutional, political and economic levels. The more dedicated the members, the better will it be for the institution or organisation. The number of possible functions of rituals, proximate or ultimate, is immense, and only specific cases may elucidate what exactly is at stake. Any analysis should be aware that there may be other effects of rituals besides those that are more directly discernible as the 'ritual concern', that is to say, the underlying structural programmes of various types of ritual (see Table 5.7). Such other effects may be political, economic, psychological or social.

Structural relations of ritual concern

When the anthropologist Arnold van Gennep coined the term 'rites of passage' (French: *rites de passage*) in 1909, the emphasis was on rituals where the element of 'passage' was clearly visible (van Gennep 1960). Upon closer inspection however, it turns out that there are movements in all rituals, even those that are concerned with confirming a 'status quo' ('Society is passing into a new year', 'NN is still our chief', 'God remains with us'). Most rituals (if not all) mark some kind of transition of subjects and objects across borders, for instance from

Table 5.7 Structural relations of ritual concern

Structural relation	General characteristics	Examples
Confirmation: keeping things as they are	Celebration of existing order in new situation/ceremonies	New Year celebrations
Transformation: changing things	Changing the nature or status of subject(s)/object(s)	Initiations of individuals in puberty rites
Attribution: giving something to something	Attribution of nature or status to subject(s)/object(s)	Hailing chiefs, anointments of priests
Removal: taking something from something	Destruction of sacrificial object, destruction of malignant object/influence	Removal of evil spirit, healing rituals
Inclusion: including something	Including someone into something/adding status by inclusion	Initiation of juveniles into adult society, becoming member of special society
Exclusion: excluding something	Rituals of protection, banning, ex-communication	Warding off evil spirits, rituals of control of heretics

profane to sacred and back, even if it is a weekly or daily ritual that marks one more year, week, day or one more prayer. The ritual concern may refer to individuals, collectives or objects and instruments – or the state of the world (e.g., greeting the sunrise). Table 5.7 is an attempt to break the possible number of the structural relations of ritual concerns down to the logical minimum.

Rituals and ritual sequences with these characteristics come in many and complex configurations. A multifaceted example could be the annual Muslim *hajj* (pilgrimage) to Mecca, which includes all these structural features. Another complex example from the more (but not wholly) secular sphere is a coronation ritual such as the transformation of a princess to a queen, through attribution of insignia and status, inclusion into a line of reigning royalty, and a confirmation of the status of the royal family and the continued existence of the institution of monarchy.

The complexity of ritual concern also shows in initiations: they are *transformative* and integrative when they change the status of individuals and install them as members of a collective, but in doing so they also confirm the endurance and value of the collective and its social institutions. Similarly, rituals concerned with the keeping of the status quo and *conservation* tend to deliberately highlight the 'mock' transition to a similar situation, and so emphasise that 'things have *not* changed'.

Frequently transitions involve transformations of subjects and objects as in sacrifices, initiations, and in crisis and healing rituals. The latter especially centre on protection from and removal of dangers and they regularly exhibit a zone of liminality, where the possibility of ritual manipulation and work-on-the-world also involves dangers if things go wrong. Such situations call for strong 'ritual control'. The Ainu bear ritual described above demonstrated this element of control: not a single drop of the bear's blood must be spilled lest things may go terribly wrong.

Generally, the more ritual control there is in a ritual the more important it is for the participants and purposes involved in it. Similarly, there are often requirements that ritual performer(s) should be in a special state to perform the proper actions. Perhaps only specially appointed ritual experts are allowed to perform the actions, or it must be done as meticulously as bordering on the neurotic.

Problems of ritual taxonomy: sacrifice

Among scholars in theology, classical studies and the earlier history of religions, as well as the first generations of anthropologists, the taxonomies and classifications of rituals were clearly influenced by the scholars' Western Christian backgrounds. A typical taxonomy of sacrifice would emulate and be an extension of the types known from the Hebrew Bible. The text of the third book, Leviticus (chapters 1–7), containing instructions for the priests and duties of the lay people, lists the basic forms of offering: burnt, peace, sin, guilt and grain or cereal. As a scientific taxonomy it is confused because it combines substances, methods of destruction, reasons and intentions, but it has still made an enduring impact. In a representative textbook for the study of religion from the 1970s the types of sacrifice (offering) are enumerated as shown in Table 5.8.

Table 5.8 Types of sacrifice/offering

Name/label	Major characteristics	Example(s)
Gift/firstling offering	Gift sacralised and offered creates and maintains bond or *Do ut des* ('I give so that you will give')	Ancient Indian (Vedic) ritual offering of butter. First bits of the crop offered to Hebrew God
Votive and thanksgiving	Offering with promise, or thanks, for health, livestock, longevity	Daily food for gods in Egyptian temples. Promises for healing at Roman Catholic pilgrim sites
'Convivial' sacrifice	'Bonding': Superhuman agent invited to take part in communal meal	Goddess Athena enjoys the scent of the ancient Greek sacrifice
Communion	The sacrificial substance identified with god and eaten/provides power	Host and communion in some Christian traditions. Totem animal eaten in some Aboriginal Australian traditions
Atonement and substitution	Apologising/compensating wrong, unclean, sinful action	Scapegoat rituals (transfer of guilt from human to animal)
Kathartic or piacular	Cleansing/evil-averting	Sacrifice to 'wash off' sins or guilt and to avoid being seen by 'evil eye'
Libation/drink-offering	Offering beverage	Ancient Indian (Vedic) offering of *soma* (sacred drink). Offering beer to ancestors in African traditions

This example of a classical listing of types of sacrifice is problematic, although not entirely incorrect, because there *are* types of ritual behaviour relating to superhuman agents that have these (quite different) characteristics and functions. A theoretically rigorous taxonomy is probably not even possible. Then again, this example of a typology of sacrifice also demonstrates how theory-dependent classifications in the study of religion are:

> So, a model of, say, 'sacrifice' will depend on how and why we detect some practice or some event as 'sacrifice'. In ancient Greece, we would have had the indigenous notion of 'thusia' – a gift to the gods as stipulated in Homer. With William Robertson Smith our model of sacrifice changed into one of community building and cultural reproduction activity. With Marcel Mauss it becomes symbolic exchange; with Stanley Tambiah it is viewed as performative action, with René Girard a kind of violence-aversive under-taking; with Pierre Bourdieu we see it as a transaction in a symbolic econ-omy, etc. The point is that no data are model-free, no model is theory-free, and conversely, no theory is without models. They come and go together. The ancient Greek conception of sacrifice was also a theory, though a folk one and an indigenous cultural model.
>
> (Jensen 2009b: 250–1)

Thus, the category of 'sacrifice' and the practices labelled by this term can be conceptualised in a number of ways, depending on theory, method and the focus of the actual investigation. The word 'sacrifice' means 'making something sacred' in and through actions directed towards communicating with agents, powers, representatives of the 'other world' to maintain bonds and contract. (The term 'offering' is often used as synonymous with sacrifice and it accent-uates the 'giving away' of something.) The overt purpose of sacrifice is to *give* something and so *communicate* by means of a symbolic transfer of resources and maintain a contract with the 'other world'. Sacrifices, with offerings of any kind, are symbolic exchanges (in an 'economy' of precious items) with the 'other world'. In 1925, the anthropologist Marcel Mauss pointed out how gifts have obliging powers and how they create mutual social bonds (Mauss 1990). Historical and anthropological records indicate how the 'other world' has multiple preferences for the exchange: anything from silent prayers, vows, flowers and the smoke of burnt offering to flagellation and martyrs can be objects of exchange. The important issue is that something is handed over and that it is something important. It may be materials for transfer and 'destruc-tion', such as food, drink or other precious symbolic objects so that they are no longer the property of the sacrificer. The range of objects offered in the world's religions is extensive: martyrs may give their own life while others may offer a relic, or flowers that represent themselves, to a saint.

It should be remembered, however, that sacrificial acts are also oblique means of communicating messages in this world to the other participants in and around the sacrificial ritual. Often the subtext reads like this: 'We, the X, offer this precious Y to the great NN because we are, and wish to remain, under the tutelage of NN. We are NN's children.' This mode of discourse is called 'auto-communication' (as noted above) because it will happen regularly, the message will already be known and acknowledged by participants, and no new information is added. It is basically like branding in advertising. Many communal rituals are like that.

Communal rituals: intention, purpose and action

In all religions of the world, existing or extinct, many (if not most) rituals are performed publicly, sometimes with very large crowds participating as performers or spectators. One may think of the Muslim Hajj to Mecca, the Easter celebration led by the Pope in the Vatican, the pilgrimages to the Ise Grand Shrine in Japan, or Kumbha Mela in India, celebrated every twelve years and sometimes with more than 10 million participants. Group or 'communal rituals' (to use the more technical term) mostly explicate common goals, apply common means and attempt to achieve common (ideal) results. Many rituals include communal recitations, songs, prayers and invocations. The salient distinction among communal rituals is whether – as programmes of action – they are mainly concerned (a) with processes of transformation or conservation or (b) with signalling identity, status and competence. Again, the question is what is the intention, evident or latent, of the ritual? It is important here to distinguish between the many possible layers in rituals. In one and the same ritual, the intention of the participant may be one of initiation, to a new social and religious status or to obtaining sacred knowledge, for the group it may be a ritual of celebrating a sacred institution or ethnic identity, and on the level of the programme of the ritual it may be one of conservation and so celebrating the unchanging nature of the ultimate sacred postulates.

Thus, even process-oriented rituals may be celebrating the unchanging, the status quo. This characteristic is found in many examples of pilgrimage and other kinds of communal rituals such as processions, festivals, cult dramas and ritual dances: what is process for the participants is conservation for the ritual programme and the social context in which it is embedded. One thing is certain, however: the actions are prescribed, fixed and stereotypical. In some cases, it may actually be demonstrated how participants' ritual coordination and bodily synchronisation influence somatic states, for instance by measuring heartbeat rates as physiological effects of synchronised arousal (Konvalinka et al. 2011). This also shows how and why marching to the beat may have emotional effects on participants and why rituals with large processions seem to have originated in the ancient state cultures such as China, Mesopotamia and Egypt: they represent the orderliness of the hierarchical and bureaucratic society. Social and political contexts have a profound influence on the size, staging and function of large communal rituals. Since antiquity, large processions have been frequent when celebrating military conquests or the inauguration of a new ruler. Today, and outside the specifically religious contexts, the same psychological mechanisms are brought into play when regimes celebrate their military and political supremacy and demonstrate their powers to their people. Rituals may be large and external but they may also be quite private and very internal.

The curious case of mysticism as 'true' religion

Mysticism, the alleged direct experience of the sacred, is and has been a vexed problem in the study of religion. A typical view of mysticism looks like the one from the *Encyclopaedia Brittanica*: 'Mysticism: the practice of religious ecstasies (religious experiences during alternate states of consciousness), together with whatever ideologies, ethics, rites, myths, legends, and magic may be related to them.'

In Christian theology, the philosophy of religion and the earlier history of religions research a good many scholars considered mysticism a special kind of sincere religion with direct (though self-reported) religious experience (e.g., Katz 2000). The confluence of inspirations from romanticism, pietistic theology and the ideas of, for instance, Friedrich Schleiermacher and Rudolf Otto, supplied the idea that individual piety and experience of the sacred were the true goals of religious observance. The philosopher and psychologist William James characteristically noted in 1902 that religion 'shall mean for us the feelings, acts, and experiences of individual men in their solitude, so far as they apprehend themselves to stand in relation to whatever they may consider divine' (James 1985: 31). Over the past century, there have been a plethora of diverse, if not confused, contribution to the subject of mysticism (Katz 2000). The status of current debate can be summed up in the claim that 'The term "mysticism" is a taxonomical black hole', and there is little agreement on the meaning of the term (Nelstrop 2016). New research attempts to tidy up the topic, such as the work of historian of religions Ann Taves (2011) and Geertz et al. (2012) will be drawn upon here below.

At a first glance, mysticism may seem to belong to i-religion because it is commonly described as a mental event, a mode of experience, but upon closer inspection mysticism emerges as a ritual process, a discipline fostered in line with a specific tradition. Religious experience does not just drop from the sky irrespective of time and place. However, in early scholarship and for a good deal of scholars, religion was considered *sui generis* (a kind of its own), and this was taken to mean that religion(s) and matters religious could and should only be explained in sui-generis religious terms because of the ontological autonomy of the sacred. This leads to methodological solipsism: only those who have (or think they have) such experiences can or are allowed to talk about them and only in a special idiom. It is difficult to see such a stance as anything but an immunisation strategy. Consequently, mysticism has been a problem for the wider study of religion. An attempt to introduce historical-critical and analytical discipline into the study of mysticism and a critical confrontation with claims of privileged and direct access to the transcendent world are called for.

Viewing mysticism not only as inner experience and intuition but also as a kind of ritual action shows how mystics follow prescribed conventional patterns that are most often fashioned over ordinary behavioural patterns. Mystical experience has the same characteristics as other types of experience: cognitive, perceptive, conative, emotional, somatic and so on, but in mystical practice they are considered to be caused directly or indirectly by external forces or beings. Thus, mystical experience is more than a mental phenomenon: it is also sensate (sight, hearing, taste, smell and touch). There may be other senses involved closely related to touch, such as temperature, pleasure or pain. Then there are the interoceptive senses of internal somatic processes and sensations such as respiration or heartbeat. Frequently, mystical experience is stimulated by ecstatic techniques with ecstatic content: a trigger, the ecstatic moment and what has been called the 'afterglow' (Laski 1961). It is a common notion in scholarship on mysticism that the ecstatic content may vary but that it mostly involves an experience of unity with the divine or a universal essence – however that might be conceived. It should not be forgotten, though, that mystical experience is *also* a social, culturally bound institution with clearly delineated goals and functions within particular societies. Mystics may use their techniques and seek mystical experiences out of gratitude or for soteriological purposes, but they may also function in society as prophets, healers, magicians, missionaries, advisers or even politicians. They can also be objects of worship such as saints. Mysticism is, in short, not only enacted inside the religious tradition in question but also deeply entrenched in society and culture.

The history of research on mysticism, whether in philosophy, theology, religious studies or the psychology of religion, has been filled with romantic and uncritical acceptance of introspective descriptions of ecstatic behaviour with the assumption that devotees gain direct or privileged access to whatever is considered sacred (Katz 2000). It has uncritically welcomed the possibility of studying the divine or universal reality based on experiencers' oral or literary descriptions. A routine error found in such research is the confusion of text with the reality it purportedly describes, and systematically ignoring the social contexts of ecstatic behaviour. Some have tried to shred the culture-specific aspects from the experience descriptions and come out with a kernel, a pure consciousness event. The early (and some contemporary) research rested on a set of assumptions: a transcendent reality exists; the transcendent reality manifests itself in certain types of religious experience; the two main types of religious experience in which transcendent reality manifests itself are the numinous and the mystical. Also, it has been maintained in this kind of theologically oriented scholarship that numinous and mystical experiences are universal phenomena found within (the so-called) world religions such as Islam, Buddhism, Christianity and Hinduism. It has also been claimed that theism (i.e. primarily Christian theism) is the form of religion that most harmoniously combines the two central types of religious experience and hence best expresses religious truth. Against this tradition, Armin W. Geertz et al. point out that ecstatic rituals *do not* offer direct or privileged access to God or the universe for two reasons:

First, because the rituals employed and the traditions within which such experiences are understood, are the primary source of the meaning and interpretation of them. In other words, possession and ecstasy are socialized practices. Second, our biology and cognition offer no direct access to anything. Even though we think that we do, in fact, have direct access, this is an illusion created by our brain.

There are four mechanisms of illusion that prevent us from direct access (although they increase our survival in natural and social environments): the first is controlled by the brain in the environment (neurobiological), the second by the body and the environment (somatic), the third by our thoughts, feelings and social relations (psychological), and the fourth by society (cultural). Thus, the ecstatic can at best be assumed to gain access to worlds constructed by the brain and society. Such access is achieved through the ritual manipulation of body, mind and social context.

(Geertz et al. 2012: n.p.)

Humans act based on their assumptions, beliefs and convictions and since human perception is largely driven by expectations. Recent work on predictive cognitive processing demonstrates how almost any kind of experience may be induced if individuals have strong expectations. (e.g., Geertz 2010; Nielbo and Sørensen 2013; Schjoedt et al. 2013; Andersen et al. 2014). This also applies to mystical experience. It is very easy to manipulate an individual's mental states through working on the body. In other words, cultural and religious systems can gain intimate access to participants' mental and emotional states. Accordingly, a redesigned research model of mysticism will hypothesise that (1) religiously informed expectations direct, modulate and even alter perceptions in specific situations; (2) religious information and social interactions are crucial in the construction of expectations; and (3) specific cultural techniques, notably but not solely ritual ones, effectively modulate both automatic predictions and more conscious expectations of events. Furthermore, expectation modulation provides a foundation for (4) culturally shared religious models used to interpret events and actions leading to the formation of shared knowledge and motivating future behaviour, and (5) expectation-aligned experiences and classifications are important in institution construction and in the allocation of religious authority (Geertz et al. 2012). The construal 'mystical' is thus an ascription; it is attributed to the psychosomatic experience, either by proponents of the mystical tradition itself or by outsiders, ranging from critics in the tradition to 'outsider' scholars.

Summing up, the differences between the new ascription oriented programme for research in mysticism and the old '*sui generis*' are clearly illustrated in Table 5.9, based on the model developed by Ann Taves in the analysis of the work on religious experience more generally (Taves 2011: 18). Taves' model explained the methodological differences between the sui-generis and ascription models of religious experience in general, but it is readily applicable to the study of mysticism.

Table 5.9 Mysticism: two attitudes in scholarship – *sui generis* versus ascription

Guiding questions	Sui-generis model	Ascription model
Are some experiences inherently mystical?	Assumes that there are some things (most often experiences) that can be viewed as inherently religious or mystical.	Assumes that things (events, experiences, feelings, objects or goals) are not inherently religious or not-religious but must be constituted as such by persons.
Should certain things always be considered mystical?	Yes. There are underlying things (again often experiences) which can or should be understood as (authentically) religious or mystical or spiritual.	No. Diverse things can be deemed religious – mysticism is a modern category – and there are diverse views regarding what should count as religious, mystical or spiritual.
What can be compared?	Religious things are compared with other religious things. Common features are often granted evidential force relative to religious claims.	Experiences are compared with other things that have some similar feature(s) whether they are viewed as religious or not.
What is the goal of comparing forms of mysticism?	To understand more about religious or mystical matters.	To understand how and why people deem things religious and to allow researchers to explore the making and unmaking of religion.
How do they relate to other modes of experience?	Mystical experience is set apart from other experiences and tacitly protected from comparison with them.	Experiences deemed religious or mystical are viewed in relation to other experiences and subject to comparison with them.

Source: After Taves (2011: 18).

Finally, consigning the sources of mysticism to culture and society takes us to the next chapter on the institutionalisation of religious belief, action, norms and values.

6   Institutions

Ethics, morality and norms in religion

'Institution(s)' is not a common index entry in books about religion. This peculiar omission overlooks the importance of institutions in social life in general as well as the value of bringing them into the study of religion at centre stage. Linking to the preceding two chapters, the topic of this chapter is how 'beliefs and representations' and 'practices and behaviours' converge and solidify into the social and cultural institutions that govern ethics, morality and norms in thought and behaviour in religious traditions. An institution can be defined as 'a network of norms, rules, and values': that is, an institution has 'deontic powers' such as duties, obligations, permissions, prohibitions and rights (Searle 2010: 8–9). Examples could be the institution of private property, the institution of marriage or the family, which typically have public, legal aspects as well as less general and more private aspects, as for instance in the family. Here, one may think of family-related traditions for what counts as proper in the family, which, again, all depends on the socio-cultural context. Ideas linked to practices are institutions and not just speculative philosophies. As the anthropologist Mary Douglas pointed out:

> It is misleading to think of ideas such as destiny, witchcraft, mana, magic as part of philosophies ... They are not just linked to institutions, as Evans-Pritchard put it, but they are institutions – every bit as much as Habeas Corpus or Hallow-e'en.
>
> (Douglas 1966: 90)

In traditional societies, religiously based normative institutions have been instrumental in governing and regulating the social system. Law was typically seen as instituted by the gods and so were the rules of social hierarchy, political power as well as morality and ethics. Right and wrong, and good and bad, were 'givens' by and from the superhuman realms of the 'other world'. It is in the very definition of traditional society that this is so: the 'Sacred Canopy' is (or was) suspended over all of life's domains, as the sociologist Peter Berger has described it (1990). Post-traditional or modern society is when and where the legitimacy of the 'other world' wanes or altogether disappears as ultimate reference. It is also where and when religion emerges as a separate sphere of society with a definite name. In religiously governed traditional societies there would mostly be no specific term equal to 'religion'. What we might call 'religion' is simply 'the way things are' in traditional society. Not so in modern society where the authority of religion fades. How and why did these changes from traditional to modern culture and society come about?

In the perspective of the study of religion, religion is not made by gods but by humans – with the peculiar twist that humans say that the gods made it. This denial of human intention (already noted by Ludwig Feuerbach) requires some explanation. Hence, the focus here is on how humans labour on the social construction and transmission of institutions, such as their religion(s), and how this happens primarily through language (or through other language-like media). In a philosophical perspective, language clearly appears as the 'ultimate artefact' for the construction of social worlds (Jensen 2009a: 402–26). The philosopher John R. Searle has worked extensively on determining the conditions for the making of social worlds in a 'philosophy of society' that will deepen our understanding of the 'structure of human civilization' (Searle 2010).

According to Searle, the most fundamental social function of human minds is that they are able to have 'collective intentionality', that is, that they are able to agree on ideas, plans, values and the status of things (2010: 42–60). Searle analyses the conditions for the creation of social objects by the use of status function declarations in the form of '*x* counts as *y*'. Less abstractly, this means, as a helpful example, that pieces of paper (or bits and bytes in a computer system) may count as money because humans agree upon it. It was not always so – money has a history – but now money is an institutional (and universal) fact. The existence of money ultimately depends on human collective intentional attitudes towards it. Humans have money and other mammals do not have money.

Marriages and cocktail parties are what they are because people agree on the rules for these events being what we think they are. Both may turn into what looks more like war scenes, but that does not alter their status. The rules of chess are agreed upon as the rules that constitute the necessary conditions precisely for that game and from these derive those rules that regulate the actual playing of the game. Searle labels these rules 'constitutive rules' because they are the conditions for the existence of the game. Similarly, there are constitutive rules for all aspects of our social worlds, where universities as well as religious traditions are very good and powerful examples of this. The second kind of rules, the 'regulative rules', tell you what to do, when driving a car or when signing up for exams, for example. The analogy with religion is stunning, although not one that philosophers make much of (e.g., 'religion' is not in the subject index in Searle [2010]).

Status function declarations of cosmic proportions arise, for example, when some imagined being is named Lord of the Universe or when someone is declared as an incarnation or messenger of such a being. It is, however, in the nature of religious traditions that the set of constitutive rules omit any direct reference to the agent that produces the declaration of the status function. It is a powerful form of linguistic practice: 'We use semantics to create a reality that goes beyond semantics, and semantics to create powers that go beyond semantic powers' (Searle 2010: 14). This is how humans can 'do things with words' and again, religion is a stunning example of the making of social ontology.

All religious traditions abound with rules, some more than others, but the basic social function of both rules and religion is to structure human life. Very few, if any, cultures have no personal names whatever: everywhere an individual becomes a social person (Latin: *persona* = 'mask') by becoming incorporated in the social world with names, status, obligations and rights that allow for actions, hopes, fears and all the rest of what matters in life. Examples of this are the functions of gender and age roles in cultures. In many places are they so important that they are considered directly sanctified in and by the religious tradition because the superhuman agents wanted it this way in primeval time and now 'they are watching'. The rules have deontic power, they make humans do and not do things: 'That is, they carry rights, duties, obligations, requirements, permissions, authorizations, entitlements and so on' (Searle 2010: 8–9). Along these lines, religion is *institutional reality* created by linguistic representation, that is, by the use of language as a creative medium. Searle's notions of 'constitutive' and 'regulative' rules, 'status function', 'declaration' and 'deontic power' are useful concepts in the understanding of the bases and functions of religious traditions. Scholars of religion are increasingly becoming aware of the theoretical potentials of this perspective (Rota 2016).

In the modern world, many institutional facts are created through political, legal or economic practice. In the histories of literate religious traditions there are some known 'authors' of religious social facts and institutions, from the king Hammurabi to Mahatma Gandhi, but in general the construction of social (and religious) institutions and worlds mainly appears in the form of subconscious collective psychological projections. Projection is the mechanism whereby subjective phenomena become treated as objectively independent and real objects:

> Projections achieve the status of collective, social reality when its propositions become widely accepted; from the time when someone suggests something till the same proposition ends as tacit and accepted knowledge there may be a long way, but that is how 'truths' are made as social facts.
>
> (Jensen 2009a: 186)

As with so many other social phenomena, and here language is a first-class example, institutions are the unplanned, and sometimes even unexpected result of group behaviours. Further, institutions can be seen as forming a kind of meta-language or 'grammar' of social norms of what is considered, for example, lawful, ethical, pious, unclean or blasphemous (Jensen 2016b). For cultural and social facts to be understandable and workable for human, some amount of order and structure is called for. It is for the scholar or the scientist to discover, describe, analyse and explain such clusters, networks or systems of cultural, social and religious facts and institutions (e.g., Bicchieri 2006).

In contrast to many social institutions, organisations consist of formalised cooperation between individuals and groups that facilitate certain kinds of action. The United Nations is an example of this. A religious group functions as an institution when it instructs its members in the appropriate world view and ethos (cf. Geertz above, p. 3) and as an organisation when some are leaders, clergy and others are 'lay-folks' – along with rules that stipulate how one may become a member. On this view, the Roman Catholic Church is both an institution (a network of norms, rules and values) and an organisation with headquarters, hierarchy and membership regulations.

Where rituals are mostly of specific duration in time, religious institutions are continuous and durable. Where rituals are usually clearly visible, institutions are more subtle and often invisible until they are articulated or 'put into action'. For example, if you have one child, the institution of children's birthday parties may be activated once a year; if you are a kindergarten teacher, it may happen almost daily. Children's birthday parties are rituals where the expectations, emotions and memories that make up the institution of 'children's birthdays' are made visible, they are activated, so to speak. In this sense, rituals are the *parole* (expression) side of the *langue* (systemic) side of social institutions – recalling here Ferdinand de Saussure's distinction of the two theoretical aspects of language. This also means that many social institutions may (a) be invisible for a long time and then become activated and visible when relevant or (b) be so common that they go unnoticed. There are, so to speak, many more social institutions than meet the eye.

Institutions in classification systems and cosmologies

Institutions in the form of classification systems regulate and govern the lives of humans, individually and collectively, and consciously as well as subconsciously (Turner 1977; Lévi-Strauss 2004). To recall Durkheim, institutions and their corresponding systems of classification are social facts that have coercive force on humans in society. Paraphrasing Claude Lévi-Strauss' dictum about 'how myths operate in men's minds without their being aware of the fact' (1969: 12), social institutions can be said to reside in human beings 'without their being aware of the fact'. Because, like myths, social institutions are 'what goes without saying' – they are simply taken for granted and their deontic powers are not questioned.

Classificatory systems are articulated in narratives, often in foundational myths, put into practice in rituals and articulated within the confines of institutions. Institutions provide us with the building blocks, that is, the norms, rules and values of a certain world view, ethos and its action patterns. Religious cosmologies are built on and around the distinction of the 'sacred and profane', which invariably involves establishing and maintaining borders between this and the 'other world'. Very illustrative examples of this come from Polynesian religious traditions with the dichotomous distinction between *mana* (special power, force or quality) and *tapu* (border, caution or dangerous), where especially the latter has become a term used in many languages across the globe: 'taboo'. Such terms as *tapu* and *mana* mark off special space, time and qualities where certain rules apply, such as attending a funeral for instance. The negative power of death is dangerous and therefore appropriate ritual actions, however insignificant they may seem to the observing eye, are of great importance – when leaving the burial place, it is Maori custom to wash hands in water to dispel the tapu dangers of death.

Among the Polynesians, the term *mana* denoted special and powerful qualities, in a person, place or thing – as a kind of symbolic capital. For instance, a Maori chief had so much *mana* that there were strict rules, *tapus*, for giving him food and touching him. Religious tradition abound with borders, cautions and dangerous matter but they may display the opposite as well: matters that are pure, special, sanctified, revered and positively powerful. Humans have a penchant for imagining things with special qualities, cognitive salience, and nothing is more apt for producing and staging such qualities than rituals. Many rituals are precisely 'extra-ordinary', special and exceptional and so they may serve to attribute extra value to particular acts, persons or objects and thereby also sanctify the institutions that enable these acts of attributions.

Institutions are located within world views and cosmologies and they are linked to particular programmes for behaviour. This is how rituals work as articulations of institutions. Institutions need not be present and evenly distributed in all minds in a group. Rather, they are external socio-cultural devices to employ at specific times and circumstances: Halloween is a good example of a small package of norms, rules and roles with restricted legal and economic consequences, and marriage a good example of a much larger package with many more ramifications. These are also examples of how institutions cut across and so can bridge various collective (cultural and social) and individual (emotional and cognitive) domains: in marriage, the parental, the legal, the social, the economic and the sexual domains become intertwined, and when and where marriage is a religious institution it also involves transcendent conditions and qualifications. As in belief, mythology and ritual, religious institutions display the remarkable ability to cross and unite various realms of the human life-world. When Lévi-Strauss wrote about the 'savage mind' in 1962 (Lévi-Strauss 2004), his point was precisely that the indigenous peoples he referred to were not 'savage'. Their thoughts about life, as expressed in myths and classification systems, were logical enough. However, when languages and cultural settings differ, the conditions for thought also differ, depending, for instance, on the available memory systems. In non-literate cultures and religions, extensive use is made of very attention-grabbing devices: 'stuff' that is good to think with and easy to remember because it is composed of both intuitive and counter-intuitive elements that come together in creative ways. Lévi-Strauss termed this process *bricolage*: what the handyman does when he works with the bits and pieces he already has at hand. In a similar manner, cosmologies and institutions are woven together in patterns that mutually reinforce them and (ideally) prevent their decay. Where there are institutions there are cosmologies and vice versa.

Cosmologies come in four distinct types, according to anthropologist Philippe Descola, based on the way they classify the relations between humans and their environments and ecologies. Descola uses the term 'ontologies', that is, 'modes of identification' based on the ideas of what the world consists of, what kinds of beings there are and how they are related. Being ideal types, the four types are animism, totemism, analogism and naturalism (Descola 2013). They each have distinct ways of world-making or 'worlding'. Animism is well known as the humans attribution of subjectivity to and personal relations with animals, plants and other elements of their surroundings. Non-humans have different physical shapes, but interiorities similar to humans – they have souls and so shamans and jaguars may change identities or the gods may visit in the shape of bear cubs. Animism is and has been found all over the world (and is the basis of all religion, Chapter 3 above). Totemism has been a vexed topic in anthropology, but here it means that a specific human group consider a species of plant or animal as their original ancestor and so they share certain qualities, descent or fate with the ancestral beings. Totemism is primarily found in Australian aboriginal cultures with complex genealogical cosmologies. Analogism is the cosmological idea that all being is fragmented into many shapes and essences with a hierarchy, the God-given 'Great Chain of Being' (or Latin '*Scala Naturae*') and with complex networks of analogies between them. Resemblances and similarities among things are being interpreted as signs of relations. Astrology, ancient and modern, 'analogic', modes of divination (cf. above), and elaborate systems of correlations such as the Chinese system of Feng Shui all draw on analogical relations between humans and the world they inhibit. Analogism was also the common European mode of thought from antiquity, through the Middle Ages and the Renaissance until the Age of Enlightenment.

The last mode of identification, naturalism, is the modern scientific world view, where human share their biological physicality with many other sentient beings, but only (?) humans have intentionality, the human type of 'interiority' is considered unique. In many religious traditions, aspects of these four modes of identification can be found in varying degree and thus the typology straightforwardly lends itself to analyses, with the caution that 'epistemology' probably would be a better term than 'ontology' for the modes of identification as they are human efforts at understanding the world. At best, they are 'cultural ontologies'.

Cognition in institutions

Examples of comprehensive, complex and resilient religious institutions may be found in the norms and systems for purity and impurity that are well known from many (if not most) religious traditions. In 1966, Mary Douglas emphasised how modern secular ideas of dirt and pollution are quite different from those found in 'primitive cultures', and yet:

> Before we start to think about ritual pollution we must ... scrupulously re-examine our own ideas of dirt. There are two notable differences

between our contemporary European ideas of defilement and those, say, of primitive cultures. One is that dirt avoidance for us is a matter of hygiene or aesthetics and is not related to our religion. The second difference is that our idea of dirt is dominated by the knowledge of pathogenic organisms.

(Douglas 1966: 36)

This was a formidable revolution in medicine, says Douglas, and we must think back to the times before bacteriology and analyse the 'bases of dirt-avoidance':

If we can abstract pathogenicity and hygiene from our notion of dirt, we are left with the old definition of dirt as matter out of place. This is a very suggestive approach. It implies two conditions: a set of ordered relations and a contravention of that order. Dirt then, is never a unique, isolated event. Where there is dirt, there is system. Dirt is the by-product of a systematic ordering and classification of matter, in so far as ordering involves rejecting inappropriate elements. This idea of dirt takes us straight into the field of symbolism and promises a link-up with more obviously symbolic systems of purity.

(Douglas 1966: 36)

Douglas continues to analyse how human perception is organised: 'Perceiving is not a matter of passively allowing an organ ... to receive a ready-made impression from without' (Douglas 1966: 36). Here she adds a classic observation by the psychologist Frederic Bartlett (in 1932): 'It is generally agreed that all our impressions are schematically determined from the start. As perceivers we select from all the stimuli falling on our senses only those which interest us, and our interests are governed by a pattern-making tendency, sometimes called schema' (Douglas 1966: 37). This view of perception as an activity dependent on practical bodily awareness is echoed and amplified in recent philosophy of cognition (Noë 2004). Bartlett additionally had the idea of what he called *prospect*, that is, the direction of development of both individual and group: not only will the past be remembered and assist in creating a stable cultural present but the future becomes imaginable and the group can project itself on to it. That is why the claim 'this is our tradition' is not vacuous but ever so strong; it organises the future. This also happens because, as Douglas notes on the ontogenetic development of individuals:

As time goes on and experiences pile up, we make a greater investment in our system of labels. So, a conservative bias is built in. It gives us confidence. We may have to modify ... but the more consistent experience is with the past, the more confidence we can have in our assumptions.

(1966: 37)

Along this line of theorising, social and cultural institutions serve as collective external memory and cognitive anchors for organising experience. Institutions become deeply fundamental for human individuals and collectives because they also contain and indicate the scripts, and schemata, for action as well as the emotions and values that they trigger. Religious institutions are ready-made formulas for thought, emotion and action handed over from one generation to the next.

Religious *tradition* literally means the 'handing over' of larger sets of religious institutions to coming generations. Like languages, traditions are multifactorial cultural and cognitive networks that humans both inhabit and exploit in their capacity as social creatures. In this more complex sense, where cognition meets culture and society, traditions consist of frames, schemata and the scripts inherent in the institutions and the narratives involved in their construction and maintenance. Then again, how narrative forms and functions are encoded in, transmitted by, and expressed in discourse are also functions of institutions. The impression that it is institutions 'all the way down' or that the networks of institutions are circular or self-generating easily emerges.

Social functions of institutions: authority, economy and power

Institutions not only regulate (have regulative rules) but they are, as Searle pointed out, composed of codifications (constitutive rules) of roles regarding gender, body, sexuality, social arrangements in the family, clan and tribe, and the statuses and hierarchies of sacralised offices. Therefore, religious institutions are inextricably linked to issues of power and authority, and, very often, the distribution of resources and wealth. In most of the world's religious traditions, religion, economy and politics have been joined together. Whatever differences there may otherwise be between religion, politics and economy, they are all systems or networks of social governance and normative cognition (Jensen 2013). It is only with the advent of modernity and (degrees of) secularisation that the differentiation of society meant that religion became less involved in economy and politics in many parts of the world. The sociologist and economist Max Weber (1864–1920) turned to the issues of religion, authority and power in his now classic sociological studies of authority (see Morris 1987; Pals 2006). Weber distinguished between three types of authority and leadership, which are also interesting for the study of religion: traditional, legal and charismatic. The 'traditional' leader has the authority (often hereditary) from the tradition, that is, from the ways things have always been. 'Legal' authority is based on systems of laws and rules, and persons who are assigned an office with authority are appointed or elected according to legal procedures and only have the authority for as long as they hold office. 'Charismatic' authority arises from the personal charisma that is attributed by followers to a leader, typically the founder or reformer of a sect or movement, who then leads by virtue of special qualities (the charisma) and not because of law or tradition. Habitually, charisma is considered intrinsic to the personality of the leader, but upon closer inspection, it becomes evident that the charismatic status is a function of the veneration of the followers. When the leader dies (or is removed) the authority structure in the movement becomes 'bureaucratic': the subsequent leader (s) who usually do(es) not have the same amount of charisma then gain their authority by having a position or an office with authority and so they gradually institute a system based on rules that becomes tradition. Weber's analysis of authority is a natural history of religious movements, new and old.

As religious traditions and institutions function in society, they are unavoidably · entangled in economy and politics. A quick glance at the ancient Egyptian pyramids attests to this, as do the edicts of the Buddhist king Ashoka (d. 232 BCE), or the functions of the Vatican in European history. Even those religious traditions that apparently give the impression of being world-rejecting are factors in society in general; groups of ascetics or monastics that live outside society are often an important segment of the total social order. For example, in the Jain communities in India, the ascetics are not just ascetics. They have religious, ritual and moral functions in relation to the lay people that also affect the economic relations in the Jain community, which is one of the most economically successful in India (Laidlaw 1995). The economic functions of religious institutions can be many and varied, ranging from decisions of which kinds of foods are produced and consumed to the distribution of alms to the poor. A list of empirical data on this issue could be virtually endless, and so there are good reasons for looking for economic relations in any specific study of matters religious (see also Chapter 7).

In many traditional societies, religious authority is involved in the allocation of resources such as hunting terrains and fishing grounds, as well as the distribution of prey, catch and crops. Economists habitually do not take much interest in religion, nor have scholars of religion in economics, and so the field of 'religion and economy' has been remarkably limited. However, economics is not only about money; it is about *resources* in general and other matters considered special and valuable. As religion happens to have very much to do with what humans care about and spend time and other resources on, different perspectives on religious practices and the efforts involved in them would most likely reveal a deep relation between '*homo economicus*' and '*homo religiosus*'. When viewed in this perspective, most religious traditions in the ancient world might be seen as insurance institutions, individual as well as collective. To take just one example, ancient Roman agricultural rituals were deeply concerned with the health of the livestock, the fertility of the land and the fate of the household, looked over by minor gods and spirits such as the Lares and Penates, who were tutelary demons and ancestor spirits (Rüpke 2016). There was no shortage of invisible agents looking after and taking care of humans and beasts, but of course they did not do so for free. Symbolic exchange, in the form of sacrifice and other respectful communication, was the order of the day (every day).

Because invisible beings ruled many of the affairs of humans who were expected to respond respectfully, it was also quite logical that rulers in this world should have close and proper relations with the 'other world'. Needless to say (almost), these relations have always played important roles in the legitimisation of power as they were based on the ultimate sacred postulates. If the cosmic and divine orders are unshakeable, so are the social orders presided over by the rulers. Rulers have traditionally represented their lands and subjects in a metonymic *pars pro toto* relation and so the well-being of the ruler could be taken as a sign of the well-being of the reign. In some southern African kingdoms, the king's health and digestion were scrupulously monitored, as this would provide information about the entire cosmic order (analogism again). Old Norse kings in Scandinavia were responsible for the crops and the economy. If the of crops did not live up to expectations, the king would face being ostracised. The rulers must be in good and close relations to the 'other world'. As the god Thor reigned over the weather, a bad crop would indicate Thor's dislike of the king. Traditionally the history of religions literature distinguishes between rulers and their roles as either (a) sacred or (b) divine. Table 6.1 is, again, an 'ideal type' diagram so some overlap may occur in actual historical examples.

In the contemporary world, the topic of the relations between religion, politics and power is resurfacing with a growing body of literature, especially on fundamentalism and terrorism. Much of the research is quite recent, spurred by events that have received extensive media coverage and led to political actions (Norris and Inglehart 2011). It should be emphasised that the contemporary situation where religion and politics are relatively easy to distinguish as separate domains in society is a historical exception. The segregation of these domains in society is a characteristic of modern society. Traditional and non-literate societies did not have such separations of domains, so when scholars now operate with these domains in historical or anthropological analyses, the distinctions are made in the scholars' interests, used in their analyses and belong to the scholars' theoretical tools and terminologies.

In the social and political sciences, research and literature on religion has mostly presented religion as the dependent variable and politics and economics as the independent variables. That is, religion is seen as resulting from and depending on political and economic causes. This view of religion is well known in anthropology and sociology as 'correspondence' or 'symbolism' theory (cf. Chapter 3). The opposite view, that religion causes political and economic effects, is habitually termed 'idealist' as it refers to (religious) ideas as the driving force in human life. As history demonstrates, in those cases where it is at all possible to distinguish between these factors, there have been many diverse economic and political pressures on religious traditions, but the ways in which traditions (as interpretive communities) have responded may well accord theoretical primacy to religion in many cases of historical change (Weber 2001). A definite conclusion or solution to the theoretical problem of the direction of causation is lacking, and for good

Table 6.1 Types and characteristics of rule

Type of rule	Characteristics	Examples
Sacred kingship (or emperorship)	Ruler *has special status/properties bestowed* by 'other world' with responsibility	Chinese emperors, Persian emperors, most African and Indo- European kings
Divine kingship (or emperorship)	Ruler *is* divine	Egyptian pharaohs, Japanese emperors, Roman emperors

reasons: the actual historical, social or anthropological data are often so complex that it is only with the actual analyses and specific questions that it is possible to delineate the direction of causation concerning certain objects, aspects and dimensions of religion. In reality, it seems that many matters related to religion can be both causal and caused. Bi-directional causality is common in biology so why should it not also be so in matters relating to religion? To try to produce an all-encompassing and final proof on this issue would be a futile undertaking. It is the 'word and object' or 'map and territory' problem once again, because the *word* 'religion' prompts us to reify conceptually and think that there is 'a thing' that is called 'religion' and that causality may then be neatly determined.

Institutions and social identity

Religious institutions are important in the control of minds and bodies: they define how humans should think and behave and so religious traditions can be seen as powerful social governance vehicles. The puzzling fact is that although many rituals and religious beliefs are not intelligible to the participants in the sense that they explicitly know what the reasons in and behind the rituals and beliefs are, the religious beliefs and rituals are meaningful to participants, simply as indicators of 'who we are' or 'what we do'. This means that, although beliefs and rituals do not carry or activate semantic content that makes explicit sense to the participants, they are still 'meaningful', that is, they are consequential, because beliefs and actions in ritual and religion function as cognitive stabilisers that enable the construction of social codes, norms and institutions as habitual. Here it becomes apparent how the semantics of religious traditions work as shared background assumptions, although the semantics (meanings) may have no direct references in the material world (Jensen 2004).

Humans share the unique ability to have goals, and to cooperate according to plans and in respect of norms and rules. (Weddings are a good modern example.) In that sense, social institutions 'make us smart' collectively when constitutive and regulative rules are internalised in participants. Social and so also religious institutions are cognitive tools with force because they 'store' and 'radiate' normative commitments that often 'crystallise' in rituals (such as weddings). Institutions in religious traditions are mental and social technologies that can be used to govern thoughts and emotions, dietary codes and sexual behaviours as well as the status of individuals or the rights of groups. The history of Hindu traditions provide ideal examples of highly complex institutionalised laws and patterns of behaviour (Olivelle and Davis 2017). Religions are 'many things', and social and cognitive governance are clearly some of those 'things'. Readers are invited to check with the traditions most familiar to them.

Highly important in religious traditions (and a major topic in the sociology of religion) are the institutions that regulate religious group membership and the relations to other groups. The relations between individuals and religious groups may take almost any shape, but they are always regulated: there are always rules that govern the prescribed relations, positive or negative. Some rules are very easy to conform to – parents having a child being baptised in a church or given a name in a Muslim community do not have to do much – whereas adults who wish to convert to a different tradition may have to go through extensive rituals, ordeals or dogmatic tests. Acts of inclusion, such as initiation rituals, may take on almost any shape but they do have some general structural features (see Chapter 5). Acts and rules of exclusion are more infrequent, but in some religious traditions, for example the Muslim, there are rather specific rules in the legal systems for defining and dealing with apostates. Some groups have extreme rules and severe punishments for apostates, and without doubt such harsh behaviours are meant to discourage members from leaving the group (Boyer 2001: 287–96).

Relations between groups may also be anything from relaxed and amiable to extremely hostile. There do not seem to be any general social mechanisms that can account for these variations, but coalition psychology likely provides the best bet. Group identity is important in most religious communities, and the religious signs and symbols such as dress, headgear or hairstyle frequently also function as signs of group identity and membership. In many cases, group institutions also provide ethnic identity. Historical examples of multi-ethnic societies have demonstrated how such religious and ethnic signalling has social functions, for instance, providing trust and distrust among groups (Bulbulia and Sosis 2011). What signals trust for the in-group very often comes to signal distrust to the out-group(s), and, as such, it is a variant of the general psychological tribal instinct. Group-adherence signalling does not seem to follow any specific rules, except that *difference* is crucial. There are groups that do rather special things, such as buttoning their shirts in the back.

In anthropology and the history of religions, totemism was for some time considered quite a special and important case of group identity: One half of the tribe may be called 'hawks' and the other half 'coyote'. Why is this? It was an enigma. When William Robertson Smith (2005) published his study in 1894 he had already contributed to the then heated debate in the UK about totemism. It was heated because totemism was imagined by many to have been the origin of religion and *that* was a heated topic when the previously approved explanations of the divine origins of religion offered by the Churches were falling into disrepute. Totemism, which was then considered the worship of animals (or plants), was thought to have been an early form of religion and a stage that all religions must have gone through. Later research treated totemism in very different ways, and the debate only ended in the 1960s when Claude Lévi-Strauss pointed out how animal symbolism was used to 'think with' in processes of social differentiation: 'We are X and they are Y'. Today, many sports teams use (mainly strong) animal 'totems' as insignia of identity.

Institutions that provide, organise and articulate identity have important functions in ideology in general and in religious traditions in particular. Ideologies, or world views, have the ability to mediate between worlds: (1) the natural, physical and material world; (2) the mental and social worlds; and (3) the ideal 'thought-of' worlds. They mediate in the sense that they can 'speak of' these different worlds and the relations between them through the use of religious symbolism with its special characteristics and functions (as noted in Chapter 4). In lives regulated by institutions, and associated rituals, humans are able to comprehend their place and fate in life. 'Who we are?' is intimately tied to 'what we do', and what we do is inextricably connected with 'what we can do' and, not least, the normative and deontic question of 'what we must do' or 'what we should do' (or not, of course). All this takes place according to the framework of institutions that govern social as well as mental life. Institutions thus also govern 'how we think'. When humans are religious, the religious interpretive frameworks take precedence and in turn govern the normative cognitive functions. That is what Clifford Geertz meant by notion of the *religious perspective*.

Intentionality in tradition and cognition

Here is a short philosophical addendum to the talk about institutions: human intentionality is always about something and about something *in relation* to something. That is, when individuals interact they (mostly) interact with something, a third entity to which they jointly refer. Such triangulation stabilises their joint action and understanding. The third entity is the set of background assumptions of shared information and in the case of religious world views this encompasses the totality of (1) the natural, physical and material world; (2) the mental and social worlds; and (3) the ideal 'thought-of' worlds. This totality sets the stage for judging the interaction of self and other against norms, rules and values, which in turn prompt expectations and judgements. The act of exchanging perceptions and conceptions thus requires a common ground on which to process the information shared. Religious traditions provide just this: norms, rules and values. Thus, even gossip is possible only against a shared, normative background.

Philosophers have pointed out how humans are inevitably involved in and depend on language, tradition, 'spaces of reason' or 'forms of life', and how human social life is only possible on the basis of social institutions (Searle 2010). Having a body and a brain is not enough – culture is what changes brains to minds. The philosopher John McDowell has cogently attacked the myth of the 'endogenous given', the idea that individual cognitive competence is based on innate capacities only. Instead, as he says, human individuals:

> must come to their cognitive task already equipped with a sense of the layout of the space of reasons, a substantive conception of what 'the constitutive ideal of rationality' requires. Now I think we should be suspicious of the thought that we can simply credit human individuals with this equipment, without benefit of anything like my appeal to initiation into a shared language and thereby into a tradition. I think the idea that this cognitive equipment needs no such background is just another outcropping of Givenness ... We must take the subjectivity and the concept of objectivity to emerge together, out of initiation into the space of reasons.
>
> (McDowell 1996: 185–6)

How is this initiation accomplished? Through language and what comes with language.

Language: the ultimate institution

In all societies throughout human history, McDowell's idea of initiation into a shared language and thereby into a tradition has meant taking part in the religious traditions, according to age, gender, status and other social criteria. As already noted, language is the primary tool that humans use when they create social institutions and act within them. Even the initiatory rituals would hardly be meaningful if not for the linguistic scaffolding organising them. Language itself is, in a sense, not just the ultimate artefact but also the ultimate institution: it is conventional, value-laden and rule-governed. Language is fundamental for religion and, traditionally, religion has been fundamental in language. In traditional cultures and societies, religion has been deeply involved in language and how language was used, and much of the vocabulary would be of a religious nature judged by modern standards. Thus, language matters deeply, as Edmund Leach pointed out on the double role of language:

> One crucial point here is that our internal perception of the world around us is greatly influenced by the verbal categories which we use to describe it. A modern urban street scene is wholly man-made and it is only because all the things in it carry individual names, i.e., symbolic labels, that we can recognize what they are. This is true of all culture and all human societies. We use language to cut up the visual continuum into meaningful objects and into persons filling distinguishable roles. But we also use language to tie the component elements together again, to put things and persons in relationship to one another again.
>
> (Leach 1976: 33)

The process of learning a new language will quickly disclose differences in word meanings and categories and so it appears quite compelling that language influences how humans think in and across cultures. The influence of culture and language on thought and cognition has been a controversial subject among linguists, anthropologists and philosophers for decades. Some, the 'culturalists' have gone so far as to suggest that language wholly determines one's world while others, the 'nativists', have denied any substantial influence of language over thought. A prudent compromise would mean that both are partly right: children have innate dispositions to learn languages but languages are different as they also comprise and initiate into specific cultural networks of norms and world views (Tomasello 1999; Deutscher 2010). What linguists and many others often seem to overlook are the religious dimensions of language in traditional society. Most language learning involves learning conventions, and not least religious conventions: norms and values, emotions and codes of conduct, as well as ethics and morality. Traditionally, language and religion come together as a big 'package' that is of crucial importance in the acquisition of culture. Developmental psychologist Michael Tomasello notes that cultural learning often comes to children by seeing and doing, but language is also of vital importance, because:

even nonliterate cultures have important domains of knowledge that are almost exclusively in symbolic format, and so they can only be transmitted symbolically – most clearly knowledge concerning things removed in space and time such as characteristics of distant relatives and ancestors, myths and some religious rituals, some knowledge of local flora and fauna, and so forth.

(Tomasello 1999: 165)

Thus, by learning language, so much more than 'just' language appears. This is also the reason many scholars who are experts on a specific religious tradition often find it difficult to translate adequately from, say, Maori to English or from German to Japanese. The meanings of words, terms and categories have their proper place in large webs of significations, and it may be very difficult to pick just one term or category out of its original context of use and say what it means in another language.

Religion, ethics and morality

All religious systems and all cultures have rules of conduct, however invisible they may be to the outside observer. Religious systems abound with such rules for although religions may seem to be concerned with the 'other world' it is, nevertheless, the fate of humans that is the first concern of religious traditions. 'Religion without rules' is a contradiction in terms as rules are what religions have always been made of (with some postmodern exceptions attempting to prove the opposite). The modes of prescribed behaviour are often imagined as a 'way' to be followed; the idea that wrongdoers are 'straying from the narrow path' is not merely a Puritan Christian invention. Muslim traditions have similar ideas, the now common term for the Islamic law, *Sharia*, originally meant 'a path' in classical Arabic. In the quranic *sura* (chapter) 45, verse 18, Allah says: 'Then We set you upon a pathway of faith, so follow it, and do not follow the inclinations of those who do not know.'

Metaphors of the 'way' abound in many religious traditions, for instance in Buddhism there is the notion of *Dhammapada*: 'The way of the dhamma (Law)' and in Japanese, Shinto means 'the way of the spirits'. In the Chinese religious traditions, the word *dao* means 'way' as well as the natural order of the universe. Also in non-literate cultures, such as Native American religious tradition, there are similar conceptions: the Hopi Native Americans in Arizona have the term 'Hopivewa', indicating the right way to be followed in life. The underlying logic generally seems to be that humans are imperfect and so need guidance and discipline. Religious traditions, and noticeably so the literate ones, present themselves as the main sources of human ethics and morality. Philosophy and philosophers have had similar concerns for millennia and still do. In many places, there is a consensus that religion is the guardian of morality and ethics. At least, all known religious traditions say so.

Moral psychology in religion: bridging innateness and enculturation

In a scientific perspective, human morality and ethics cannot originate in the 'other world'. If religious ideas are human ideas, a different explanation is called for – most likely an evolutionary one. Recent advances in moral psychology research suggests that human morality is broadly based on a set of five evolved moral foundations. Moral psychologists Jonathan Haidt and Craig Joseph demonstrate how innate moral dispositions and normative ethics and morality come together as a biological *and* socio-cultural phenomenon. Thus, enculturated humans have innate 'moral intuitions' as well as learned 'moral reflections' (Haidt and Joseph 2007). Moral reflection is integral to religious traditions and so religion seems to exploit and build upon existing human moral intuitions and dispositions. Therefore, it appears to be the other way round: religious moral reflection is not the (single) source of human morality, but, on the contrary, religion is the culturally evolved outcome of innate human moral psychology. Humans are cooperative animals and cooperation demands fairness and other means of regulation, thus moral psychology spills over into politics and economics (Haidt 2012).

According to Haidt and Joseph, two moral psychological foundations are universal. The first is concerned with harm versus care: humans have a deeply rooted tendency to protect and care for their own. The second is concerned with fairness and justice: humans do not like 'free-riders' who want to join the party without contributing. Haidt and Joseph identify these two foundations as 'individualising' because they care for and protect individuals. In their view, however, morality covers more than the conditions for individuals. Their findings are highly interesting for the study of religion for, as they point out, traditional societies also care deeply about pollution, taboos, sex, ancestors and gods. Thus, in addition to the two 'individualizing foundations', Haidt and Joseph list three additional 'binding foundations': One that concerns 'in-group' loyalty with a basis in 'coalitional psychology'; a second involves 'authority and respect' stemming from primate hierarchy, and the third relates to 'purity and sanctity' based on the uniquely human emotion of disgust. These three binding foundations emphasise sociality and the collective (Haidt and Joseph 2007: 382). As any scholar of religion will know, most religious traditions care very much about matters that relate to these five foundations of evolved intuitive morality. Haidt and Joseph's notions that 'moral thinking is for social doing' and that 'morality binds and builds' support the views of Durkheim from more than a hundred years ago. Now the question is how the innate moral dispositions mesh with social and cultural factors. Here are some brief notes on how this may be accomplished.

The anthropologist Edwin Hutchins developed the concept of 'distributed cognition' because, in his view: 'human cognition is not just influenced by cultures and society ... it is in a very fundamental sense a cultural and social process' (1995: xiv). Hutchins' main idea was to 'move the boundaries of the cognitive unit of analysis out beyond the skin of the individual person' (1995: xiv) and explore 'cognitive properties of systems that are larger than an individual' (1995: xv). Hutchins' notion of 'distributed cognition' discloses some important cognitive (and emotional) functions of social institutions. Social, cultural and religious institutions are systems 'larger than the individual'.

The 'outside-in' processes of learning and reproducing such systems are complex. There are various explanations of how this may be achieved but it is obvious that role-playing, imitation and language play important roles. In a deep sense, culture is constitutive of mind. A simple example demonstrates how complex the interplay between brain, mind, culture, language and society is: how do we learn to identify a promise, that is, the act of promising something? It involves performing an act, including speaking and using the right words, representing and monitoring the act, remembering comparable past acts, imagining future acts and evaluating the act in relation to prevailing norms. All that requires cultural and normative cognitive competence. The evolution of normative cognitive governance depended on creation of external symbolic social systems (Donald 2001). Religious traditions are such comprehensive symbolic social systems. Social, cultural and religious standards are external symbolic props that humans live by, in action, cognition and emotion.

Humans have intuitive affective reactions to most events and 'things' in their life-world. Recent advances (even) in the behavioural sciences show how humans are guided by 'intuitive primacy' much more than by rational reflection. Patterns of emotional reaction are the subjects of reflection in religious traditions as they aim to provide 'emotional governance': how to feel and administer the proper emotions about the ancestors or the family, how to feel reverence to the priest, the scripture or the prophet, when and how to express which emotions in rituals. Emotion is often the most crucial factor in human social behaviour and the regulation of emotions is an important aspect of the functions of religious institutions (Corrigan 2008, 2017).

'Policing', or 'God is watching you'

Religion, ethics and morality have always been fundamentally intertwined and the gods, ancestors and spirits have always had a keen eye to human behaviour – some of them have 'full strategic knowledge' (Boyer 2001: 150–67). Religion, morality and social control come together – and that may spill over into politics and economics. Complex societies need 'big gods' to keep score (Norenzayan 2013). In the ancient Indian Vedic hymn to the god Varuna, it is told how he watches over human conduct, judging what is good and evil and punishing wrongdoers by ensnaring them in his nooses with which he binds all liars. With 1,000 stars as his eyes and spies, he was omniscient as a moral judge: when two persons conversed, Varuna was the invisible third. There is no way of escaping his sight and so his omniscience secures the social order. In the qur'anic *sura* 50, 'Qaf', Allah proclaims in verse 16 that 'It was We who created Man, and We know what dark suggestions his soul makes to him: for We are nearer to him than his jugular vein.' Such proximity should create the optimum condition for moral policing.

The conception of moral rulings and their implementation is not restricted to literate religious traditions. Shamans among the Inuit in Greenland performed a ritual where the *Angakoq* (shaman) journeyed to the bottom of the sea, to meet Sedna, the Sea Woman, and tidy her hair. The moral plot of the underlying narrative is that the animals have become caught in her hair and so they are not available for humans because, as the shaman is able to disclose, members of the community have forgotten to think 'heavy thoughts'. As soon as the Angakoq has tidied Sedna's hair and returned from his spirit journey, the participants in the shamanic seance confess and reveal broken taboos. Then the animals return, and hunting and fishing resumes. In this way, the shamanic ritual restores not only moral order but the natural, social and cosmic orders as well. This is an unmistakable example of ritual work-on-the-world. Morality is important because humans live by it.

Purity systems as religious institutions

Given the importance of purity systems and rules in most cultures and religions, it is remarkable how little attention this subject usually receives. Besides the classic work by Mary Douglas (1966), William Paden's introduction to the field of comparative religion is a noteworthy exception (1994: 141–60). Well-known and widespread examples of the importance of religious purity institutions are the Islamic system of Tahara and the comparable Jewish kosher system, but almost every religious tradition has rules and regulations concerning what is proper for humans and their gods. Many scholars have sought to explain such systems as resource management or as results of avoidance of germs and disease. Although such explanations may be valid in particular cases, the systems are in general *not* rationalistic; they are symbolic and largely arbitrary. However, that is not how it appears to the 'consumers' of the systems because, when such systems are being reproduced through generations, they typically become what is 'natural', even when the systems contain quite intricate rules for control of the body and its functions (Reinhart 1990: 18–20). While such rules visibly regulate food, dress and the body, there are other dimensions as well. Purity systems are also used to signal information. The anthropologist Arjun Appadurai applied this perspective in his now classic research on Hindu food in South Asia and introduced it this way:

> When human beings convert some part of their environment into food, they create a particularly powerful semiotic device. In its tangible and material forms, food presupposes and reifies technological arrangements, relations of production and exchange, conditions of field and market, and realities of plenty and want. It is therefore a highly condensed social fact. It is also, at least in many human societies, a marvelously plastic kind of collective representation. Even the simplest human cuisines, as Lévi-Strauss has suggested, encode subtle cosmological propositions.
>
> (Appadurai 1981: 494)

Appadurai then notes and analyses how the social, cultural and religious practices that relate to food are used in ethnic and political contexts. Food relates closely to most everyday practices, to social status and to the whole of the classification system as well as to morality and aesthetics. Food encodes what is emotionally important, for instance as feared or avoided. Moreover, and not least, gender roles are involved: in many cultures, only women should transform foodstuff into edible food. In most cultures, food is much, much more than just nutrition (Counihan 1999). Most religious purity systems focus intensely on the human body, its secretions and, especially, matters that relate to sex and gender. The social construction of gender is probably as old as language and symbolism in general. Nowhere have anthropologists or historians found societies who were not preoccupied with these issues, and nowhere have they found societies without (some form of) religion. It comes as no surprise, then, that values and norms of 'body-politics' and religion have merged in (probably) all societies. In one way or the other, all religions are about sex.

In some religious traditions, the dualist ideas about body and soul seem to make up a zero-sum game: the less the body and its needs are heeded, the more spiritual the ideology or practice appears. In the Hindu tradition, the ideal of the ascetic *sannyasin* is a lucid example of this principle: a holy man that has left all behind in his final stage of life. Monks, nuns and other ascetic practitioners everywhere articulate these principles through their behaviours. Asceticism is and has been considered a sign of 'godliness' in many times and places (e.g., Freiberger 2016). Even in today's modern world, many who are drawn towards spirituality and spiritual practices also adopt frugal and ascetic lifestyles and thus turn their back on materialism. The historian of religions Gavin Flood suggests that asceticism is best understood as an 'internalisation of tradition', where the life script of the individual ascetic is brought into harmony with the deep narrative of the religious tradition, and so the ascetic performance also functions as a kind of memory of the tradition. Ascetic performance is simultaneously an eradication of the individual will and an affirmation of the will to be an ascetic (Flood 2004). Religion, religious institutions and religious traditions are, in this perspective, discipline, discipline and discipline. Religious institutions are social, yes, but they are also *in bodies*, a fact that demonstrates the startling ability of religious institutions to tie together abstract ideas, forms of behaviour, material objects, minds, bodies, subsistence, resources and power. Humans use religious institutions to make worlds and they use them to regulate worlds and in so doing they regulate their own selves and lives.

7 Religion today

Modernity, postmodernity and secularisation

It is the intention of this chapter to present, though only loosely, some recent developments that have affected the status and functions of religious traditions and what that may entail to the understanding of religion in general. While some traditions survive *where* they have been and *as* they have been for a long time, others have undergone major transitions, some have become extinct and new ones have arisen. The recently changed conditions, with globalisation, migration, increased literacy and electronic media, have profoundly influenced many forms and expressions of religion. Under all circumstances, and in spite of what many (e.g., Marx and Freud, see above) have wished for, religion has not gone away. In some places, it might seem that religion has more or less disappeared. On closer inspection, however, it appears that religion has *changed* (Davie 2013). In many parts of the world, religion is no longer the 'sacred canopy' that was once suspended over the totality of human existence. Instead, bits and pieces of religious world views have dissipated into other domains of society, culture and the human mind (see Berger 1990, and below).

In a large part of the modern Western world, the general view of religion was that it would fade away and lose influence in important spheres of life, such as economics, law and politics. *Secularisation* was the dominant sociological hypothesis about the decline of religion, and it was common in public discourse, the media and in the academy during most of the twentieth century (Dobbelaere 2009). The processes of secularisation have been robust in some parts of the world and less so in others and it has affected some sections and functions of societies more than others. The potential future developments are of course difficult to forecast, but modern lifestyles could point in the direction of increasing secularisation on a global scale (Bruce 2013). Some societies (e.g., Scandinavian) seem to thrive without much religious tradition as other social institutions and organisations have taken over some of the traditional functions of religion (Zuckerman 2010). However, secularisation has not won entirely. If, for instance, banking and the world of finance do not seem to depend much on religious traditions (ethics and morality), other spheres, such as primary education, continue to have close links to religion and tradition. The views concerning gender, family, children, sex, food and purity, and 'decency' in general are long-lived deep structures in culture and society. Some things change more than others, and there is more implicit religion in modern culture and society than meets the eye (Bailey 2009).

The development of the study of religion is itself a telling example of these mechanisms. For instance, in Denmark, which is one of the least religious countries in the world according to statistics, the non-confessional teaching about religion is a compulsory subject in the secondary education system because of the historical, anthropological and philosophical importance of knowing and understanding something *about* religion. In many other European countries, however, the teaching *of* religion (more than teaching *about* religion) is entrusted to religious institutions or to church-approved institutions of education. In still other countries, there is so much religion that there is no need to study it; people are either immersed in the tradition or oppose it vigorously. Both attitudes are, however, not the same as studying it in a critical scholarly manner, as should have become evident through this book.

More recent historical events, traditionalist or fundamentalist revivals, have questioned the validity of the secularisation thesis and the presumed uniform fate of religion in the modern world. Max Weber spoke about the 'disenchantment' of the world as mythic world views waned and the scientific world views took over as explanations of the world. Historian of religions Robert Yelle characterises the semiotic dimensions of the historical processes of secularisation or disenchantment as:

- the decline or sequestration in particular genres of densely symbolic discourses such as myth, ritual and magic;
- the decline of a symbolic, allegorical, or typological view of the world, and the gradual ascendancy of realism, literalism, or a prosaic view of the world;
- the shift away from a conviction in the natural or non-arbitrary status of signs, or from a 'magical' theory of language, and the ascendancy of the idea that the sign is arbitrary and bears no essential connection to that which it represents;
- the rise of scientific projects for the purification of language from errors, and the substitution of a perfect, rational, or universal language.

(Yelle 2013: 4–5)

However, this process is changing in some ways and in some places where the notion of 're-enchantment' is becoming increasingly noticeable – at least for the role of religion in more personal spheres of human existence, such as in 'spirituality' (see below). Looking back to the decades around the year 1900, there was little room for religion beyond the personal sphere among the philosophers and intellectuals behind the 'modern turn'. The term 'modern' took on the meaning of emancipation from tradition, and so religious authority was increasingly discredited as legitimately influential on other spheres of life other than the personal, emotional or existential. The modern, and so post-traditional, world is composed of increasingly separate domains of social, economic and political activity (Bellah 1991). Scientific knowledge must no longer pass the tests of religious authorities and similarly, political and economic matters are rarely driven or governed by religious motivations. Modernity, and especially late modernity (1960s onwards), is characterised by a high degree of societal differentiation and segregation, that is, the segments of society have becoming ever more separate with their own rules and rationales – they become self-sustaining and self-generating systems. Modern social theorising and thus theorising about religion in late modernity is turning out to be theories of systems – in the plural. This also means that religious life may thrive in pockets of societies that are otherwise highly secularised. Religion becomes one system in itself and with a certain autonomy and immunity in relation to other social systems. This is a process of compartmentalisation (Luhmann 2013).

In such cultural climates, religion mostly only matters for people when and where they need to do something religious: having their children baptised, having church weddings or whatever the tradition may offer in an otherwise secularised social setting. Where literalist fundamentalism and pietism once reigned in the Danish Lutheran Church, there is now (with some exceptions) an exceptionally soft theology with a form of Christianity reinterpreted in terms of existentialist philosophy (as Paul Tillich above). Very few interpret and understand the Bible as literally true and divine. Theologians publicly deny the existence of Heaven and Hell and reinterpret these *topoi* (places) symbolically as conditions of human behaviour. Heaven is 'here on earth', provided humans think about their responsibilities towards fellow human beings. The language of the Bible is shed of its mythical chaff and becomes the kernel of a 'deflationary' theology that offers an existential 'essence' in an age of science. As a matter of fact, this mode of religion borders on 'post-religion' as religion transforms into ethics and so on, culminating in the welfare state where religious social belonging loses importance for most people (Zuckerman 2010).

In some financially less fortunate parts of the globe, the situation is entirely different, and this suggests an inverse ratio between welfare and religion – and thus more religion with less welfare. Christianity was previously very much a phenomenon of the northern hemisphere, but today the most fervent Christian populations exist in the south, especially in Africa and Latin America. In these cases, traditional forms of Christianity have changed and intensified (Jenkins 2011). In other circumstances, religious traditions move with populations as a result of labour migration and other aspects of globalisation (Vásquez 2011). Many religious traditions have spread to areas where they were previously unknown. This happened with the migration-based spread of Islam in Europe during the past half century in countries with populations with no previous (colonial) encounters with Muslim religious traditions. In some of these countries, the indigenous religion had also been in decline over decades so a general understanding of what was happening was largely absent. This sometimes turned into a 'culture shock' (Caldwell 2010).

Other new religious encounters derive from the operations of missionary movements, especially Christian. In fact, Pentecostal Christian movements have made great impacts during the past half century and can now lay claims to affiliation from some 500 million people in especially Africa, Asia and Latin

America. The sociological reasons for such success are apparent because 'Pentecostalism's flexible networks, vigorous sociability, and egalitarian disregard of race, class, ethnicity, and, within limits, gender, explains much of the tradition's appeal among the displaced and impoverished of the developing world' (Hefner 2009: 154).

This economic, political and sociological explanation of religious responses to deprivation and exclusion has its merits, but a more psychological explanation of the religious dimensions of the ritual practices would also emphasise Pentecostals' enthusiastic experience of direct contact with the divine.

Religion and politics

The relations between religion and politics quite often emerge as heated topics in today's media. Religion is frequently associated with terrorism and violence, but this is unmistakably a slanted presentation that is produced at least in part by a bias in and of the media for the sensational, things that stir up the cognitive and emotional 'threat detection' mechanisms. Nevertheless, it is just as evident that religion and politics go hand in hand in many places and in many ways. The 'religion and politics' relations range from Muslim fundamentalists discouraging people from voting in democratic elections to basing educational politics on the traditional values of Confucianism. As cognitive, emotional and behavioural governance, religion can be used for almost any purpose, good and bad. For reasons of space, it is possible here to take only a brief look at the impact of religion in politics– others do so in depth (e.g., Bruce 2003; Turner 2013). In history and in most parts of the present-day world, religion has always been a political and or ethnic resource. In Saudi Arabia, the Qur'an *is* the constitution. In many places, many things are changing but the directions of change are not always predictable. Such an issue as, for instance, the impact of Islam in the contemporary Western world is extremely complicated as it involves religion and politics on many levels and in many functions (Amir-Aslami 2013).

In many Western countries and societies, the battles between science, politics, education and religion were fought for decades in the nineteenth and twentieth centuries. The outcome has become one of *entente*: a peace treaty where each sphere in society takes care of its own system and its functions. This is a difficult area, however, because although some countries have deliberately separated religion and politics ('church and state') in their constitutions, politicians often and freely refer to religious convictions and values. Many of the more recent post-colonial nations (such as India) have also chosen to become explicitly secular in terms of politics to curb the possible disruptive forces that might arise from political aspirations of religious traditions, especially where these also relate to ethnic or class affiliations. Religious symbolism may be used politically in unification processes, as when Archbishop Desmond Tutu coined the term 'Rainbow Nation' for South Africa, which, according to statistics, is one of the most religious countries in the world and where the different religious ideologies have large political mobilising potentials.

Today, there are, as ever before, openly visible alliances between political and religious powers, systems or leaders. Political influences may also be found in less obvious connections, especially when and where the influence of religions has faded, either in whole countries or in domains of society. In politics, religion-like phenomena may be more implicit than explicit (Bailey 2009). There are also many ways in which religions and the uses of religion appear in the political sphere. Literal readings of ancient and sacred myths and other texts in combination with nationalist ideology may produce startling results such as when the Indian prime minister Mahendra Modi pronounced in 2014 that 'We worship Lord Ganesha. There must have been some plastic surgeon at that time who got an elephant's head on the body of a human being and began the practice of plastic surgery.'

Myth-making permeates political discourse and, in conjunction with ideological beliefs, it is a very widespread and typical way of making political events understandable in a religious population. Even Fidel Castro made use of religious terminology when trying to make his brand of socialism appeal to the Cuban people. The presidents of the USA often refer to God in their speeches, but noticeably not to any particular god. The religion they so 'practise' has been labelled 'civil religion', a notion coined by the philosopher Jean-Jacques Rousseau (1712–78), who tried to find a secular substitution for the functions of religion with similar moral and ethical values, but without revelation and the Church. The inspiration from Rousseau was profound in Durkheim's attempts (see Chapter 1) to discover which social institutions might take the place and role of religion as social glue and become the warrants of morality and ethics in modern industrial and post-traditional society. In 1967, the sociologist Robert Bellah published an analysis of the inauguration speech of President John F. Kennedy and noticed the particular ways in which religion and religious imagery were used to foster enthusiasm in the nation by appealing to God and the idea that Americans should do God's work. As Kennedy said, 'Let us go forth to lead the land we love, asking His blessing and His help, but knowing that here on Earth God's work must truly be our own.' As Bellah then notes:

> Considering the separation of church and state, how is a president justified in using the word 'God' at all? The answer is that the separation of church and state has not denied the political realm a religious dimension. Although matters of personal religious belief, worship, and association are considered to be strictly private affairs, there are, at the same time, certain common elements of religious orientation that the great majority of Americans share. These have played a crucial role in the development of American institutions and still provide a religious dimension for the whole fabric of American life, including the political sphere. This public religious dimension is expressed in a set of beliefs, symbols, and rituals that I am calling American civil religion. The inauguration of a president is an important ceremonial event in this religion. It reaffirms, among other things, the religious legitimation of the highest political authority.
>
> (1967: 3)

Certainly, the secular substitutions for religion may be many, but considering the multifariousness of 'the thing called religion', this is no surprise. The most common substitute in a market-oriented world is most probably money. Even the study of religions may be politically less innocent that it aspires to be. Research project funding is a case in point. (McCutcheon 2005).

The political importance of religion relies on the fact that most religious traditions serve(d) as collective markers of identity and, often, ethnicity, with all that this may include in terms of religious belonging, conflict, violence, war, radicalisation and terrorism (Atran 2011). Any endeavour to explain (at least partly) these important symbolic functions of religion will have to take into account a number of factors: geography, history, economy, social conditions and social psychological mechanisms. The construction of in- and out-groups using religious affiliation and symbolism is and has been widespread, and religion is most like the primary ethnicity-forming tool. Recent research in evolutionary social and coalition psychology demonstrates how the mechanisms of 'group-ishness' work and where they come from (Boyer 2001: 287–96). Further, theories of terror management hypothesise that humans have an innate awareness of mortality. This may generate a sense of urgency and necessity of defending world views (e.g., religious or political) that furnish the world with meaning, order and permanence. Social psychology experiments demonstrate that subjects who are primed with a sense of mortality become more vengeful towards criminals (Lieberman 1999). Religious groups that live in high-tension and high-risk surroundings may thus have a propensity to develop more radical and violent thoughts and behaviours. Also, as Boyer notes, 'Fundamentalist violence too seems to be an attempt to raise the stakes, that is, to discourage potential defectors by demonstrating that defection is actually going to be very costly, that people who adopt different norms may be persecuted or even killed' (2001: 295). Anyone who wants to be on the 'safer' side will make sure to display the right signs, wear the right clothes or burn the right flags. Fundamentalist religio-political behaviour is, for these very reasons, often very frenzied and noisy: not only to scare the enemy but more so to discipline the ranks.

New age, spirituality and reinventing religions without 'religion'

Fortunately, religious traditions, individual religiosity and spirituality – the more recent addition to the range of religion – may also foster benevolent behaviours. Religious convictions and practices may help individuals and groups to cope in life, in identity formation, by offering salient and valid life narratives or an ambiance of compassion. New modes of religiosity appeal to so many individuals in the modern world that established religion is perceptibly giving way to *spirituality* (Heelas and Woodhead 2005). The dominant feature of contemporary religiosity and spirituality in the post-traditional world is that religious belief and behaviour are now much more freely chosen by individuals, and many movements are (consequently) very active in recruiting new members (Clarke 2009: 723–817). Here are but a few notes on a range of resources that relate to New Age, spirituality, holism, healing and mindfulness meditation, to name the most frequent and widespread of these currents. There are so many, and so varied, views on spirituality that it is difficult to present an adequate overview here (the number of shelves devoted to these issues in any bookshop will prove this). If religion is difficult to define, then 'spirituality' is an even more muddled concept; there is very little agreement on what 'it' means (Paloutzian and Park 2013: 26–9). Fortunately, scholarly resources are available (e.g., Lewis 2004). Two 2017 polls showed that 18 per cent of the US population considered themselves to be 'spiritual but not religious' (Parsons 2018:18). It seems that humans not only want but also need to believe and that apparently some of the conventional sources are not able to supply the spiritual goods that 'consumers' in the market now desire. This has created new religious marketplaces (Gauthier and Martikainen 2013).

In many late modern and postmodern societies there is a marked tendency towards 'DIY religion', that is, to build or bring your own mode of religiosity and spirituality by assembling spiritual world views from the bits and pieces available and as a form of spiritual *bricolage*. There is also an increased tendency to listen to one's own inner voice as the genuinely truthful first-person authority more than an acceptance of established tradition. The idea that what feels right is what *is* right has become a common mode of spiritual authentication. In 1985, the sociologist Robert Bellah and colleagues described how religion in America had moved from being integrated and publicly expressed, as in newly settled New England, to becoming disparate and individualistic. They coined the now sociologically established term 'Sheilaism' by giving voice to a young woman, Sheila Larson, as the personalised generalisation of this tendency:

> I believe in God. I'm not a religious fanatic. I can't remember the last time I went to church. My faith has carried me a long way. It's Sheilaism. Just my own little voice … It's just try to love yourself and be gentle with yourself. You know, I guess, take care of each other. I think He would want us to take care of each other.
>
> (Bellah et al. 1996: 221)

Bellah and his colleagues saw Sheilaism as a common expression of some aspects of American religious life (originating more in California than in Galilee) in forms of anti-dogmatic, anti-moralistic but still ethical and humanitarian religion. It is a religion 'for Sheila', it is individualistic, personal, and it does not require the reading of sacred texts or worshipping a deity. There is no Church of Sheilaism, but the Durkheimian question remains whether it is a moral community. In some ways it is, but more as a set of institutions (ideas, norms, values) that the individual may subscribe to rather than join as a member of an organisation. This is the major difference to conventional religion: the membership is more of a 'grid' type than of a 'group' type and thus it is more of a cognitive and emotional phenomenon than a social one (Douglas 2003). Similar conditions hold for many other 'spiritualities of life' (Heelas 2009). With the Internet, new possibilities have opened up. Many traditional religions and religious organisations are on the Internet while new religions that are only on the Internet also appear. Like most other religions, these appear as mixtures of something old, something new and something borrowed. The Internet does make communication easier but it does not substantially change the contents of religious formations (Bunt 2009). Their impact and effects history will judge.

Individualism is the key impulse in most of the new modes of religiosity and this to such an extent that individualism can be said to have become the 'new conformity'. The sociologist Peter Berger saw this already in 1967 and it has accelerated ever since (Berger 1990). Remember that the one truly determining factor for individuals becoming religious is living in environments where there are more religious people. This looks like a circular argument, but it is true. The same seems to hold for spirituality: it spreads like an 'epidemiology of representations' (Sperber 1996). Esotericism, paganism and witchcraft all have as common denominators attitudes of non-conformity, anti-establishmentism and anti-authoritarianism – although with a twist, as these currents of thought seem to create their own authorities (compare with Max Weber's notion of charisma above).

Still, highly valued in most new religious contexts are subjectivity, anti-rationalism and anti-logic, all devalued as belonging to old and stifling tradition (see, e.g., Parsons 2018). New Age and spirituality-oriented world views display much eclecticism, syncretism and a high degree of *bricolage*; in anything from theosophy to Scientology (and what came after), many kinds of beliefs and representations become blended with subsequent cognitive and epistemic incongruities, inconsistencies and discrepancies. Some of these movements are modern examples of the fact that religious systems are not always *seamless* systems but rather to be conceived of as networks, conglomerates, clusters of religious beliefs and practices – contemporary examples of syncretism (Leopold and Jensen 2004). Anyone with an interest in the histories of these ideological formations would benefit from studying Hellenistic religions, Western esotericism and Hindu traditions, as much of the belief contents of the new modes of religiosity are derived from these other traditions (Stuckrad 2005). However, from many adherents' point of view such creativity is precisely the great blessing, because now old truths have come to life again.

Humans have the remarkable ability to be 'in more minds' than one, and this is eminently demonstrated when otherwise rational non-believers are drawn to the irrational, unusual and occult practices of modern magic and witches, among pagans, druids and initiates of esoteric mysteries (Luhrmann 1989). The 'messy' conditions and circumstances concerning membership and organisation that are found in relation to witchcraft, shamanism and paganism are no more tidy in the research on many of these topics (Pizza and Lewis 2009). This is partly because the subject matter is often being (re-)presented by its own adherents and advocates, and so with a level (or lack) of scholarly integrity that is considered problematic by others in the academy. Some 'insider' scholars are, or make, their own sources and so they may not be adequately distanced or critically analytic. They are caretakers more than critics or, as an analogy, poets more than literary critics. Representatives of these alternative world views are apt to point out the plain fact that theologians have always represented the creeds to which they belonged. That is true, but most theologians did not pretend to be secular critical scholars *of* religion (like the literary critics); they were and are theologians who *make* religion (like poets produce poetry). Depending on one's normative view, this may be seen as an advantage or the opposite, but blurring genres is not always a blessing.

The dissipation of 'something religious' where there is no religion

There is also a range of socio-cultural phenomena in which we see dissipations of traditional religious elements and functions into other domains of differentiated and segregated late modern or postmodern society. Noticeably, bits and pieces, motifs and mythemes of religious narratives, myths and cosmologies are widespread in the entertainment industry: in the media, in literature, in film and television, and in computer games. Theme parks are built around and on the foundations of classic fairy tales, moral and ideological universes; the popular imagination is governed by age-old mythical structures and by deeply embedded basic religious structures concerning norms, values, hierarchy and purity. For instance, many movies that wish to attract audiences by presenting daring sex and infidelity are really about the sanctity of the family as an institution. Marriages are still 'made in Heaven'.

Sports are as ritualistic as ever, their stars become heroes, and popular music has its idols. Where adolescents were once initiated into tribal lore and prepared for adult status and responsibilities, they are now under the constant influence of market mechanisms that sell attractive identification objects and offer peer-group attachment styles through merchandise and entertainment. In this way, the social and cognitive mechanisms of tribalisation as known from most religious traditions' insistence on solidarity with in-groups, with belonging, and with ethnic symbolic marking are being reproduced 'incognito'. In this way, adolescents are introduced to a lifestyle as consumers. There is no special initiation rite with ordeals, no special priesthood with authority, and no special and vital tribal knowledge to be remembered and passed on to the next generation, and, finally, there are no immediately visible sanctions for failing. Thus, initiation into consumer society becomes a comfortable commodity, de-ritualised, invisible, and so it is not even conceived of as a mode of initiation; it has just become 'what goes without saying' in the same manner as myths and institutions 'operate in men's minds without their being aware of the fact' (Lévi-Strauss 1969: 12). Nevertheless, the psychological conditioning and the social pressures are there. Television advertising on children's channels is a case in point. Advertising often employs the same basic cognitive mechanisms as those that are activated in magic and religious modes of representation. Also, 'story-telling' as corporate identity formation has become widespread in business management, and 'spirituality' is introduced in what is so benignly termed 'human resource management' in attempts to make business appear more 'human' than it is. The appeal to 'spirituality' should thus warrant a world view that includes more than just the material. In several kinds of psychotherapy, elements of Buddhist mindfulness meditation are increasingly being employed in more holistic methods of treatment. Religious elements, structures and functions seem to pop up continuously as applicable measures when 'models for life' are called upon. The reservoirs of norms and values in contemporary society are deeply indebted to their pre-modern forms. Modes of normativity, whether moral, ethical, aesthetic or political, are being reproduced in the contemporary social and cultural worlds in ways that are similar to ways in which religious traditions were disseminated and reproduced: both consciously in instruction and subconsciously in unnoticed emulation. Often, in these social processes, critical analyses will disclose how projections spread in the epidemiologies of representations and how 'truths' are made as social facts.

What will the future bring?

Now as then, religious traditions are made up of elements – of 'things'. In 1912, Durkheim wrote on the emergence of a religion as a social formation: 'When a certain number of sacred things sustain relations of coordination and subordination between them, forming a system that has a certain unity but does not enter into any other system of the same kind, this set of beliefs and corresponding rites constitutes a religion' (2001: 40). Now, Durkheim found the data for his theory of the elementary forms of religion in what he considered the most enduring and clear-cut shapes and functions of religious traditions, namely in Australian Aboriginal religions. Religions have changed in history, of course, and sometimes quite significantly, as in the Axial age, around the middle of the first millennium BCE. As noted earlier, this idea of an Axial age was invented by the philosopher Karl Jaspers (1883–1969). The Axial age phenomenon sees fundamental changes in a range of religious and philosophical traditions towards ethical and moral concerns, from ancient Greece and Israel across the Eurasian continent to India and China and mostly accompanied by the advent of literacy. The Axial age notion and the historical changes it refers to have been treated by several scholars, but recently and prominently by the sociologist Robert Bellah in a momentous work (2011). In this era, we find the bases for the rise of the major scriptural traditions in the history of religions, changing from more ancient forms of practice of 'bloody rituals', such as those that worried Zarathustra, to the ethical precepts and moral instructions that were to follow in these literate traditions. Ideas about individualism, ethical universalism, asceticism, monasticism, sublimated symbolic sacrifices, 'anti-establishment' ideology, an emphasis on transcendence and redemption became prominent in these traditions that were changed forever. Although some religious traditions became extinct (e.g., the ancient Greek), others became the heirs of these changed traditions: Christianity and Islam to mention two now universal traditions. A different kind of revolution in religion took place with the Protestant

Reformation in Christianity. There were, of course, theological motivations, but perhaps even more important were the adoption of the recently invented printing technology and the use of local vernacular language as the medium of religious communication – not forgetting the power-related political and economic measures to curb the influences of the Roman Catholic Church. At any rate, the changes were so profound that there could be reason to speak of a 'second axial age', not so much specifically located in time but rather in the logical transformation of religious traditions under pressure from new technologies and correlated social formations.

However, that all happened a long time ago and one may ask the question 'What happens now?' In the theorising about religion in the academy, there are indications of new developments as seen above in the previous sections, but these trends in research are not groundbreaking. It is still very much the same subject matter that is studied – most likely because that *is* what is 'out there' (Stausberg 2009). As demonstrated above, religious formations continue as more or less religious and as more or less integrated. Some traditions appear to be very robust, but changes are inevitable. Electronic media will offer new possibilities of religious affirmation as well as of religious criticism. Whether things go in one or the other direction, both have in common that they proceed from increased levels of reflection. This might be the beginning of a third axial age, which is also tied to new technology. For instance, young Muslims may use electronic Qur'ans to become their own religious authorities, or people in remote areas may be able to communicate with like-minded dissidents around the globe and affirm their disbelief. Religious minority groups who have been persecuted and silenced may set up websites that give them a voice to the world, to be heard and reflected upon. Such changes in the life of traditions will undoubtedly lead to increased reflection. If there is any *one* direction in the future of religious traditions, I would think that it is *this* one of increased reflection. Some individuals may then opt for inclusion in non-reflective religious groups, but then even that has been a result of reflection and decision. However, for a long time to come many may become and remain members of groups simply because they are born into the groups. Then, reflection may set in later. Peter Berger's 'heretical imperative' is more alive than ever; all over the globe people are aware that there are more ways of being human than their own traditional (Berger 1980).

In the course of history, religious traditions have been ways of world-making and of assuring the persistence of modes of behaviour; they have provided cognitive governance and been the warrants of normative cognition. Some of these socio-psychological functions may be taken over by other institutions in society, but it is unlikely that *all* those elements that make up religious traditions will disappear. The emotional, cognitive, cultural, social and political (etc.) functions and institutions that were the characteristic features of more traditional forms of religion may become more separated in the future. Most likely there will, be new compositions of 'things religious', and they may not all form a system that has a certain unity, as was common in Durkheim's era. Postmodernity, *bricolage*, syncretism and hybridity will most likely not go away. With postmodernism change has become the permanent condition of the world. This is also true in the world of religion and that is new as religion has always been a conservative social force in the history of humanity. In the future, religions might take on many different and until now unseen shapes and functions. That may become the end of religion as we now know it. Time alone will tell.

8 A brief conclusion

Dear reader, I apologise, but you might actually have begun reading here. As a way of concluding, I shall shift the voice from the commonly elided academic subject to the first person 'I' and round up the ideas and ambitions of this book in a more personal manner. I wrote this book as a typological *phenomenology of religion* and have attempted here to set up an inventory and a classificatory systematisation of the elements, functions and structures of religion. I wanted answer the question of the book's title by demonstrating how religion is not one 'thing'; rather 'it' (the general abstract category) and they (religious traditions) are composed of many 'things' in varying proportions. It is the business of a typological phenomenology of religion to identify, describe, analyse, interpret, explain and understand these 'things' and their combinations and so it forms the backbone of the study of all religions and of religion *in general*. There is, as we saw above (p. 72), a different path of research that is also called phenomenology that studies religious experience, but that is a separate and different enterprise, although one that falls within the confines of the general study of religion.

During the twentieth century, the phenomenology of religion and comparative religion fell into some disrepute. Christian theologians who valued the uniqueness of their traditions were wary of the comparative enterprise and scholars of specific traditions (mostly philologically astute) were critical of comparisons of matters that appeared clearly different and so irrelevant. After the Second World War, the academic climate in the study of religion became increasingly particularistic and empiricist. Comparative and general studies were commonly criticised as super- ficial, finding similarities more than differences, decontextualising the phenomena studied, producing comparisons that were descriptive and not explanatory, with generalisation driven by theological agendas and (lastly for now) the accusation that 'comparativists' find phenomena according to their own imagined or invented patterns. My own reaction was one of puzzlement, and I thought that if the phe- nomena that interest scholars of religion were, as critics opined, incomparable and non-generalisable, then the study of religion would remain an intellectual and academic impossibility. However, 'proof by existence' tells us that it is not so although many comparative investigations were, admittedly, muddled exercises. Then, in 1993, I published an article on the possibility of rethinking the phenom- enology of religion as a comparative and classificatory discipline (Jensen 1993).

The conclusion of the study was positive: the comparative study is not impossible. It only has to be done in a sensible manner. After a decade of thinking and reading I published a book on the theoretical and philosophical conditions that would have to be met in a 'new comparativism' (Jensen 2003). I compared the study of religion, its history and problems to anthropology and linguistics and found that the problems for the comparative and general study of religions were in principle no worse than those in other humanities subjects with global ambitions. Another decade later and a half later of teaching these matters, I have set out to demonstrate *how* it can be done. The degree to which it succeeds depends, of course, on the reader's responses to this volume.

Religions, being human social and cultural creations, are like languages in some respects, and the study of religion somehow resembles linguistics. In spite of many vexing and unsolved questions in linguistics (as in the study of religion), all languages have some kinds of sounds, 'words', sentences, rules of grammar and syntax and conventions for humans communicating meaningfully. The same should hold for the study of religion: that there are kinds of 'things' that can be compared. Durkheim expressed it the other way round: 'Since all religions are comparable, all species of the same genus, they all share certain essential elements' (2001: 6). So, it boils down to what we can say about the elements, the 'things', and how they may be studied. Here is a recent suggestion by the historian of religions Ann Taves who advocates a 'building block' approach; one that I wholeheartedly endorse:

> Religions and spiritualities are composite formations, or in Durkheim's terms, wholes made up of separate and relatively distinct parts. Focusing our attention on 'special things' takes our attentions away from 'religion' in the abstract and refocuses it on the component parts or building blocks that can be assembled in various ways to create more complex socio-cultural formations, some of which people characterize as 'religions' or 'spiritualities' or 'paths'. A building block approach to religions ... strikes me as a more promising way forward in the study of religion than continuing to wrestle with defining the abstract concept of 'religion'.
>
> (Taves 2011: 162)

This volume may be seen precisely as a catalogue of those blocks; call it a 'componential approach'. And so, here is a list of abstract *universals* found in all religions: imagination, experience, intentionality, narrative, discourse, classification, cognitive governance, emotion regulation, action, behaviour, roles, social control, authority, hierarchy, institutions, power, economies, exchanges, reciprocity, sanctity, sociality and world-making and then more. *All this* goes against the idea of religion as a primitive notion; that is, a notion, or a phenomenon, which cannot be broken down into constituent parts and elements. In this volume, I have tried to demonstrate how religion and religions can be understood and analysed in terms of the constituent components and their compositionality, that is, how they are assembled and function in human life.

Cultural, discursive and ideological formations are all social, but when they shape into religion they tend to become 'special', concerning some 'things' that are highly valued, respected and revered by the members of the religious groups. By now, we know that religions are so much more than belief as they concern bodies, practices and 'emplacement' (Vásquez 2011). Religion is 'in space' so to say, not in inner space nor in celestial space, but in places *on earth*. As most other 'things' on earth, religion can be compared and generalised in pursuit of knowledge of things human. It is true that it is the scholars, and not so much the members of religious traditions, who make the 'comparables', 'generalisables' and 'universals' in their comparisons and generalisations. That is because it is the scholars who want to know *what religion is as a human creation*. That is, again, because human creations are important to humans. As much as I agree with Pascal Boyer on many issues here is one where I dissent. Boyer talks about humans as 'complex biological machines' who produce religion when 'they manage to give airy nothing a local habitation and a name' (2001: 330) – as if religions were unimportant. Although the general and abstract concept of 'religion' is made up by scholars as a second-order datum, we must realise that we are comparing matters that are *real enough*:

> We do not compare things-in-themselves. The old idea that there were phenomena with essences that would manifest themselves is now extinct. Instead, the items that we compare are the products of scholarly activity... and in that sense they are made up. But so are law, government, money and many other things that we consider real enough to worry about.
>
> (Jensen 2008: 160–1)

So, to the question 'What is religion?' there is at least one important answer: something that is real enough to 'worry about', that is, some *thing*, an object to study and to interpret, explain and understand. And that *is* possible.

References

Allen, S. (1991) *The Shape of the Turtle: Myth, Art and Cosmos in Early China*, Albany, NY: SUNY Press.

Alles, Gregory D. (1996) *Rudolf Otto: Autobiographical and Social Essays*, Berlin: Walter de Gruyter.

Ambasciano, L. (2019) *An Unnatural History of Religions: Academia, Post-Truth and the Quest for Scientific Knowledge*, London: Bloomsbury.

Amir-Aslami, A. (2013) *Islam and the West*, New York: Enigma Books.

Andersen, M., *et al.* (2014) 'Mystical Experience in the Lab', *Method and Theory in the Study of Religion*, 26(3): 217–245.

Appadurai, A. (1981) 'Gastro-Politics in Hindu South Asia', *American Ethnologist*, 8(3): 494–511.

Assmann, J. (2009) *The Price of Monotheism*, Stanford, CA: Stanford University Press.

Atran, S. (2002) *In God We Trust: The Evolutionary Landscape of Religion*, Oxford: Oxford University Press.

Atran, S. (2011) *Talking to the Enemy: Violent Extremism, Sacred Values and What it Means to Be Human*, London: Penguin.

Atran, S. and A. Norenzayan (2004) 'Religion's Evolutionary Landscape: Counter-intuition, Commitment, Compassion, Communion', *Behavioral and Brain Sciences*, 27: 713–770.

Bailey, E. (2009) 'Implicit Religion', in P. B. Clarke (ed.), *The Oxford Handbook of the Sociology of Religion*, Oxford: Oxford University Press, pp. 801–816.

Barth, F. (1990) *Cosmologies in the Making: A Generative Approach to Cultural Variation in Inner New Guinea*, Cambridge: Cambridge University Press.

Barthes, R. (2000) *Mythologies*, London: Vintage. Originally published in French in 1957.

Bascom, W. R. (1965) 'The Forms of Folklore: Prose Narratives', *Journal of American Folklore*, 78: 3–20.

Bell, C. (1992) *Ritual Theory, Ritual Practice*, Oxford: Oxford University Press.

Bell, C. (1997) *Ritual: Perspectives and Dimensions*, Oxford: Oxford University Press.

Bellah, R. N. (1967) 'Civil Religion in America', *Dædalus, Journal of the American Academy of Arts and Sciences*, 96(1): 1–21.

Bellah, R. N. (1991) *Beyond Belief: Essays on Religion in a Post-Traditionalist World*, Berkeley, CA: University of California Press.

Bellah, R. N. (2011) *Religion in Human Evolution: From the Paleolithic to the Axial Age*, Cambridge, MA: Harvard University Press.

Bellah, R. N., R. Madsen, W. M. Sullivan, A. Swidler and S. M. Tipton (1996) *Habits of the Heart: Individualism and Commitment in American Life*, Berkeley, CA: University of California Press.

Benedict, R. (2005) *Patterns of Culture*, New York: Mariner Books. First published 1934.

Berger, P. L. (1980) *The Heretical Imperative: Contemporary Possibilities of Religious Affirmation*, New York: Doubleday.

Berger, P. L. (1990) *The Sacred Canopy: Elements of a Sociological Theory of Religion*, New York: Anchor Books. First published 1967.

Bering, J. M. (2006) 'The Folk Psychology of Souls', *Behavioral and Brain Sciences*, 29(5): 453–462.

Bering, J. M. (2012) *The Belief Instinct: The Psychology of Souls, Destiny, and the Meaning of Life*, New York: W. W. Norton.

Bicchieri, C. (2006) *The Grammar of Society: The Nature and Dynamics of Social Norms*, Cambridge: Cambridge University Press.

Bloom, P. (2004) *Descartes' Baby*, New York: Basic Books.

Bloom, P. (2007) 'Religion Is Natural', *Developmental Science*, 10(1): 147–151.

Bloom, P. (2012) 'Religion, Morality, Evolution', *Annual Review of Psychology*, 63: 179–199.

Boyer, P. (1996) 'Religion as an Impure Subject: A Note on Cognitive Order in Religious Representation in Response to Brian Malley', *Method and Theory in the Study of Religion*, 8(2): 201–213.

Boyer, P. (2000) 'Functional Origins of Religious Concepts: Conceptual and Strategic Selection in Evolved Minds', *Journal of the Royal Anthropological Institute*, 6: 195–214.

Boyer, P. (2001) *Religion Explained: The Evolutionary Origins of Religious Thought*, New York: Basic Books.

Boyer, P. (2010) 'Why Evolved Cognition Matters to Understanding Cultural Cognitive Variations', *Interdisciplinary Science Reviews*, 35(3–4): 377–387.

Boyns, D. and S. Luery (2015) 'Negative Emotional Energy: A Theory of the "Dark-Side" of Interaction Ritual Chains', *Social Sciences*, 4(1): 148–170.

Bruce, S. (2003) *Politics and Religion*, Cambridge: Polity Press.

Bruce, S. (2013) *Secularization: In Defence of an Unfashionable Theory*, Oxford: Oxford University Press.

Bruner, J. (1986) *Actual Minds, Possible Worlds*, Cambridge, MA: Harvard University Press.

Bulbulia, J. and R. Sosis (2011) 'Signalling Theory and the Evolution of Religious Cooperation', *Religion*, 41(3): 363–388.

Bunt, G. R. (2009) 'Religion and the Internet', in P. B. Clarke (ed.), *The Oxford Handbook of the Sociology of Religion*, Oxford: Oxford University Press, pp. 705–720.

Caldwell, C. (2010) *Reflections on the Revolution in Europe: Immigration, Islam and the West*, London: Penguin.

Campany, R. F. (2018) '"Religious" as a Category: A Comparative Case Study', *NUMEN*, 65(4): 333–376.

Capps, W. H. (1995) *Religious Studies: The Making of a Discipline*, Minneapolis, MN: Fortress Press.

Clarke, P. B. (ed.) (2009) *The Oxford Handbook of the Sociology of Religion*, Oxford: Oxford University Press.

Cole, M. (1998) *Cultural Psychology: A Once and Future Discipline*, Cambridge, MA: Harvard University Press.

Collins, R. (2004) *Interaction Ritual Chains*, Princeton, NJ: Princeton University Press.

Corrigan, J. (ed.) (2008) *The Oxford Handbook of Religion and Emotion*, Oxford: Oxford University Press.

Corrigan, J. (ed.) (2017) *Feeling Religion*, Durham, NC: Duke University Press.

Counihan, C. M. (ed.) (1999) *The Anthropology of Food and Body: Gender, Meaning and Power*, London and New York: Routledge.

Cox, J. (2010) *An Introduction to the Phenomenology of Religion*, London: Continuum.

Damasio, A. (2000) *The Feeling of What Happens: Body, Emotion and the Making of Consciousness*, London: Vintage.

Davie, G. (2013) *The Sociology of Religion: A Critical Agenda*, London: Sage.

Deacon, T. (1997) *The Symbolic Species: The Co-evolution of Language and the Human Brain*, Harmondsworth: Penguin.

Descola, P. (2013) *Beyond Nature and Culture*, Chicago, IL: University of Chicago Press.

Deutscher, G. (2010) *Through the Language Glass: Why the World Looks Different in Other Languages*, London: Arrow Books.

Diener, E., L. Tay and D. G. Myers (2011) 'The Religion Paradox: If Religion Makes People Happy, Why Are So Many Dropping Out?' *Journal of Personality and Social Psychology*, 101(6): 1278–1290.

Dobbelaere, K. (2009) 'The Meaning and Scope of Secularization', in P. B. Clarke (ed.), *The Oxford Handbook of the Sociology of Religion*, Oxford: Oxford University Press, pp. 599–615.

Donald, M. (1991) *Origins of the Modern Mind: Three Stages in the Evolution of Cognition and Culture*, Cambridge, MA: Harvard University Press.

Donald, M. (2001) *A Mind So Rare: The Evolution of Human Consciousness*, New York: W. W. Norton.

Douglas, M. (1966) *Purity and Danger: An Analysis of the Concepts of Pollution and Taboo*, London: Routledge & Kegan Paul.

Douglas, M. (2003) *Natural Symbols: Explorations in Cosmology*, London and New York: Routledge. First published 1970.

Douglas, M. (ed.) (1973) *Rules and Meanings: The Anthropology of Everyday Knowledge*, Harmondsworth: Penguin.

Dubuisson, D. (2003) *The Western Construction of Religion: Myths, Knowledge, and Ideology*, Baltimore, MD: Johns Hopkins University Press.

Dubuisson, D. (2016) *Religion and Magic in Western Culture*, Leiden: Brill.

Dupré, J. (1993) *The Disorder of Things: Metaphysical Foundations of the Disunity of Science*, Cambridge, MA: Harvard University Press.

Durkheim, É. (2001) *The Elementary Forms of Religious Life*, trans. C. Cosman, Oxford: Oxford University Press. Originally published in French in 1912.

Eidinow, E. (2019). 'The (Ancient Greek) Subject Supposed to Believe' *NUMEN* 66 (1), 56-88.

Eliade, M. (1987) *The Sacred and the Profane: The Nature of Religion*, San Diego, CA: Harcourt. First published 1957.

Engler, S. (2004) 'Constructionism Versus What?' *Religion*, 24(4): 291–313.

Evans-Pritchard, E. E. (1956) *Nuer Religion*, Oxford: Oxford University Press.

Evans-Pritchard, E. E. (1966) *Theories of Primitive Religion*, Oxford: Oxford University Press.

Farias, M. and J.Barrett (2013) Special Issue: New Trends in the Cognitive Science of Religion, *International Journal for the Psychology of Religion*, 23(1).

Fauconnier, G. (1997) *Mappings in Thought and Language*, Cambridge: Cambridge University Press.

Fauconnier, G. (2003) *The Way We Think*, New York: Basic Books.

Flood, G. (2004) *The Ascetic Self: Subjectivity, Memory and Tradition*, Cambridge: Cambridge University Press.

Frankenberry, N. K. and H. H. Penner (1999) *Language, Truth, and Religious Belief: Studies in Twentieth-Century Theory and Method in Religion*, Atlanta, GA: Scholars Press.

Frazer, J. G. (1993) *The Golden Bough* (abridged version), London: Papermac. First published 1922.

Freiberger, O. (2016) 'Asceticism', in R. A. Segal and K. von Stuckrad (eds.), *Vocabulary for the Study of Religion*, Leiden: Brill.

Freud, S. (1961) *The Standard Edition of the Complete Psychological Works of Sigmund Freud*, vol. XXI: *The Future of an Illusion, Civilization and its Discontents, and Other Works*, ed. J. Strachey, London: Hogarth Press. Originally published 1927–31.

Fujiwara, S. (2017) 'The Reception of Otto and Das Heilige in Japan: In and Outside the Phenomenology of Religion', *Religion*, 47(4): 591–615.

Gauthier, F. and T.Martikainen (2013) *Religion in Consumer Society*, Farnham: Ashgate.

Geertz, A. W. (2010) 'Brain, Body and Culture: A Biocultural Theory of Religion', *Method and Theory in the Study of Religion*, 22(4): 304–321.

Geertz, A. W. (2011) 'Religious Narrative, Cognition and Culture: Approaches and Definitions', in A. Geertz and J. S. Jensen (eds), *Religious Narrative, Cognition and Culture: Image and Word in the Mind of Narrative*, London: Equinox, pp. 9–29.

Geertz, A. W. (2013) 'Whence Religion? How the Brain Constructs the World and What This Might Tell Us about the Origins of Religion, Cognition and Culture', in A. W. Geertz (ed.), *Origins of Religion, Cognition and Culture*, London and New York: Routledge, pp. 21–85.

Geertz, A. W. and J. S. Jensen (2011) *Religious Narrative, Cognition and Culture: Image and Word in the Mind of Narrative*, London: Equinox.

Geertz, A. W., J. Sørensen, U. Schjødt, K. L. Nielbo and M. Andersen (2012), Research project proposal: 'Mysticism, Magic, and Miracles', Aarhus University (personal communication).

Geertz, C. (1973) *The Interpretation of Cultures*, New York: Basic Books.

Guthrie, S. E. (1993) *Faces in the Clouds: A New Theory of Religion*, Oxford: Oxford University Press.

Haidt, J. (2012) *The Righteous Mind: Why Good People are Divided by Politics and Religion*, London: Allen Lane.

Haidt, J. and C.Joseph (2007) 'The Moral Mind: How Five Sets of Innately Prepared Intuitions Guide the Development of Many Culture-Specific Virtues and Perhaps Even Modules', in P. Carruthers, S. Lawrence and S. Stich (eds.), *The Innate Mind*, vol. III, Oxford: Oxford University Press, pp. 367–391.

Hall, D. (1997) *Lived Religion in America: Toward a History of Practice*, Princeton, NJ: Princeton University Press.

Harris, P. L. (2000) *The Work of the Imagination*, Oxford: Blackwell.

Heelas, P. (2009) 'Spiritualities of Life', in P. B. Clarke (ed.), *The Oxford Handbook of the Sociology of Religion*, Oxford: Oxford University Press, pp. 758–782.

Heelas, P. and L. Woodhead (2005) *The Spiritual Revolution: Why Religion Is Giving Way to Spirituality*, Oxford: Blackwell.

Hefner, R. W. (2009) 'Religion and Modernity Worldwide', in P. B. Clarke (ed.), *The Oxford Handbook of the Sociology of Religion*, Oxford: Oxford University Press, pp. 152–171.

Hinde, R. A. (1999) *Why Gods Persist: A Scientific Approach to Religion*, London and New York: Routledge.

Honko, L. (1984) 'The Problem of Defining Myth', in A. Dundes (ed.), *Sacred Narrative: Readings in the Theory of Myth*, Berkeley, CA: University of California Press, pp. 41–52.

Hood, R. W., P. C. Hill and B. Spilka (2009) *The Psychology of Religion: An Empirical Approach*, New York: Guilford Press.

Hughes, A. (2017) *Comparison: A Critical Primer*, Sheffield: Equinox.

Hultkrantz, Å. (1957) *The North American Indian Orpheus Tradition: A Contribution to Comparative Religion*, Stockholm: The Ethnographical Museum.

Hume, D. (2008) *An Enquiry Concerning Human Understanding*, Oxford: Oxford University Press. First published 1748.

Humphrey, C. and J. Laidlaw (1994) *The Archetypal Actions of Ritual: A Theory of Ritual Illustrated by the Jain Rite of Worship*, Oxford: Clarendon Press.

Hutchins, E. (1995) *Cognition in the Wild*, Cambridge, MA: MIT Press.

James, W. (1985) *The Varieties of Religious Experience*, Harmondsworth: Penguin. First published 1902.

Jenkins, P. (2011) *Next Christendom: The Coming of Global Christianity*, Oxford: Oxford University Press.

Jensen, J. S. (1993) 'Is a Phenomenology of Religion Possible? On the Ideas of a Human and Social Science of Religion', *Method and Theory in the Study of Religion*, 5(2): 109–133.

Jensen, J. S. (1999) 'On a Semantic Definition of Religion', in J. Platvoet and A. Molendijk (eds.), *The Pragmatics of Defining Religion*, Leiden: Brill, pp. 409–431.

Jensen, J. S. (2001) 'Universals, General Terms and the Comparative Study of Religion', *NUMEN*, 48(3): 238–266.

Jensen, J. S. (2003) *The Study of Religion in a New Key: Theoretical and Philosophical Soundings in the Comparative and General Study of Religion*, Aarhus: Aarhus University Press.

Jensen, J. S. (2004) 'Meaning and Religion: On Semantics in the Study of Religion', in P. Antes, A. W. Geertz and R. R. Warne (eds.), *New Approaches to the Study of Religion*, vol. I, Berlin: Walter de Gruyter, pp. 219–252.

Jensen, J. S. (2008) 'On How Making Differences Makes a Difference', in W. Braun and R. T. McCutcheon (eds.), *Introducing Religion: Essays in Honor of Jonathan Z. Smith*, London: Equinox, pp. 140–162.

Jensen, J. S. (2009a) *Myths and Mythologies: A Reader*, London: Equinox.

Jensen, J. S. (2009b) 'Conceptual Models in the Study of Religion', in P. B. Clarke (ed.), *The Oxford Handbook of the Sociology of Religion*, Oxford: Oxford University Press, pp. 245–262.

Jensen, J. S. (2009c) 'Religion as the Unintended By-product of Brain Functions in the "Standard Cognitive Science of Religion Model"', in M. Stausberg (ed.), *Contemporary Theories of Religion: A Critical Companion*, London and New York: Routledge, pp. 129–155.

Jensen, J. S. (2009d) 'Explanation and Interpretation in the Comparative Study of Religion'. *Religion*, 39: 331–339.

Jensen, J. S. (2011a) 'Revisiting the Insider-Outsider Debate: Dismantling a Pseudo-Problem in the Study of Religion', *Method and Theory in the Study of Religion*, 23(1): 29–47.

Jensen, J. S. (2011b) 'Epistemology', in M. Stausberg and S. Engler (eds), *The Routledge Handbook of Research Methods in the Study of Religion*, London and New York: Routledge, pp. 40–53.

Jensen, J. S. (2013) 'Normative Cognition in Culture and Religion', *Journal for the Cognitive Science of Religion*, 1(1): 47–70.

Jensen, J. S. (2016a) 'Cloning Minds: Religion between Individuals and Collectives', in C. Bochinger and J. Rüpke (eds.), *Dynamics of Religion: Past and Present*, Berlin and Boston, MA: de Gruyter, pp. 290–303.

Jensen, J. S. (2016b) 'How Institutions Work in Shared Intentionality and "We-Mode" Social Cognition', *Topoi: An International Review of Philosophy*, 35(1), 301–312.

Jensen, J. S. (2016c) 'Narrative', in M. Stausberg and S. Engler (eds.), *The Oxford Handbook of the Study of Religion*, Oxford: Oxford University Press, pp. 290–303.

Jensen, J. S. (2017) '"Religion Is the Word, but, What Is the Thing – If There Is One?" On Generalized Interpretations and Epistemic Placeholders in the Study of Religion', *Historia Religionum: An International Journal*, 17–28.

Jensen, J. S. (2019) 'Scholarly Imaginations – and Modes of Their Comparability', *Method and Theory in the Study of Religion*, 31(1), 23–33.

Kahneman, D. (2011) *Thinking, Fast and Slow*, New York: Farrar, Straus & Giroux.

Kant, I. (2009) *Religion within the Bounds of Bare Reason*, Indianapolis, IN: Hackett. Originally published in German in 1793.

Katz, S. T. (ed.) (2000) *Mysticism and Sacred Scripture*, Oxford: Oxford University Press.

King, R. (1999) *Orientalism and Religion: Post-colonial Theory, India and the Mystic East*, London and New York: Routledge.

Kippenberg, H. G. (2002) *Discovering Religious History in the Modern Age*, Princeton, NJ: Princeton University Press.

Konvalinka, I. *et al.* (2011) 'Synchronized Arousal Between Performers and Related Spectators in a Fire-walking Ritual', *PNAS*, 108(20): 8514–8519.

Kreinath, J., J. Snoek and M. Stausberg (eds) (2008) *Theorizing Rituals: Classical Topics, Theoretical Approaches, Analytical Concepts*, Leiden: Brill.

Laidlaw, J. (1995) *Riches and Renunciation: Religion, Economy, and Society Among the Jains*, Oxford: Clarendon Press.

Lakoff, G. and M. Johnson (1980) *Metaphors We Live By*, Chicago, IL: University of Chicago Press.

Larson, J. (2016) *Understanding Greek Religion*, London and New York: Routledge.

Laski, M. (1961) *Ecstasy: A Study of Some Secular and Religious Experiences*, New York: Greenwood Press.

Lawson, E. T. and R. N. McCauley (1990) *Rethinking Religion: Connecting Cognition and Culture*, Cambridge: Cambridge University Press.

Leach, E. (1976) *Culture and Communication: The Logic by Which Symbols Are Connected – An Introduction to the Use of Structuralist Analysis in Social Anthropology*, Cambridge: Cambridge University Press.

Leopold, A. and J. S. Jensen (eds) (2004) *Syncretism in Religion*, London: Equinox.

Lévi-Strauss, C. (1969) *The Raw and the Cooked: Introduction to a Science of Mythology*, vol. I, Harmondsworth: Penguin. Originally published in French in 1964.

Lévi-Strauss, C. (2004) *The Savage Mind*, Oxford: Oxford University Press. Originally published in French in 1962.

Lewis, J. R. (2004) *The Oxford Handbook of New Religious Movements*, Oxford: Oxford University Press.

Lieberman, J. D. (1999) 'Terror Management, Illusory Correlation, and Perceptions of Minority Groups', *Basic and Applied Social Psychology*, 21(1): 13–23.

Lisdorf, A. (2004) 'The Spread of Non-natural Concepts: Evidence from the Roman Prodigy Lists', *Journal of Cognition and Culture*, 4(1): 151–173.

Luhmann, N. (2013) *A Systems Theory of Religion*, Stanford, CA: Stanford University Press.

Luhrmann, T. M. (1989) *Persuasions of the Witch's Craft: Ritual Magic in Modern Culture*, Cambridge, MA: Harvard University Press.

Malinowski, B. (1992) *Magic, Science, Religion and Other Essays*, Long Grove, IL: Waveland Press. First published 1948.

Martin, L. H. and D. Wiebe (2014) 'Pro- and Assortative-Sociality in the Formation and Maintenance of Groups', *Journal for the Cognitive Science of Religion*, 2(1): 1–57.

Marx, K. (1977) Introduction to *A Contribution to the Critique of Hegel's Philosophy of Right*, Cambridge: Cambridge University Press. First published in German in 1843.

Marx, K. and F. Engels (1973) *The German Ideology*, New York: International Publishers. First published in 1845–6.

Mauss, M. (1990) *The Gift: Forms and Functions of Exchange in Archaic Societies*, trans. Mary Douglas, London and New York: Routledge. First published in French in 1925.

McCauley, R. N. and E. T. Lawson (2002) *Bringing Ritual to Mind: Psychological Foundations of Cultural Forms*, Cambridge: Cambridge University Press.

McCutcheon, R. T. (2003) *The Discipline of Religion: Structure, Meaning, Rhetoric*, London and New York: Routledge.

McCutcheon, R. T. (2005) *Religion and the Domestication of Dissent: Or, How to Live in a Less than Perfect Nation*, London: Equinox.

McDowell, J. (1996) *Mind and World*, Cambridge, MA: MIT Press.

Metzinger, T. (2009) *The Ego Tunnel: The Science of the Mind and the Myth of the Self*, New York: Basic Books.

Meyer, M. and R. Smith (eds) (1994) *Ancient Christian Magic: Coptic Texts of Ritual Power*, San Francisco, CA: Harper.

Michaels, A. (2015) *Homo Ritualis: Hindu Ritual and Its Significance for Ritual Theory*, Oxford: Oxford University Press.

Morris, B. (1987) *Anthropological Studies of Religion: An Introductory Text*, Cambridge: Cambridge University Press.

Needham, R. (1973) *Belief, Language and Experience*, Oxford: Blackwell.

Nelstrop, L. (2016) 'Mysticism', in R. Segal and K. v. Stuckrad (eds.), *Vocabulary for the Study of Religion*, Leiden: Brill.

Nielbo, K. L. and J. Sørensen. (2013) 'Prediction Error during Functional and Non-functional Action Sequences: A Computational Exploration of Ritual and Ritualized Event Processing'. *Journal of Cognition and Culture*, 13(3–4): 347–365.

Nielbo, K. L., U. Schjødt and J. Sørensen (2013) 'Hierarchical Organization of Segmentation in Non-functional Action Sequences', *Journal for the Cognitive Science of Religion*, 1(1): 71–97.

Nietzsche, F. W. (2003) *The Antichrist*, in *Twilight of the Idols and The Anti-Christ*, London: Penguin. Originally published in German in 1895.

Noë, A. (2004) *Action in Perception*, Cambridge, MA: MIT Press.

Norenzayan, A. (2013) *Big Gods: How Religion Transformed Cooperation and Conflict*, Princeton, NJ: Princeton University Press.

Norris, P. and R. Inglehart (2011) *Sacred and Secular: Religion and Politics Worldwide*, Cambridge: Cambridge University Press.

OlivelleP. and D. R. Davis (eds) (2017) *The Oxford History of Hinduism: Hindu Law – A New History of Dharmasastra*, Oxford: Oxford University Press.

Otto, R. (1923) *The Idea of the Holy: An Inquiry into the Non-Rational Factor in the Idea of the Divine and Its Relation to the Rational*, trans. J. W. Harvey, Oxford: Oxford University Press. First published 1917.

Paden, W. E. (1994) *Religious Worlds*, Boston, MA: Beacon Press.

Paden, W. E. (2016) *New Patterns for Comparative Religion: Passages to an Evolutionary Perspective*, London: Bloomsbury.

Pagels, E. (2003) *Beyond Belief: The Secret Gospel of Thomas*, New York: Random House.

Paloutzian, R. F. and C. L. Park (2013) *Handbook of the Psychology of Religion and Spirituality*, 2nd edn, New York: Guilford Press.

Pals, D. L. (2006) *Eight Theories of Religion*, Oxford: Oxford University Press.

Paper, J. (2005) *The Deities Are Many: A Polytheistic Theology*, Albany, NY: SUNY Press.

Parsons, W. B. (ed.) (2018) *Being Spiritual but Not Religious: Past, Present, Future(s)*, London and New York: Routledge.

Patton, K. C. and B. C. Ray (2000) *A Magic Still Dwells: Comparative Religion in the Postmodern Age*, Berkeley, CA: University of California Press.

Peacock, J. L. (2001) *The Anthropological Lens: Harsh Light, Soft Focus*, 2nd rev. edn, Cambridge: Cambridge University Press.

Pezzoli-Olgiati, D. (2016) 'God/Goddess', in R. Segal and K. v. Stuckrad (eds.), *Vocabulary for the Study of Religion*, Leiden: Brill.

Pizza, M. and J. R. Lewis (eds) (2009) *Handbook of Contemporary Paganism*, Leiden: Brill.

Plotkin, H. (2003) *The Imagined World Made Real: Towards a Natural Science of Culture*, New Brunswick, NJ: Rutgers University Press.

Powell, R. and S. Clarke (2012) 'Religion as an Evolutionary Byproduct: A Critique of the Standard Model', *British Journal for the Philosophy of Science*, 63(3): 457–486.

Preus, J. S. (1987) *Explaining Religion: Criticism and Theory from Bodin to Freud*, New Haven, CT: Yale University Press.

Purzycki, B. G. et al. (2017) 'the Evolution of Religion and Morality: A Synthesis of Ethnographic and Experimental Evidence from Eight Societies', *Religion, Brain and Behavior*, 8(2): 101–132.

Pybus, T. A. (1954) *The Maoris of the South Island*, Wellington: Reed Publishing.

Rappaport, R. A. (1999) *Ritual and Religion in the Making of Humankind*, Cambridge: Cambridge University Press.

Reinhart, A. K. (1990) 'Impurity/No Danger', *History of Religions*, 30(1): 1–24.

Rota, A. (2016) 'Religion as Social Reality: A Take on the Emic-Etic Debate in Light of John Searle's Philosophy of Society', *Method and Theory in the Study of Religion*, 28 (4–5): 421–444.

Rowlands, M. (2010) *New Science of the Mind: From Extended Mind to Embodied Phenomenology*, Cambridge, MA: MIT Press.

Rüpke, J. (2016) *On Roman Religion: Lived Religion and the Individual in Ancient Rome*, Ithaca, NY: Cornell University Press.

Rüpke, J. and D. M. B. Richardson (2018) *Pantheon: A New History of Roman Religion*, Princeton, NJ: Princeton University Press.

Saler, B. (2015) 'Religion, Concept of', in R. A. Segal and K. Von Stuckrad (eds.), *Vocabulary for the Study of Religion*, Leiden: Brill.

Saussure, F. de (2012) *Course in General Linguistics*, Wellington: Forgotten Books. Originally published in French in 1916.

Schilbrack, K. (2014) *Philosophy and the Study of Religions: A Manifesto*, Chichester: Wiley Blackwell.

Schjødt, U. (2011) 'The Neural Correlates of Religious Experience', *Religion*, 41(1): 91–95.

Schjødt, U., H. Stødkilde-Jørgensen, A. W. Geertz, T. E. Lund and A. Roepstorff (2011) 'The Power of Charisma: Perceived Charisma Inhibits the Frontal Executive Network of Believers in Intercessory Prayer', *Social Cognitive and Affective Neuroscience*, 6: 119–127.

Schjoedt, U., *et al.* (2013) 'The Resource Model and the Principle of Predictive Coding: A Framework for Analyzing Proximate Effects of Ritual', *Religion, Brain and Behavior*, 3(1): 79–86.

Schleiermacher, F. (1996) *On Religion: Speeches to Its Cultured Despisers*, ed. R. Crouter, Cambridge: Cambridge University Press. Originally published in German in 1799.

Schwitzgebel, E. (2010) 'Belief', in E. N. Zalta (ed.), *Stanford Encyclopedia of Philosophy*, Stanford, CA: Stanford University Press. Available at http://plato.stanford.edu/entries/belief/ (accessed December 2018).

Searle, J. R. (2010) *Making the Social World: The Structure of Human Civilization*, Oxford: Oxford University Press.

Segal, R. A. (1999) *Theorizing About Myth*, Amherst, MA: University of Massachusetts Press.

Slingerland, E. (2008) *What Science Offers the Humanities: Integrating Body and Culture*, Cambridge: Cambridge University Press.

Smith, J. Z. (1987) *To Take Place: Toward Theory in Ritual*, Chicago, IL: Chicago University Press.

Smith, J. Z. (2004) 'A Matter of Class: Taxonomies of Religion', in *Relating Religion: Essays in the Study of Religion*, Chicago, IL: University of Chicago Press, pp. 160–178.

Smith, W. R. (2005) *Lectures on the Religion of the Semites*, Chestnut Hill, MA: Adamant Media Corp. First published in 1894.

Sørensen, J. (2004) 'Religion, Evolution and an Immunology of Cultural Systems', *Evolution and Cognition*, 10(1): 61–73.

Sørensen, J. (2007) *A Cognitive Theory of Magic*, Lanham, MD: Altamira Press.

Sperber, D. (1996) *Explaining Culture: A Naturalistic Approach*, Oxford: Blackwell.

Spiro, M. (2017) *Burmese Supernaturalism*, London and New York: Routledge. First published 1978.

Stausberg, M. (2011) 'Comparison', in M. Stausberg and S. Engler (eds.), *The Routledge Handbook of Research Methods in the Study of Religion*, London and New York: Routledge, pp. 21–39.

Stausberg, M. (2013) 'Textbooks in Review: Introductions to the Psychology of Religion', *Religion*, 43(2): 135–150.

Stausberg, M. (ed.) (2009) *Contemporary Theories of Religion: A Critical Companion*, London and New York: Routledge.

Sterelny, K. (2018) 'Religion Re-explained', *Religion, Brain and Behavior*, 8(4): 406–460.

Strauss, D. F. (2012) *The Life of Jesus, Critically Examined*, Wellington: Forgotten Books. First published in 1835.

Strenski, I. (2015) *Understanding Theories of Religion*, 2nd edn, Malden, MA and Oxford: Wiley-Blackwell.

Stuckrad, K. von (2005) *Western Esotericism: A Brief History of Secret Knowledge*, London: Equinox.

Swanson, G. E. (1960) *The Birth of the Gods: The Origin of Primitive Beliefs*, Ann Arbor: University of Michigan Press.

Tambiah, S. J. (1990) *Magic, Science, Religion, and the Scope of Rationality*. Cambridge: Cambridge University Press.

Taves, A. (2011) *Religious Experience Reconsidered: A Building-Block Approach to the Study of Religion and Other Special Things*, Princeton, NJ: Princeton University Press.

Thomas, K. V. (2003) *Religion and the Decline of Magic*, London: Penguin Books.

Tillich, P. (1957) *Dynamics of Faith*, New York: Harper & Row.

Tomasello, M. (1999) *The Cultural Origins of Human Cognition*, Cambridge, MA: Harvard University Press.

Tuckett, J. (2016) 'Clarifying Phenomenologies in the Study of Religion: Separating Kristensen and van der Leeuw from Otto and Eliade', *Religion*, 46(1): 75–101.

Turner, B. S. (2013) *The Religious and the Political: A Comparative Sociology of Religion*, Cambridge: Cambridge University Press.

Turner, J. H., A. Maryanski, A. K. Petersen and A. W. Geertz (2017) *The Emergence and Evolution of Religion: By Means of Natural Selection*, London and New York: Routledge.

Turner, M. (1996) *The Literary Mind: The Origins of Thought and Language*, Oxford: Oxford University Press.

Turner, T. (2008) 'Structure, Process, Form', in J. Kreinath, J. Snoek and M. Stausberg (eds.), *Theorizing Rituals: Classical Topics, Theoretical Approaches, Analytical Concepts*, Leiden: Brill, pp. 207–246.

Turner, V. W. (1977) *The Ritual Process: Structure and Anti-Structure*, Ithaca, NY: Cornell University Press.

Tylor, E. B. (1871) *Primitive Culture*, London: John Murray.

Van Gennep, A. (1960) *The Rites of Passage*, Chicago, IL: University of Chicago Press. First published 1909.

Vásquez, M. A. (2011) *More than Belief: A Materialist Theory of Religion*, Oxford: Oxford University Press.

Wagner, R. (2005) 'Mana', in L. Jones (ed.), *Encyclopedia of Religion*, 2nd edn, vol. VIII, New York: Macmillan Reference, pp. 5631–5633.

Weber, M. (2001) *The Protestant Ethic and the Spirit of Capitalism*, London and New York: Routledge. First published in 1904.

Whitehouse, H. (2000) *Arguments and Icons: Divergent Modes of Religiosity*, Oxford: Oxford University Press.

Wiebe, D. (1991) *The Irony of Theology and the Nature of Religious Thought*, Montreal: McGill-Queen's University Press.

Wiebe, D. (1999) *The Politics of Religious Studies: The Continuing Conflict with Theology in the Academy*, New York: St Martin's Press.

Wilson, D. S. (2002) *Darwin's Cathedral: Evolution, Religion, and the Nature of Society*, Chicago, IL: University of Chicago Press.

Wittgenstein, L. (1993) *Philosophical Occasions, 1912–1951*, ed. J. Klagge and A. Nordmann, Indianapolis, IN: Hackett.

Wulff, D. (1997) *Psychology of Religion: Classic and Contemporary*, New York: John Wiley & Sons.

Wynn, M. (2008) 'Phenomenology of Religion', in E. N. Zalta (ed.), *Stanford Encyclopedia of Philosophy*, Stanford, CA: Stanford University Press. Available at http://plato.stanford.edu/entries/phenomenology-religion (accessed October 2013).

Xygalatas, D. (2012) *The Burning Saints: Cognition and Culture in the Fire-Walking Rituals of the Anastenaria*, London: Equinox.

Yelle, R. A. (2013) *Semiotics of Religion: Signs of the Sacred in History*, London and New York: Bloomsbury.

Zuckerman, P. (2010) *Society without God: What the Least Religious Societies Can Tell Us about Contentment*, New York: New York University Press.

Zuesse, E. M. (1992) *Ritual Cosmos: The Sanctification of Life in African Religions*, Athens, OH: Ohio University Press.

Index